Theory and History
Series Editor: Donald MacRaild

Published

Empiricism and History	*Stephen Davies*
Social Theory and Social History	*Donald M. MacRaild and Avram Taylor*
Marxism and History	*Matt Perry*
Postmodernism and History	*Willie Thompson*

Further titles are in preparation

Theory and History Series
Series Standing Order
ISBN 0–333–91921–1 paperback
(*outside North America only*)

You can receive future titles in this series as they are published by placing a standing order. Please contact your bookseller or, in case of difficulty, write to us at the address below with your name and address, the title of the series and the ISBN quoted above.

Customer Services Department, Macmillan Distribution Ltd, Houndmills, Basingstoke, Hampshire RG21 6XS, England

---

Social Theory and Social History

Donald M. MacRaild and Avram Taylor

First published 2004 by
PALGRAVE MACMILLAN
Houndmills, Basingstoke, Hampshire RG21 6XS and
175 Fifth Avenue, New York, N.Y. 10010
Companies and representatives throughout the world

PALGRAVE MACMILLAN is the global academic imprint of the Palgrave
Macmillan division of St. Martin's Press, LLC and of Palgrave Macmillan Ltd.
Macmillan® is a registered trademark in the United States, United Kingdom
and other countries. Palgrave is a registered trademark in the European
Union and other countries.

ISBN 0–333–94747–9 paperback

This book is printed on paper suitable for recycling and made from fully
managed and sustained forest sources.

A catalogue record for this book is available from the British Library.

Library of Congress Cataloging-in-Publication Data
MacRaild, Donald M.
    Social thoery and social history / Donald M. MacRaild
and Avram Taylor.
        p. cm. — (Theory and history)
    Includes bibliographical references and index.
    ISBN 0–333–94747–9 (paper)
        1. Social history—Philosophy. 2. Historical sociology. I. Taylor, Avram,
1962– II. Title. III. Series.

HN28.M335 2004   2004048873
306'.09—dc22

10 9 8 7 6 5 4 3 2 1
13 12 11 10 09 08 07 06 05 04

Printed in China

To our mothers, Wendy MacRaild
and Irene Rebecca Taylor

Contents

Conclusion

Acknowledgements

This book has been enriched by the our experience of teaching social history and social theory to undergraduate students. So, we would first like to thank all our students, past and present who have helped shape the contents of this volume. We would also like to thank David Martin at the University of Sheffield, and Lorna Goldsmith and Alan Harvey at the University of Northumbria for their comments on earlier drafts of this work. Finally, thanks are due to Terka Acton for her constant support and encouragement during the writing process.

Introduction

▶ The need for theory in historical explanation

Several years ago a colleague began teaching a course on the Fascist period in Italy. There was nothing unusual about the content of the course in itself. It was to look at the rise of fascism in Italy, the reasons for Mussolini's accession to power, and various aspects of Italian society during the period of the Fascist regime itself. Such a course is quite typical of the specialised options any undergraduate might expect to study in a university today. As a way of introducing the topic, the tutor decided to ask the students what type of regime Mussolini's dictatorship was. Was it an authoritarian dictatorship, a Fascist regime or a totalitarian state? What do we mean by terms like 'fascist' or 'totalitarian?' he asked. How can we offer a definition of 'fascism' that can encompass all the movements and regimes characterised as 'fascist'? Is the 'totalitarianism' concept a valid one? Is it right to bracket together regimes as different as Nazi Germany and Stalinist Russia? These are, you might think, perfectly legitimate questions to begin such a course with. The students did not agree. One particularly vociferous member of the group complained that 'this was not proper history, and it wasn't what they came to university to study'. Other members of the group agreed with the dissident student, and the unfortunate tutor felt obliged to defend his introduction of conceptual issues into the course.

Did this student have a point? Surely history is about what happened, not about constructing models of different types of societies or social phenomena. Why had the tutor not just got on with the serious business of telling them what happened in Italy before Mussolini came to power, giving them the 'facts' about the political crisis that led to the appointment of Mussolini as prime minister in 1922? This seemed to be what the students wanted from the session. On the other hand, though, surely we cannot study something without first knowing what it is we are looking at. Any scholar needs to be able to use language precisely. Biologists need to know that 'appearances notwithstanding, the whale is not a fish', as E.H. Carr observed when pondering a slightly different question of historical philosophy.[1] However, how do biologists know that a whale is not a fish? By having quite clear criteria for categorising fish and mammals, and by observing that the whale in no way fits into the category 'fish'.

So how is this relevant to the study of the Italian dictatorship of Mussolini? Fascism began in Italy, and Italy was the first Fascist state, so how can there be any need to discuss the nature of the regime? Mussolini's regime proclaimed itself to be 'Fascist' so why should there be any need for further debate? There are problems to be considered though. Consider to what extent the ideals of the Fascist movement were realised during the period of the regime. Can the regime be said to embody those ideals? If not, then can it be said to be truly 'Fascist'? The regime has often been characterised as 'totalitarian', but we cannot label it as such without an adequate definition of the term. Historians have even questioned whether Fascist Italy and Nazi Germany belong together, and whether the differences between the two regimes did not outweigh the similarities.

This is not the place to go into the answers to any of these questions, but the mere fact that they are questions of historical importance raises issues about how we are to approach history, and what its ultimate purpose is. It suggests that we need some kind of explanatory framework for looking at the societies we wish to study as historians: that we cannot just 'plunge in' and begin to look at the 'evidence'. On the other hand, you may still be asking yourself whether we do need to consider such issues. Surely there are 'common-sense' definitions of any concept we may wish to employ as historians, and we all instinctively know the meaning of terms like 'class', 'nation state', 'nationalism' or 'fascism'? Are there not commonly accepted definitions of these terms that do not need to be unpacked, which historians can employ in their everyday language without the need for further intellectual gymnastics?

Take one of the most basic conceptual tools of a historian: 'class'. Now think about it for a moment. You might feel it is obvious what class any particular individual belongs to, and that there is no need for any further discussion of the point. The working class, for example, comprised those who work with their hands and perform manual labour – doesn't it? Well, consider the case of eighteenth-century artisans who not only used tools or machinery to produce goods, but also owned the tools or machinery they worked with, and were thus working for themselves. Were they working class? If they were self-employed, does that not mean that they belonged to a different class from those who really did have nothing but their own labour power to sell? Take the problem into the present day. What about the issue of manual labour? Look at contemporary society and consider how easy it is to identify a working class. If we consider workers on a production line in a car factory, then we do not have too much of a problem, they are creating wealth for an employer, and performing manual labour, so they are obviously working class. What about some of the workers in jobs who are more characteristic of late twentieth-century employment: those people who work in the service sector, for example? Does being a receptionist, a secretary or a telephone salesperson make an individual a member of the working class? Is working in a burger chain manual labour? Do such workers 'make' burgers, or just hand them over to the customer? Does assembling a burger constitute an act of 'adding value' to raw materials?

Such problems of historical explanation require recourse to a body of knowledge that is usually referred to as 'theory'. The sociologist Anthony Giddens sees theory as crucial to sociology because it constitutes 'an attempt to identify general properties which explain regularly observed events'. He also suggests that 'While theories tend to be linked to broader theoretical approaches, they are also strongly influenced by the research results they help generate.'[2] Theory thus enables structured generalisations about the world: in other words, to move beyond descriptions of particular places and times, and towards a discussion of general properties of particular social phenomena. The type of phenomena under discussion could be anything at all, from a model of Fascist movements and states, to a concept of social revolutions, or a schema with different types of society existing at different historical periods. Theory is particularly important in explaining historical change. However, while the introduction of theory into history has the potential to solve many problems, it has also been the source of much controversy. The first area of controversy is indicated by Giddens' statement that theory is 'an essential element of all sociological work'. Most of the theory that historians employ originated in the social sciences, and there are those who feel that it should stay there. Some historians are still sceptical about the use of concepts borrowed from the social sciences within their discipline. Others reject the possibility of ever generalising about the course of history at all, or even ever knowing the truth about the past. The use of theory by historians is a comparatively new problem, as John Tosh points out. 'For most historians up to the end of the nineteenth century this was not in practice a major problem since their interest tended to be confined to political and constitutional history; accordingly some notion of the body politic was all the conceptual equipment they required.' But Tosh also claims that the more recent trend for breaking down historical enquiry into sub-specialisms demands 'an ever greater capacity to think in terms of abstractions'.[3] As the scope of the discipline has expanded, so has the number and type of questions posed by historians.

Let us just think for a moment about history as a discipline. History as a subject is characterised by debate. That debate is not about the chronicle of events. It is about the way we interpret those events. Historians do not argue about whether the Battle of Hastings took place in 1066 or 1067. The debate about the French Revolution does not centre on when it took place, historians argue about the significance of it as an event; its time is important only for what it tells us about the state of society and politics at that point. For example, was the revolution caused by the rise of new class (the bourgeoisie) within France? Often historians are concerned with identifying the causes of an event. Probably the most commonly asked questions at all levels of historical study relate to the causes of the First and the

Second World Wars. Usually a historian will assign several causes to the same event. But as E.H. Carr says: 'The examination candidate who, in answering the question, "Why did revolution break out in Russia in 1917?", offered only one cause would be lucky to get a third class.'[4] The historian thus deals with a multiplicity of causes. Often the historian will identify a number of levels of causation: economic, political, ideological and personal. This raises the problem of how those different levels of causation relate to each other. Is one of greater significance than another? How are we to cope with the vast number of causal factors that contribute to the making of any single event?

It is obviously being argued here that the use of theory can help historians to deal with the complex nature of the problems they study. However, if our dissenting students from the seminar on Fascist Italy were still with us, perhaps they would still not be convinced by this argument. They may still wish to raise objections to the introduction of theory into the discipline. The (by now exasperated) students might ask, why can't historians just stick to the facts? Why don't historians just tell us what happened during the Industrial Revolution, or the French Revolution? Why will they not just agree on an interpretation of why the Second World War broke out, and stick to it? Well, the short answer is: all historians are biased and the individual bias of the historian has an effect on the type of history they will write. Think about any armed conflict. For example, it may not be surprising to learn that English, French and German historians have different interpretations of the Battle of Waterloo, or the First World War. National sentiment can often play a role in a historian's interpretation of events. But that is not the only type of bias a historian can display. Political bias is of crucial importance in the type of history a historian will produce. It is also of crucial importance in the type of theory they will favour or adopt. This is equally true of historians who claim to be 'objective', 'non-theoretical' or 'professional'. Historians who claim to have no ideological standpoint are, in fact, operating a kind of professional confidence trick on their readers (whether they are aware of it or not). This is merely a way of smuggling in their own beliefs under the cover of 'objectivity'. So theory is not an adjunct, or an optional extra, to 'real' history. It is an intrinsic part of the process of historical writing. Neither should it be seen as some kind of obstacle, or a way of merely making a difficult subject more complicated. The use of theory can actually help us to explain the events that we study. The increased interest in the use of theory in historical explanation is linked with the other main concern of this book: the expansion of social history.

▶ The expansion of social history

Although various definitions can be offered, social history essentially involves an expansion of the historian's range of concerns beyond the activities of social and political elites.[5] By the nineteenth century, historians were beginning to display a greater concern with the social and the economic. During the twentieth century, this broadening of historical interest began to bear fruit. First, with the attempt at writing a 'total' history by the *Annales* School in France, then through the post-war expansion of social history in Britain, which drew its inspiration as much from Marx as from the French scholars. Social history is characterised by a concern with describing the experience of various social groups. An initial focus on class has been followed by an attempt to integrate the experiences of women, and also different ethnic groups into the writing of history. As the range of the social historians' concerns expanded, so did the range of methodologies and theoretical approaches they employed. The borrowing of approaches and techniques from the social sciences led a number of commentators to discuss the growing 'convergence' between history and the social sciences, and this is an issue that we will be considering at length in this book.

The two main features of the development of history in the twentieth century are the increasingly **interdisciplinary** nature of historical enquiry, and the fragmentation of the discipline into a number of sub-disciplines. Historians have become more willing to borrow from other disciplines, whether that involves the construction of **counterfactual** models of economic development, or a focus on the 'thick description' of other cultures.[6] The scope of historical enquiry has also expanded dramatically. The relatively narrow focus of nineteenth-century historians on political and diplomatic history, and the biographies of 'great men' was challenged in the twentieth century with the consolidation of economic and social history as sub-disciplines. The process of fragmentation did not stop there. As Peter Burke puts it: 'In the last generation or so the universe of historians has been expanding at a dizzying rate.'[7] **Metanarratives** of the nation, which dominated nineteenth-century writings, have been pressured in from the broadest and the narrowest perspectives: on the one hand, from new emphases upon global approaches; and, on the other hand, from assertions of the importance of localities and regions. In due course, moreover, as Burke also points out, new sub-disciplines themselves soon fragmented: 'Social history, for example, became independent of economic history only to fragment, like some new nation, into historical demography, labour history, urban history, rural history, and so on.'[8]

The proliferation of sub-disciplines as well as the constant changes of emphasis within them, have also made it very difficult to draw clear distinctions between the various branches of history. For example, it is not always easy to identify clear differences between economic and social history. In addition, there are significant new categories, such as cultural history, that have further blurred boundaries. A survey of the specialist journals can be a good way to gain an appreciation of the expansion of the discipline in recent years. Many of these 'new' titles are concerned with social history topics. To merely list some notable examples: *History Workshop*

Journal, *Urban History*, *Immigrants and Minorities*, *Oral History*, and, of course, *Social History*, all fall into this category. While other, more general, journals regularly carry articles depicting aspects of social history. In addition, social historians have concerned themselves with an increasingly wider range of topics. An earlier focus on social conditions and labour history has now given way to an increasing diversity of subject matter, which cannot be exhaustively described here. Social historians are concerned with topics such as education, sport and leisure, reading habits, crime and deviance, and the growth of towns. They have become increasingly concerned with recapturing the experience of a number of different social groups, not just that of different social classes, but also the experiences of women, immigrants and minorities, and those who have been viewed as 'outsiders' by mainstream society: for instance, as a result of their sexuality, or because they were classified as insane.[9] Thus the expansion of social history in recent decades is to be welcomed, as it has opened up many new areas of historical inquiry and rejuvenated the discipline. At the same time, though, it has led to an increasing fragmentation of the discipline, as well as leaving many questions of historical explanation unresolved.

▶ The developing relationship between social theory and social history

This book seeks to outline some of the main developments within both social theory and social history, and to discuss the complex relationship between the two. As well as being a discussion of prominent examples of both types of work, it is also a reflection on the nature of the task that confronts both historians and sociologists. Any survey, such as this, must inevitably involve a large element of selectivity, and the personal views of the authors plays a part in regard to both the choice of examples, and the discussion of the theoretical issues in this volume. This element of bias has to be acknowledged at the outset, although we have also sought to cover as many significant historians and sociologists as possible, regardless of our own feelings towards them. The text in general is intended as a gateway to a wider body of scholarship, and it is hoped that some of the ideas presented here will lead to other writings, thus suggestions for further reading are presented throughout.

Chapter 1 deals with the development of social history, particularly the core question: 'what is social history?' The shape of this chapter is broadly chronological; but it seeks to construct a thematic consideration of our study of the social dimensions of past societies. It will also consider the links between economic and social history, and assesses how the discipline has grown and changed since the Second World War. One consistent feature of social history has been its 'present-mindedness', or its insistence that the present gives history its relevance. The growth of **history from below** is largely a result of this wider social concern. The new directions in social history outlined earlier are also discussed in more detail in this chapter. Chapter 2 provides an overview of the critical engagement between history and sociology over the past 50 years or so. Historians have borrowed increasingly from sociology, while social scientists have increasingly identified their practice with history. However, this has not ended controversy about the relationship between the two disciplines, and this chapter will discuss the attitudes of both historians and sociologists to this question. It will also consider the nature of the hybrid discipline, historical sociology, and discuss different examples of this genre.

In Chapter 3 we continue the consideration of the interplay between history and the social sciences concentrating upon large-scale, comparative and 'total' thinking. The desire to work on a broader canvas has taken a number of forms, and also created a number of difficulties. Attempts at grand-scale historical thinking embrace a wide range of scholarship: from Marx's theory of **historical material-ism**, and the notion of 'total history' most closely associated with Braudel, to attempts at comparative history. This chapter makes a case for the importance of comparative history, particularly as a necessary complement to the increasing specialisation of historical research. Chapter 4 discusses the significance of social structure and human **agency** in both historical and sociological explanation. The chapter offers a reflection on the significance of the role of individuals, social structures and the unintended consequences of action within the historical process. It considers the way in which this issue has been presented within the work of a number of social theorists. This survey takes in the work of the founding fathers of sociology (Marx, Durkheim and Weber), later theorists such as Norbert Elias and Anthony Giddens, as well as **poststructuralist** thinkers such as Michel Foucault. It asserts the central importance of class as a structural factor within the historical process, while also acknowledging that other factors, particularly ethnicity and gender, have to be considered alongside it. The significance of class, gender and ethnicity is then discussed in relation to the three classic Marxist epochs (ancient society, feudal society and capitalist society).

Chapter 5 alights on the later streams of writing that emerged as social history, 'new social history' and 'cultural history' jockeyed for supremacy. The chapter's main aim is to explain, through the use of examples, the relationship between the newer turn towards the cultural and the older forms of Marxist-inspired history of the 1960s. This returns us to a discussion of the two historical traditions that have been central to the text as a whole: Marxist social history in Britain, and the *Annales* School in France. The turn to the 'cultural' in historical interpretation can, in many ways, be seen as a development of pioneering works of the *Annales* School and the British Marxists. Both approaches embody a desire to understand the mentality of the 'common people' in different eras of history. In recent years, the influence of anthropological models, and poststructuralist thinkers, has become more prominent in the writing of cultural history. Driven by perspectives from linguistics and the philosophy of history, the new cultural history has challenged the fundamental premises of historical scholarship in a way that the *Annales* and the British Marxists clearly did not. This returns us to another issue of central concern to this text: the **postmodern** challenge to historical studies.

Many students of history, and historians themselves, are uneasy about the relationship between theory and history. It is being argued here that theory is not an adjunct, or an optional extra to, 'real' history. It is an intrinsic part of the process of historical writing. The use of theory by historians has become more widespread as history has moved beyond the mere presentation of a narrative, and the questions that historians ask have become more complex. This is partly due to the expansion of social history that took place in the twentieth century. While this has immensely enriched the discipline of history, it has also led to the increasing fragmentation and specialisation of the discipline. This ever-increasing diversity within the discipline has left unresolved the question of how the various levels of historical explanation relate to each other. The nature of the historical process means that it is very difficult to offer a pat resolution to this problem. However, this book seeks to explore the complex relationship between social theory and social history, as the authors feel that an awareness of this issue is the key to a deeper understanding of the process of historical change.

1 Cinderella Gets Her Prince? The Development of Social History

When in 1962 Harold Perkin reviewed the academic position of social history at that time, he could have had no idea how far things would proceed in the next 40 years. 'Social history is the Cinderella of English historical studies', he argued 'Judged by the usual criteria of academic disciplines, it can scarcely be said to exist: there are no chairs (i.e. professorships in social history) and, if we omit local history, no university departments, no learned journals, and few if any textbooks.'[1] This was not the case, however, with Cinderella's 'second eldest sister', economic history, whose scope was well defined and whose invitation to the ball was always open. Economic history, established in the early years of the twentieth century by such luminaries as George Unwin and John Clapham, enjoyed direct links to the historical mainstream. Clapham, for example, was an apostle of the economist, Alfred Marshall, and of Lord Acton. Economic history thus enjoyed a degree of acceptance – and acceptability – which social history was slow to acquire. Economic history existed beyond question, with universities providing a home to ensure its permanency. Whereas social history, even at the time Perkin was writing, lay at the edge of the discipline; it was experimental and inchoate, lacking the clear objectives and methodologies enjoyed by economic history.

Now we are at a curious crossroads in social history. Since the early 1960s, departments of economic *and* social history have risen and fallen in many universities; chairs have been established so long that many are now filled with cultural historians, whose subject area has in some ways outmanoeuvred social approaches; academic journals are to be found in most countries, with prestige and gravitas conferred upon them by the quality of what they contain. Perkin, interestingly enough, was writing just one year before the appearance of one of social history's landmark publications: E.P. Thompson's classic study of the English working class.[2] Thompson's preface contained a statement about the meaning of social history, and about the author's desire to invest historical enquiry with social concern, that was to change the face of the discipline.[3] *The Making* was not, of course, the first social history, and Thompson was not the first social historian. Yet, the 1960s represented

9

a landmark as well as a caesura – a period when the Vietnam War and Civil Rights campaigns, among other movements, provided a political frame for Bendetto Croce's now hackneyed truism: 'all history is contemporary history'. Before the 1960s could provide this contrast between Perkin's diffidence and Thompson's assertiveness, however, a long train of historians presented themselves as critics of a non-social, political, events-orientated approach.

At the heart of any discussion of the rise of this type of historical study lies the question 'what is social history?' This has already been given some attention in the Introduction. One of the sub-themes to this chapter, then, is the way in which both the question and potential answers to the question have changed over time. Whilst we commonly associated social history with particular forms of sociology (or at least with theory-driven writing in the modern period, particularly since 1945) we should also notice deeper strains wherein ideas supported the quest to know the social world. While social history is traditionally considered to be a relatively new branch of the discipline, focused upon recent Marxist scholarship, many of the key aspects of the ideas and philosophies underpinning it have a much older vintage than this might imply. However, Enlightenment theorists who began to ask big questions about the nature of society did not conceive of the construction of a social history of human society in the way it subsequently took shape.

▶ Ideas, philosophy and the roots of social history

As all strains of modern historiography owe a great debt to the revolution in ideas of the eighteenth century, we should not be surprised that antecedents of social history can also be located there. This is not to say that histories of ordinary people and their lives, of crime, or of working-class women, emerged at this time. The level of engagement was rather loftier than that: what the eighteenth century provided was the development of ideas about society as an organic whole, which in turn helped to prepare the ground for totalising theories which followed, most prominently those of Karl Marx (1818–83), and Friedrich Engels (1820–95). By thinking philosophically about the nature of culture and society, and by giving greater credence to men's actions, and less to those of God, Enlightenment thinkers created a space for secular accounts of the development of Man. Giambattista Vico (1668–1744), Italian philosopher and Professor of Rhetoric at Naples University, first clearly articulated this developing of an appreciation of human action in the development of human society. He challenged the pre-eminence of Cartesian science, arguing that the human world was intelligible to Man alone because it was of Man's construction, whilst countering that only God could comprehend the natural world because He had created it. Vico had established a kind of precedent, and it would be developed by eighteenth-century philosophers, such as Kant and Hegel, who themselves sought to appreciate the nature of society and human evolution in the broadest historical terms.

In the eighteenth century, there were no disputes between sociologists and his torians, because sociology did not exist as a separate discipline and history was not taught in universities. The philosophical foundations of sociology as a discipline were laid during this period with the Enlightenment. The first attempts to write a history of societies and economies in the West, date from this time. Outside the West, the fourteenth-century Islamic scholar Ibn Khaldun created the first known attempt to write a theoretical and **empirical** work of structural history. However, this work was not known in the West until the nineteenth century, and its importance has only really been recognised since the 1960s.[4]

It is certainly worth stressing the role of continuity and connection in historical inquiry, because links between seemingly older and more modern forms of knowl edge crop up time and again. Not only this, particular concerns in historical enquiry also reflected the societies in which the ideas were formulated. Early social history really emerged as a kind cultural history – not the type of history we would today conceptualise as 'cultural', but as part of the idea of a cyclical trend in social and cultural development.[5] Here, the philosophical precursors of economic history were most notable for their aim to rationalise and understand the nature of the economy, and its social effects, in the eighteenth century and the historical forces that were determining the erosion of agricultural forms by the development of urban industrial societies.

Changing contemporary social circumstances clearly influence views of the past. As Eric Roll says of early economists (using words applicable to any type of thinker): 'the economic structure of any given epoch and the changes which it undergoes are major influences on economic thinking'. Thus, he contends, 'Few people would doubt that the economic thought produced in a community in which slave labour predominates is different from that which either a feudal society, or one based on wage-labour, brings forth.'[6] So it was for the thinkers of the eighteenth century a time of great change. Beginning with the work of Adam Smith in the 1750s, and continuing with that of John Millar and Adam Ferguson, what became known as the Scottish historical school began to develop an explanation of economic and social change built on the society that surrounded them and a desire to appreciate its historical antecedents.[7] Classic among these efforts to explain the nature of economy and society was Adam Smith's *Wealth of Nations* (1776), which provided a study of economic development that would be hugely influential upon Karl Marx, whose massive study, *Capital*, shares Smith's appreciation of the importance of history. Marx himself acknowledged the importance of Scottish philosophy and its 'embryonic historical materialism',[8] which he would develop later.

In France, at about the same time, Montesquieu was seeking the laws of social and historical development and a classification of societies. Montesquieu influenced his contemporary, A.R.J. Turgot, the French **physiocrat**, who developed a theory of the stages of economic development, focusing on the issues of land and capital, echoing in broad terms the work of the Scots.[9] These eighteenth-century writers are best described by the contemporary term 'philosophical' historians.[10] They wrote social theory that drew heavily on historical examples before the creation of disciplinary boundaries, as we know them today. In eighteenth-century Europe, as **mercantilism** declined, the origins of money and capital wealth assumed an important position in philosophy. Such thought can also be seen as forerunning economic history.

The unity of the rational and the **empirical** was the distinctive intellectual feature of this period. This involved the application of the methods of the natural sciences to the social world. With the exception of Giambattista Vico, who was unknown during the period of the Enlightenment, Montesquieu made the first attempt in modern times at constructing a philosophy of society and history. He was the first thinker to utilise what sociologists call **ideal types**, although he did not refer to them as such. He identified forms of government called republic, aristocracy, monarchy and despotism that can only be seen once we go from the detail of their actual existence to a recognition of the underlying principles behind them. An ideal type is formed by exaggerating particular features of a historical phenomenon to an extreme and leaving out other accompanying features. No actually existing social phenomenon will conform exactly to the features of an ideal type. It should be noted that scholars who construct an ideal type, such as that of fascism, are in no way suggesting that it is a desirable form of government. What such an enterprise involves is identifying the common features of, for instance, Fascist movements and regimes so a model of fascism can be constructed that will contain elements from them all, while still allowing for the differences between them.[11] Although he did not invent the concept, it was Max Weber who first used the term ideal type to describe this means of generalising about societies. Weber acknowledges his debt to Marx, in particular, in formulating this concept. The use of ideal types has since become a fundamental part of sociological practice.

If the growth of early forms of economic and social history occurred in the eighteenth century, against a backdrop of an increasing rapidity of societal change, the same point can be amplified for the nineteenth century. The twin pressures for change deriving from the French and Industrial Revolutions did more than test ideas of social change: they shook them violently. Individual thinkers, such as Hegel, who were caught up in the turmoil of revolutionary France, were shaken by 20 years of incessant fighting in Europe; radical thought became more popular, and to a greater degree possible and permissible. Ideas about the majority of people – the ordinary folk, the embryonic working class – began to set new challenges for those charged with the interpretation of society. Sidney Pollard put it more starkly when he claimed: 'The Age of Innocence died with Condorcet' (1743–93),[12] the French mathematician and philosopher, whose abstract beliefs in 'metaphysical concepts as "Justice" or "Natural rights"' waned in and after the revolutionary period. A new consensus began slowly to emerge, which concluded that 'Society was more complex than had been thought, and a new foundation had to be laid for a credible system of social laws.'[13] Ideas such as these embraced a broad new approach to society, one that could encompass men such as the positivist philosopher and Utopian, Henri Saint-Simon (1760–1825) – who, like Hegel, also suffered personally during the turbulent 1790s and early 1800s – and the fathers of modern socialism, Karl Marx and Friedrich Engels. In these early works of social theory, in which the French Revolution had helped to define the concept of 'social' and 'society', metaphors from biology were being introduced, with human beings viewed as akin to cells and organs in 'super-organism'.[14]

Although the philosophical foundations of sociology as a discipline were being laid in the eighteenth century, it was Auguste Comte (1798–1857) who first used the term 'sociology' to describe the science of society in 1830. The word first appeared in English in 1843.[15] Comte, who had been an assistant to Saint-Simon,[16] was originally a philosopher and is generally regarded as the founder of positivism, though his old master's ideas, if less weighty than Comte's, were also **positivist**. **Positivism** is a belief that phenomena are governed by unchangeable, impersonal laws, which is the purpose of science to discover. So Comte hoped to establish sociology as a science that would reveal the laws governing society. This would then enable us to control our own destiny.[17] This much Comte inherited from his mentor Saint-Simon, who 'had no doubt that man's social future is as law-governed as his past ... The laws of history are the laws of destiny, which will inevitably conduct society to a determined end'.[18]

One of the most important developments, captured in the divide between the philosophies of Saint-Simon and Marx and Engels, was the movement away from Utopian visions of human society and towards a more analytical framework. If human lives were governed by impermeable laws of development, as Comte would have us believe, or if society aspired to some ideal state manufactured outside human **agency**, as might be ascribed to Saint-Simon, then the socialism, or communism, described by Marx and Engels, relied upon human agency in the form of class struggle. Marx and Engels were actually very critical of Utopian perspectives. Engels attacked Utopians such as Saint-Simon, Fourier and Robert Owen because 'not one of them appears as a representative of the interests of that proletariat, which historical development ... had produced'.[19] For Engels, 'modern socialism is, in its essence, the direct product of the recognition, on the one hand, of class antagonisms, existing in the society of to-day ... [and] on the other hand, of the anarchy existing in production'.[20] Such words were echoed again in Marx and Engels' work, perhaps most memorably enunciated by the former: 'The history of all hitherto existing society is the history of class struggle.'[21] This emphasis – quite different from that of the Utopians, and developed in criticism of them – would prove to be a foundation stone for what was to be a heavily (though not exclusively) Marxist-inspired social history.

▶ Silencing the 'drum and trumpet'? early social history traditions in Britain

Less than committed to continental positivism, and largely unwilling to follow the logic of Marxism towards the study of the working class, mainstream academic history in Britain continued to be dominated by traditionalist 'high' perspectives. Events and their main *dramatis personae* held centre stage. Walk-on parts were available for those ordinary people – mainly men – who burst on to the scene now and then: Wat Tyler, for example, or the thousands of archers who won the Battle of Agincourt.

There were those who dissented from this rather narrow conceptualisation. One historian who offered such a challenge, and who would come to be seen as the founding father of English social history, was J.R. Green (1837–83). His most famous work, *A Short History of the English People* (1874), demonstrated that some Victorians at least were concerned with the classes of people closest to the hearts of Marx and Engels. Green argued that his book was a departure from 'drum and trumpet' history; that he offered an attempt to write history from a perspective other than that of monarchs, statesmen, generals and battles:

> The aim of the following work is defined by its title; it is not a history of English Kings or English conquests, but of the English people ... I have preferred to pass lightly and briefly over the details of foreign wars and diplomacies, the personal adventures of kings and nobles, the pomp of courts, or the intrigues of favourites, and to dwell at length on the incidents of that constitutional, intellectual, and social advance, in which we read the history of the nation itself. It is with this purpose that I have devoted more space to Chaucer than to Cressy [the Battle of Crécy, 1346], to Caxton than to the petty strife of Yorkists and Lancastrians, to the Poor Law of Elizabeth than to her victory at Cadiz, to the Methodist revival than to the escape of the Young Pretender [Bonnie Prince Charlie].[22]

A step forward, certainly: but it was not so much a change of philosophy as of emphasis. Green relied upon the same types of records as F.W. Maitland or Lord Acton might use: official, institutional documents. Green may have shared with Marx and Engels an interest in economic history and peasant revolts, as opposed to high politics and statecraft, but his concern was not politically motivated, and his history did not get down very far among the 'real' people. Green was in many respects an institutional historian. Moreover, recent scholars have accused him of **anachronism**, because of the present-minded emphasis he placed on his analysis of the past. His work lacked the theoretical framework, which might have developed (as later historians developed it) through a dialogue with the embryonic social sciences, not least with the works of Comte and Marx. But this is not what historians in England in the 1870s thought was important in studying the past.

Green's stress upon events affecting ordinary people, if not upon the lives of common people themselves, must be seen in the context in which the author himself was writing. The second half of the nineteenth century saw the emergence of a truly widespread industrial economy, and while social unrest was less evident than in the 1820s or the 1840s, and though the working class sought more to accommodate than to crush capitalism, one impact of modern urban and industrial society was a social critique, which questioned political institutions and the unequal sharing of economic resources. The growth of welfare capitalism from the 1890s was one measure of a growing concern about the dichotomy between wealth generation and wealth distribution. Britain was a great imperial power, yet the people were often hungry, ill-housed or unemployed. Moreover, as Britain's industrial pre-eminence was gradually eclipsed by America and Germany amid fears about growing international competition, critics of capitalism became more audible. Much of the criticism from the intellectual Left, particularly from the Fabians, a group founded in London in 1884 by Sidney and Beatrice Webb.

At the same time, and undoubtedly partly as a response to these wider socio-political issues, the discipline of economics was beginning to emerge in a more contemporary form. The 'English Historical School' of economic thought, as it became known, worked against the political economists, these creators of general laws, and instead looked to a greater **empirical** depth. Interestingly, they also sought answers to contemporary social problems, rather than merely laws to explain economic systems.[23] In the words of Thorold Rogers, one of mid-Victorian Britain's most notable economic historians, and an early pioneer of labour history:

> The older dogmatism of this science or philosophy, after being for a long time distasteful, has latterly been shown to be untrue. Many of the formularies which were accepted as axiomatic truths by the disciples of Ricardo and Mill are found to be as incorrect as they are unsatisfactory. Besides, it is not enough for the economist to predict, he is expected to suggest the remedies for the evils under which society is labouring, or yield the social questions up to the socialist.[24]

Economic history, which was almost indistinguishable from social history, thus developed and changed through reflections upon recent historical phenomena, particularly the Industrial Revolution. The implications of this for the writing of social history were strong. Industrialism had created a class that sought social and political power through industrial action and voting rights. Yet still this class suffered, next to its masters, despite an enormous growth in national wealth.

The contempt that social reformers felt for the Industrial Revolution was given a new, cataclysmic articulation in 1884 in a hugely influential series of lectures by Arnold Toynbee:

> The Industrial Revolution was a period as disastrous and terrible as any through which a nation ever passed; disastrous and terrible because side by side with a great increase in wealth was seen an enormous increase in pauperism; and production on a vast scale, the result of free competition, led to a rapid alienation of classes, and to the degradation of large bodies of producers.[25]

Toynbee's words were to preface a period of sustained work on the lives of ordinary people. A generation of writers followed Toynbee and offered pessimistic assessment of industrialism: from the works of Sidney and Beatrice Webb (who founded the London School of Economics in 1895) to the social surveys of London and York carried out by Charles Booth and Seebohm Rowntree.[26] The works are correctly characterised as early sociology or social science; the subject matter was contemporary – Booth and Rowntree, for instance, the living conditions of the East End of London and of York, respectively. Their findings, which demonstrate the widespread and deep-rooted nature of poverty, prompted criticisms of late-Victorian and Edwardian society.

This school spawned a series of influential books, including studies by the Webbs themselves as well as by another husband and wife team, J.L. and Barbara Hammond.[27] In their studies of trades unions and workers, the Webbs and the Hammonds were seeking to analyse the Industrial Revolution in terms of its impact upon the standards of living, individuals' lives and the creation of a working class. For the Hammonds, the focus of the historian of the Industrial Revolution should be upon the way in which the commercial and industrial capitalists affected the lives of ordinary people. More than that, the power relations of the Industrial Revolution necessitated organisation among workers to ensure wealth, and the owners of wealth, were controlled. As the Hammonds stated, in one of their most famous works of social history: 'For the working classes the most important fact about wealth was that it was wealth in dangerous disorder, for unless these new forces could be brought under the control of the common will, the power that was flooding the world with its lavish gifts was destined to become a fresh menace to the freedom and happiness of men.'[28] If this attack on capitalists explained the socialism and labourism of the Hammonds' own day, and to some extent vindicated their own politicised reading of social change, there was also an attempt in their work to capture the essential character of society under new systems of production. As ever, the image was bleak:

> Hence it was that amid all the conquests over nature, that gave its triumphs to the Industrial Revolution, the soul of man was passing into a colder exile, for in this new

world, with all its wealth and promise and its wide horizon of misery and hope, the spirit of fellowship was dead. [29]

Such pessimistic assessments of industrialism were bolstered by government surveys, which pointed to the abject position of a large part of the working class, while a challenge to the political consensus of the time was offered by journalists, social comment novels and tracts, such as Andrew Mearns' *The Bitter Cry of Outcast London* (1883) and Jack London's *People of the Abyss* (1903), which captured the poor living conditions and low wage levels of a disconcertingly large part of the British population. This body of work, all told, was neither social nor economic history as we know it: it was socially oriented economic investigation. These early works were characterised by a spirit of exploration, and sometimes involved the author 'going undercover' to investigate the poor.[30] Nevertheless, they did offer a genuine attempt to tie together economic processes and social consequences, and attempted wholeheartedly to understand the impact of industrialisation. In so doing, these works were offering a preface to what would become a thriving area within social and economic history: that of labour history, with its central concern about the organisations, lives and social protests of the working classes, as well as laying the foundations for British **empirical** sociology.

A common view among its practitioners was that economic history was the *most* important sub-discipline because it sought to report on those issues that mattered most to past societies. This stress echoed Marx's view, outlined in his expositions on **historical materialism**, that the economic basis determined other aspects of society. Whilst economic historians did not need to be Marxists (and indeed often were not) to expound such a view, there were also economic historians who, while stressing the value-added importance of economic history as a discipline, also shared the views of the likes of the Webbs and the Hammonds that a history of society had, as part of its purpose, an engagement with the present. An important early twentieth-century practitioner of economic history, George Unwin, explained where his chosen form of historical enquiry fitted into the broadcloth:

> History is an account of the things that mattered most in the past, and it derives its chief interest from the assumption that those things were largely the causes of what matters to us now. And, if the things that matter most are the same now as then, the assumption seems natural.[31]

Not only that, Unwin also stressed the influence of contemporary issues:

> But if what matters most to us now is ... class conflicts and the interests of Labour, we are driven to re-explore history, and to dig for these aspects of the past beneath the political surface, where we shall certainly find them ... The deeper reason [for

adopting this approach] is to be found in the belief that, behind what seemed to matter most to the historians, we are getting at what really mattered most to most people in the past, and that these things are causally connected with what matters most to most people today.[32]

If that is the purpose of economic history, then the essence of historical research is social concern and the outcome of that research is an understanding of society at large. As well as sharing a viewpoint with social historians and critics of his day, Unwin was also foregrounding much more recent work, which stressed the popular dimension of the past, not least the approach called '**history from below**', which is associated with the British Marxists of the post-1945 generation. Yet, his conception of social history fell well short of today's: for Unwin's social history sounds more like the study of culture. For him, social history was an 'ideal' that 'should be concerned with Life, Truth and Beauty – with the energizing souls of men in community'. He saw economic and political history as 'concerned with means to social ends'.[33] But the Unwinian perspective, with its strong social concern, did influence *bona fide* economic historians. H.L. Beales, for example, maintained a life-long concern for the social dimensions of the Industrial Revolution. Writing almost 40 years after the first edition of his short study of the process of industrialisation, Beales offered a telling rebuke to economic history that lacked the social aspect:

> Perhaps it is not just the habit of riding on my particular hobby-horse which impels me to say that the analysis of the industrial revolution is still made too much in economic terms. When I read, say, Rostow's discussion of the 'first take-off – the British Industrial Revolution (1783–1802)' and the 'take-off into self-sustaining growth', I admire the ingenuity, but ask questions which will seem to be irrelevant to the purist in economic history.[34]

And Beales went on to discuss the evils of landownership in Ireland ('skilfully but unconvincingly explained away by some of the classical economists') and the Highland Clearances, with their 'legacies of pauper emigration, indentured labour, disturbed labour supplies, and disturbing participation in labour agitations'.[35] In other words, he went on to stress the social aspects of societies affected by economic realities.

An alternative political stance, if not an entirely variant view of the importance of economic history, was most clearly captured in the work of the pre-eminent economic historian of the first half of the twentieth century, J.H. Clapham.[36] Clapham's major methodological contribution was to shift the emphasis on the history of industrialisation away from cataclysmic upheaval, or 'revolution', to the notion of gradual or organic change. Clapham saw less to be pessimistic about in Britain's passage to economic superiority in the nineteenth century. He sought to shift emphasis from the social impact of industrialisation, to the great staple industries – cotton, coal, iron and steel and shipbuilding – which were viewed as central to the history of industrialism. As a result, the technologies of the Industrial Revolution and the entrepreneurs who invented and implemented them came to the fore. If not merely a matter of celebration and eulogy, the names of Richard Arkwright, James Watt, Henry Bessemer, George Stephenson and I.K. Brunel, and the spinning jenny, steam engines, steel smelting, trains and ships they brought to public fame, became more important to historians.

Clapham's methodology was directly linked with that of his mentor, Lord Acton, and the **empiricist** school. As Clapham himself asserted: 'Economic history is a branch of general institutional history, a study of the economic aspects of the social institutions of the past. Its methodological distinctiveness hinged primarily on its marked quantitative interest; for this reason it is or should be the most exact branch of history.'[37] Clapham stressed the precision of quantitative aspects of economic history. In stressing this mathematical dimension, he was distancing himself from the early social critics of industrialism, such the Webbs and Hammonds. For Clapham, 'Every economic historian should have acquired what might be called the statistical sense, the habit of asking in relation to any institution, policy, group or movement the questions: how large? how long? how often? how representative?'[38] In making this point, Clapham was asserting what continues to be a defining difference between economic and social approaches. Clapham used the term 'social historians' with contempt, criticising followers of this style who 'too often followed a familiar literary (i.e. non-quantitative) tradition'.[39] He reserved particular contempt for their failure to use available statistical evidence for the balance of wage and prices (particularly Bowley's and Siberling's indices). That these very sources would remain hotly contested for more than half-a-century did not stop Clapham expounding their superiority over the politically motivated literary approaches of the likes of the Hammonds and the Webbs. In fact, in developing this critique of social history, its methods and motivations, Clapham was laying down charges against this approach to the past, which would continue to echo in the reasoning of later critics who also approached the discipline from the political right. This position was articulated clearly and forcefully in the 1980s by Jonathan Clark, who wrote that under certain conditions 'social history is made to seem the sort of history that socialists write'.[40]

Sitting aside from Clapham, and in many ways above the early social history school, were writers such as R.H. Tawney (1880–1962), Professor at the London School of Economics. Tawney was an historian, economist and philosopher who met Thorold Rogers' criteria of suggesting remedies for social evil. While Tawney's main interest was with medieval and early modern history and moral philosophy of capitalism, his first major study, an economic history of the impact of enclosures on peasant life, provided vital historical context for his later works on the morality of capitalism.[41] Tawney's concern with the development of exploitation and the growing of wealth over labour, chimed clearly with what was by 1912, when he was writing, a sustained social criticism of capitalism and its development. Tawney reached new heights of critical clarity in one of his most famous works, *The Acquisitive Society* (1921), in which he argued that the emergence of liberalism and secularism had freed capitalism from moral obligation.[42] Tawney upheld the ideal of a functioning society as a higher form of social being than the acquisitive society he recognised around him. His position was that human society had lost its cognisance of the true purpose of industry. '[T]he meaning of industry is the service of man', he wrote, and under such a viewpoint 'all who labour appear honourable'.[43] 'But' he continued,

> when the only criterion which remains is that of wealth, and an Acquisitive Society reverences the possession of wealth ... So wealth becomes the foundation of public esteem, and the mass of men who labour, but who do not acquire wealth, are thought to be vulgar and meaningless and insignificant compared with the few who acquire wealth by good fortune, or by the skilful use of economic opportunities.[44]

Tawney's viewpoint made him an influential political thinker in Labour Party circles; but, for our purposes, we can clearly see a link in his work between social criticisms and socio-economic history. As would repeatedly be the case, social thought required an historical context upon which to build.

Tawney's next and perhaps most famous work, *Religion and the Rise of Capitalism* (1926), had as its central theme the withdrawal of Christian ethics from social and economic life during the rise of the capitalist order.[45] This book drew inspiration from the work of Max Weber.[46] Whilst Tawney described the malaise of morality in modern British society, he again echoed Thorold Rogers by also suggesting remedies to present social ills, as can be seen in one of his later works, *Equality* (1931). Whilst his works were at once studies in economics, history and philosophy, they were bound together by a strong social awareness. If not social histories in the conventional sense, his books did convey a strong appreciation of the wealth and privilege that was holding society together, and of what the author believed might replace it: Christian socialism. Moreover, in terms of period, Tawney's interest in the early modern years reflected what was at that point (and for many years afterwards) an obsession among historians with the concept of the several centuries pre-1750 as the anvil upon which modern capitalist society was forged.[47]

Despite the stinging criticisms of social history flowing from the pen of J.H. Clapham, the more literary (and socialistic) approach to the past, as conceived by the Webbs and the Hammonds, continued to attract many luminaries. G.D.H. Cole was one such writer. Cole was an important thinker in Labour circles, along with his colleagues, Tawney and Harold Laski, the three half-mockingly referred to as the 'red professors'. Cole, like the Webbs and Hammonds, was also part of a husband and wife team, with his partner, Margaret Cole.[48]

The insistence among social historians such as these that the present gave history its relevance can be seen in the way the writing, though clearly historically located, nevertheless reached into the present to offer its assessments. Cole was the most prominent labour historian of his day, and was helping to maintain a thread of interest in the working class that ran from Toynbee and the Webbs to E.P. Thompson, Eric Hobsbawm and beyond. In *The Common People*, the authors questioned the material circumstances of the working class. Their tone was not apocalyptic, but they had a message for present politicians. Despite all improvements of the twentieth century, they were still able to characterise 'two nations' standing against each other after the Second World War. The contrast was not, they admitted, as stark as it had been 100 years before. Moreover, they saw a beacon of hope in the first majority Labour government, returned in 1945. Cole and Postgate conclude this edition of their book in a powerful and political way that would have infuriated Clapham:

> Full employment, high direct taxation of large incomes, subsidising of basic foods and improved social services were narrowing very greatly the immense gulf between the actual standards of living of the rich and the poor; and under the new Labour Government were to continue to do so, until about 1949 or 1951 at least. But there has been no equivalent change in the distribution of property.[49]

This reads almost like a party manifesto. And its central message was clear. Because governments had not radically addressed that most vital source of privilege and property, arguing: 'the great majority of those who died still had almost nothing to leave to their successors'.[50]

British scholarship waited nearly seventy years for a social history following the work of J.R. Green in the 1870s. The author of this new work was George Trevelyan, who in 1941 published *English Social History*. Here the author articulated a view of history, which posited a direct challenge to Victorians such as E.A. Freeman who saw history as 'past politics'. In deliberate contrast, for Trevelyan 'social history might be defined negatively as the history of a people with the politics left out'.[51] He was certainly committed to the correct ordering of explanation in history. To him, the explanatory logic ran thus: 'Politics are the outcome rather than the cause of social change.'[52] Trevelyan's conception of history, however, was very different from Cole and Postgate's. It was a history with the politics left out; but it was also, to some degree, apolitical in style. It lacked the genuflection to Marx and ignored the darker aspects of the past. Trevelyan did not formulate a history with class struggle as a central plank. His 'social' was really 'cultural'. He wrote of the Industrial Revolution as a series of inventions, and his interests in art, books and drama fill up many pages. His reading of social conditions, and particular standards of living, owed more to John Clapham than to the Webbs and the Hammonds. Yet, Trevelyan, writing at a time when economic history was growing apace as a distinctive sub-discipline, was aware of the connection between the 'social' and the 'economic'. His introduction to *English Social History* also displays an appreciation of the parallel existence, at any given time, of continuity and change. Trevelyan recognised that both 'old' and 'new' elements of society needed to be appreciated. 'Sometimes, in forming a mental picture of a period in the past', Trevelyan argued, 'people seize hold of the new feature and forget the overlap with the old'.[53] For example, Trevelyan continued: 'students of history are often so much obsessed by the notorious political event of the Peterloo Massacre that they often imagine the Lancashire factory hand as the typical wage-earner of the year 1819; but he was not; he was only a local type, the newest type, the type of the future.'[54] This draws our attention to the importance of both continuity and change in historical explanation.

▶ 1945 and after

Much of what has occurred in the historiography of social history since 1945 we will seek to examine in much greater depth in later chapters. Here, we simply offer a sketch of some major routes, convergences and divergences. There can be no doubting that historical enquiry both expanded in scope, and yet became ultimately more fragmentary, as the discipline gained adherents in universities, which in their increasing numbers of professional historians, became sites of scholarship in a way unimaginable in the nineteenth century. 'By 1972', we are reminded, 'economic and social history had replaced biography and religious history as the largest categories after political history in the very conventional *Revue historique* [a leading French journal]'.[55]

Terms such as 'new economic history', 'new social history', 'cultural history' (and then 'new cultural history') demonstrate something of the range of historical research. Yet, the cogency of these different sub-spheres of activity is attested by the quality of research, the methodological innovation, and the theoretical adeptness produce by some of the key practitioners. Equally, once we begin to examine the sub-disciplines closest to our umbrella concept 'social history', we begin to realise that perhaps each instance is not so much sheared off the body of historiography as interconnected through a latticework of shared philosophical concerns, even if methods and sources might contrast considerably. To give a very recent example: Keith Wrightson's path-breaking analytical synthesis of early modern economic life sets him very clearly at the interface of the 'new social history' (of which he is a key proponent) and economic history.[56] Wrightson's 'social' concern is acute, drawing in vast array of personal testimony in order to capture the way *real* people felt about their economic lives; yet, at the same time, his is an economic history sensitive to the importance of determining streams of continuity and change within past societies.[57] The 'new social history' maintained a sharp analysis of social categories and social change, but with a focus upon key continuities, and less stress upon Marxist principles. Arriving at Wrightson's sort of social history – and indeed developing his kind of readable, not overly mathematical economic history – requires an appreciation of the various schools of endeavour from which this latest generation of historians has been able to draw from.

If we remember Unwin's admittedly somewhat determinist point about the essential importance of economic factors in the past, it will come as no surprise that, for the later period, it is impossible to separate the 'social' and the 'economic' forms of history. The key journal in economic history, *Economic History Review*, carries the subtitle, *A Journal of Social and Economic History*, just as the core journal of the new Marxist social history, established in 1952, with the title *Past and Present*, inflated the importance of theoretical (in this case Marxist) history by its own subtitle (later dropped): *A Journal of Scientific History*. This suggestion that, on the one hand, economic historians were (indeed are) concerned with the 'social' aspects of the past, is bolstered by the claim made by the Marxist founders of *Past and Present*, that social history, with its core theoretical underpinnings, was scientific. If history's scientificity was merely measured by the mathematical modelling of reliable statistical data (i.e. facts), then economic history might itself lay claim to the subtitle ring-fenced by *Past and Present*. If by science, however, we mean the discovery of laws to explain and predict patterns of occurrences (e.g. historical change), then it would be the inheritors of nineteenth-century positivists such as Marx (who claimed that his theories were scientific). However, just as science and scientificity cannot be bound by a single definition, neither can the line between social and economic histories be drawn with incontrovertible surety. This blurring, the multifacetedness, has been a feature of the broad areas of economic, social and cultural history in the past half-century: this despite Perkin's tentative views of the early 1960s with which we opened this chapter.

Class, gender and 'History from Below'

E.P. Thompson's *Making of the English Working Class* is usually viewed as a turning point in British social history, but the impact of the book, and the ideas contained within it, reverberated far beyond these shores and touched other areas of scholarship. Thompson was also influential in the Society for the Study of Labour History, which was formed in the early 1960s and provided a meeting point for a variety of scholars and activists whose conception of social history leant heavily upon the Labour movement in its broadest sense, focused on working-class life, and showed a keen interest in the political and economic struggles of trades unions.[58] The importance of Thompson's work ran beyond the excellence of *The Making* itself. Even critics marvelled at its erudition and range. Thompson brought together a new culturalist approach to class, in which **economic determinism** – so long an epithet levelled at Marxists – was not allowed to get in the way of the idea that ordinary men (particularly men) were active in the creation of their own identities and politics. This preferencing of cultural over economics announced a new approach to social history that will be examined in Chapter five. For now, it is important to flag the importance of what Thompson had done: in *The Making*, he had offered a sustained treatment of **'history from below'**.[59] Following George Rudé, whose work on crowds was vital, and alongside Hobsbawm, whose study of European social protest movements linked well with his work, Thompson set an agenda that put ordinary people at the centre of the stage.[60] Later, Thompson's work would influence writers on Indian nationalism, South American popular protest and a plethora of others.[61] He also impacted upon the work of **Marxist-humanist** scholars in America, notably Eugene Genovese, who wrote on slavery, and Herbert Gutman, and his followers, whose concern was with industrial workers and American capitalism.[62] An array of Marxist social historians was thus influenced by the work of the British Marxists, and a broader tradition of social historians. Gutman was in no doubt as to how these authors changed labour history: 'In Great Britain', he wrote, 'the guideposts fixed by Sidney and Beattrice Webb have been shattered by labour and social historians such as Asa Briggs, Eric Hobsbawm, Henry Pelling, Sidney Pollard, George Rudé, Brian, J.F.C. and Royden Harrison, among other scholars who have posed new questions, used new methods, and dug deeply into largely neglected primary materials'.[63]

The 1960s also saw an intersection of social and gender history. The context for the flowering of interest in women's history is provided by the political struggles of the women's movement in this period, when, as with labour history, contemporary issues and struggles prompted a reconsideration of the necessary historical context for such dramas. The revolution in understanding of working-class *males*, which accompanied the works of the British Marxists, had not been matched by a growth in concern about the larger part of that class, *women*. Building upon a tradition of women's history dating to Ivy Pinchbeck's classic work,[64] women historians of the 1960s and early 1970s began to sketch out the big issues, which would help to frame increasing numbers of detailed studies in the following years.

That women were also coming to the fore in the work of family historians, and historical demographers, provided additional impetus. But the key aim was to ensure that women were not treated as partial two-dimensional domestic objects, as could happen when household and motherhood were emphasised at the expense of other elements of women's lives.[65] Scholars of this pioneering generation strove to put the gender into history – that is, to understand the power relationships between the sexes that placed women in an inferior social position. Labour history and gender fused somewhat in the 1970s in the History Workshop (a project with a journal of the same name, dedicated to socialist and feminist perspectives). The output of these historians included many important collections of essays, as well as the articles and discussion pieces included in the journal, which was founded to support the group's work.

Equally, power relations, taboos and social ostracism were also being explored in the later 1960s and early 1970s, with the subject of witchcraft as especially important. Led by pioneers such as Alan Macfarlane a large literature has now developed on the witch craze of the seventeenth century, focusing on the county of Essex, in particular, for which records are particularly rich. From such studies we learn about the victimisation of particular types of women, with accusations of witchcraft usually levelled by those with a grievance against particular types of women.[66]

Thus we can see that, from the 1960s, social history was hardly monolithic or singular. Its range and breadth, whilst a strong point, is also potentially its Achilles' heel, because it defies more than a federation of philosophies and methods, and thus is unlike economic history.

Social history and 'the New Economic History'

The 1960s were also noteworthy for a further fracturing of social and economic history, not least with the advent of the 'new economic history', sometimes called 'econometrics' or (in rather self-regarding style) 'cliometrics'.[67] An interest in quantification was in part a reflection of what technology would allow: although computers were more cumbersome in the 1960s than now, they were available. Moreover, we can see in cliometrics the rejection by many American social and particularly economic historians of the influence of British and French social historians and of Marxism. Quantifying evidence appealed on numerous levels to American scholars whose society rejected European ideas, particularly communism and the association of social conflict with social class. It has also been argued thus: 'quantification holds great appeal for many historians working in the American pragmatic tradition because of its resemblance to the **empiricism** of nineteenth-century science'.[68] Whilst American social history developed its own dynamic with regard to attempts to quantify social performance among groups in American society, this approach to the past was part of a much larger debate about historical techniques, which at first, drew its keenest acolytes among economic, not social historians.

The reduction of economic history to 'a search for understanding of the nature of economic activity in the past',[69] reached its driest end point in the 1960s with the work of R.W. Fogel. Fogel's study of the importance of railroads in nineteenth-century America considered that such forms of transport had a much less dramatic impact upon economic growth than previous economic historians such as

Schumpeter and W.W. Rostow had imagined.[70] Fogel raised the issue of **counter-factual analysis** – that is, the use of a method that seeks to establish what might have happened if certain variables had been different or absent: what might have happened to economies if, for example, railroads had never been built. Fogel's answer was that canals, waterways and roads would have coped with much of the traffic, to the extent that the economy would not have been affected to more than the tune of about 6 per cent in total. Fogel teamed up with Stanley Engerman to apply similar techniques to America's 'peculiar institution', slavery.[71] Driven by an overwhelming confidence in the ability of cliometric techniques to command and analyse greater bodies of data than ever before, slavery became a laboratory for the latest scientific techniques in the discipline. Engerman and Fogel believed they could show that slavery was rational because it was economically viable. They also suggested conditions for slaves were no worse than for free white workers. Despite their faith in this new science, Engerman and Fogel's experiment was taken apart by a group of historians who devoted an entire volume to demolishing their study, *Time on the Cross*.[72]

Population, demography and the family

The growing interest in social history in recent decades has meant the opening up of new fields of enquiry. One of the most important of these, historical demography or the study of past populations, in some ways captures the division between economic-type and social-type approaches to the past. Historians, like social theorists, have long appreciated the importance of population, but as a determinant and a result of social change. In this regard, historical demography shares an interest with nineteenth-century figures such as Thomas Malthus and Friedrich Engels. While Malthus was most concerned with the possibly calamitous effects of unchecked population growth, Engels was interested in the vitality of population issues to the course of human history.[73] He wrote:

> According to the materialist conception, the determining factor in history is, in the last resort, the production and reproduction of immediate life. But this itself is again a twofold character. On the one hand, the production of the means of subsistence; … on the other, the production of human beings themselves, the propagation of the species.[74]

The rapid rise of populations in Europe and North America since the eighteenth century has correctly fascinated historians, drawing them towards an assessment of the trajectory of those populations with the unrealised fears of Malthus and the exhortations of Engels ringing in their ears. Population history, moreover, offers us a keen insight into the merging and the separation of disciplines. Historical geographers, sociologists, social historians, economic historians, biologists, anthropologists and many others have helped to make the study of past population a major area of academic enquiry.[75] Much of the most important work has been associated with the Cambridge Group for the History of Population and Social Structure (founded in 1962).[76] The work of the founders focused on the influence upon populations of birth and mortality rates, and the age at which people married. Moving away from perspectives that stressed medical intervention and invention as crucial to the growth of population, these historians have demonstrated conclusively that age of marriage – with its affect upon fertility rates – is the crucial variable governing population growth in the period since the eighteenth century. Whilst the Cambridge group has by and large been interested in long-run changes in the size and structure of population, their work has had an enormous impact upon social history. By reconstituting family and parish histories over long periods of time – that is, by using all available demographic data to measure as much as is possible of past populations over significant historical time – these historical demographers have much increased our understanding of the past and have, in turn, enhanced our ability to study social relations, family life and economic history.[77] In Britain the pioneering work, which captured broad streams of approaches to the family, social structure and historical change was that of Peter Laslett, whose famous book inspired a generation of scholars working in the field of social history.[78]

The long-run statistical analysis of population patterns was part of a much wider appreciation of the social history of past societies. Whilst demographers were using official sources to generate statistics to look at population change over time, others were beginning to work in related fields, such as the history of the family. Families and households are, of course, vital components of populations that are viewed at the local, parish or community, level; and this prompted historians to consider further subdivisions in the history, such as childhood, old age and death. Pioneers such as the amateur French social historian, Philippe Ariès, argued that a sense of childhood did not exist in the Middle Ages, and that children went from infants to miniature adults at the age of seven or thereabouts.[79]

Lawrence Stone also pioneered new approaches to the history of such subjects, and tried to change the way we looked at the family in particular. His study of wealthy families in the early modern period, using their household and personal records, received critical acclaim in some fields, vitriolic attacks in others.[80] Stone's book has been attacked for its Whiggish charting of the development of the modern family. Stone detected in his sources a shift in families' values from deferential and patriarchal medieval attitudes to the 'affective individualism' – relations based on love and affection for close family – encouraged by modern social and economic relations. Stone also argued for the flourishing of patriarchal nuclear forms of the family in the early modern period, as extended family links and communal ties were said to have been replaced by increasing genuflection to the nation, monarch and Church. Stone contended that, from the mid-seventeenth century, there emerged a 'closed domesticated nuclear' family, which eventually came to be dominant in the eighteenth century. Both Ariès and Stone used the 'sentiments' (non-statistical, non-quantitative) approach to family and social roles to challenge demographers, though Stone's stress upon the dominance of the nuclear family has been refuted by subsequent research. Impersonal relations may have become more important in modern societies, but links to extended families remained important.

Urban and social histories

The linkage between studies such as Stone's on the family or Wrigley and Schofield's on population is forged by their attempts to bring a broader aspect of past society into our view-finder; to help us know more about things and in different ways. Both types of work, though quite different, are structured by the idea of historical change impacting upon people, and by a need to know the dynamic of past society in terms of continuity and change – a theme common enough in historical writings. A link is also apparent in that each of these approaches privileges particular aspects of past society over others. Again, it is not at all uncommon for the economic historian to prefer the economic explanation, or for the political historian to stress political elements, and so on. What historical demographers and family historians did, however, was to open up new areas of enquiry. This is a case of historians doing what Asa Briggs, another notable social historian, exhorted them to do: 'examine in detail social structure and change in the most meaningful units'.[81]

Briggs was concerned with urban history – an urban history that Marwick asserts was made possible by developments in historical demography.[82] It is certainly true that the new-found interest in demographic data (as well as the computing revolution which enabled the data to be analysed more quickly), prevalent in both social and economic history, spurred on those interested in charting human experience in the towns and cities of the Industrial Revolution. This is not to say that a concern with the urban world was entirely a post-1960s invention, or that it occurred in isolation in Britain. In fact, the most important historical studies of urban history were initially conducted by sociologists of the 'Chicago School' from the early twentieth century, with their interests in setting the social problems of urban America set into historical context. They drew upon the works of the German sociologist, Georg Simmel.[83] This approach ran in confluence with the growing number of studies of immigrants in American society. Stressing at first the differences between rural peasant life in Poland and urban life in America, the massive works of sociologists William I. Thomas and Florian Znaniecki became hugely influential on later social historians and historical sociologists, not least Oscar Handlin, whose histories of immigrants in Boston, and then of the Irish in Boston, continued to stress the destabilising social and psychological effects of migration upon rural Europeans.[84] Yet, the idea that migration between rural to urban environments led to social dislocation and pathological behaviour has been corrected by more recent studies, which suggest continuities in social and human interaction despite migration. This work dovetailed with pioneering studies of social mobility in America, conducted by Stephan Thernstrom. The results, which focused on Massachusetts, exploded myths about equality of opportunity in America, demonstrating that mobility rates were far lower than imagined.[85]

Some of these concerns in social history, first developed in the United States, were introduced to Britain by pioneer urban historians, who began to examine the urban environment as a proper site for understanding the structures of society and their impacts upon social organisation and human life. The area of urban history even generated its own journal, *Urban History*, and it continues to be an area of innovation in the wider areas of social and economic history.[86] Historical sociologists, such as Michael Anderson and Lynn Hollen Lees, utilised historical demography to great effect in their nineteenth-century urban histories. Anderson for Preston, and the study of industrial growth, migration and kinship;[87] Lees, for a more sociological account of the formation of sub-communities by migrants.[88] Lees particularly used perspectives on urban and migration studies developed by scholars in her native United States, to generate a holistic model of social change. Focusing upon Victorian London, and particularly the Irish migrant community there, she deployed statistical material generated from decennial censuses to frame wider social questions, and to support the analysis of political and socio-cultural dimensions of past society.

'New Social History'

What is sometimes called the 'new social history' comes closer to cultural history than any previous form of social history. Less prescribed by Marxist ideology than earlier forms of post-war social history, though far from abandoning the organising principles of theory – Marxist or otherwise – new social historians borrow from E.P. Thompson's rich cultural reading, the more *Annaliste* conventions of Keith Thomas, as well from the important *Annales* cultural historians themselves. New social history stresses much more the mental frameworks and collective psychological impacts of human life in the past.[89] One of the great markers in British cultural history, Thomas's *Religion and the Decline of Magic* (buttressed by several of his other works), charted the progress from the less rational mindset of humans in which magic was believed in to the more ordered, apparently more structured, world where religions shaped central beliefs with codified collective **mentalities**. The stress upon the idea that human society 'progressed' from primitive to modern states of mind – from magic through religion to secular rationalism – has caused consternation among those who promulgate the past on its own terms, but this does not down-play the enormous erudition and complexity of books such as Thomas's, and the important leap forward he pioneered with this hybridisation of cultural and social histories.

The 'new social history' has produced works that are recognisably drawn from traditional approaches to social history, despite moving the field forward in terms of methodology, approach and explanatory stress. One of the foremost historians in this area, Keith Wrightson, captures the nature of society, and, by extension, the things of interest to social historians, brilliantly:

> Society is a process. It is never static. Even its most apparently stable structures are the expression of an equilibrium between dynamic forces. For the social historian the most challenging of tasks is that of recapturing that process, while at the same time discerning long-term shifts in social organisation, in social relations and in the meanings and evaluations with which social relationships are infused.[90]

Wrightson's study of seventeenth-century society is true to this conceptualisation, seeking to demonstrate the things in society which change and those that are sub-ject to continuity. By a close reading of personal testimony from around the coun-try, Wrightson is able to demonstrate the way in which social and economic change lay across the country like a patchwork quilt: uneven and varied from place-to-place. 'The impact of social change ... presents itself to the historian as a series of localized social dramas', Wrightson argued. And he went on:

> In the levelling of an enclosure or the staying of a load of grain, the prosecution of a witch, the conflict attending the putting down of a popular festival or the sup-pression of alehouses, we find revealed the tensions generated by the economic, administrative and cultural developments of the day. Such incidents, redolent of underlying processes of change, provide our surest indication of the gradual process of social transformation.[91]

It is noticeable that Wrightson views elements of conflict, or possible conflict, as those incidents and processes that measure or promote change. Yet, the sense of this dynamic is delivered in a way that is very different from the earlier generation of Marxist social historians, such as Thompson. Moreover, Wrightson's stress upon the local dynamic goes against Thompson, to some degree, and offers readings that might be used by critics of Marxist interpretations of class struggle in the period of Industrial Revolution. In an important essay examining the geographical dimen-sions of the Industrial Revolution, Jack Langton argued against Thompson, and others who formulated historical analysis in terms of class, preferring to see mod-ern society maintaining and strengthening local bonds and customs through migration to and fro, rather than imagining the creation of a monolithic working class, characterised by its homogeneity across regions and cultures.[92] The reality is that Thompson's stress on class and Langton's suggestion of the diehard nature of localism come together in Wrightson's argument for a creative balance between the old and the new on numerous levels of society, and across historical time.

'The New Cultural History'

The cultural history approach, as an outgrowth of Marxist-inspired social history, has led to an expansion of interests and periods of study. As with the *Annales* School, cultural historians have shown a greater interest in the social lives and behaviour patterns of ordinary people, laying less emphasis upon the class struggle dynamic which had featured in the Marxist medieval history of Rodney Hilton, or the studies of popular politics and belief in the seventeenth century by Christopher Hill. More recent works, which sit at the juncture of social and cultural history, stresses such important, though perhaps less politically radical subject matter such as eating habits and consumption patterns. Even where cultural historians stress factors which might contribute to political activity, such as the now huge area of reading culture, the stress is more upon language, communication and shared mental frameworks, and vividness of daily culture, rather than upon the move towards the next revolutionary protest.[93] In the sense that it was once driven by Marxist concerns to evaluate the narratives of political protest, social history has certainly changed considerably – to the point, in fact, where it sees much of its analytical meaning invested in cultural history.

► **Conclusion**

This sketch of numerous social history traditions is far from exhaustive. A number of the themes will be revisited in later chapters, and, where relevant, this has been indicated in the text. The chapter aimed to demonstrate how social history changed over time, growing out of social concerns about the Industrial Revolution, developing alongside (and sometimes in conflict with) economic history. Certain strains of continuity were also suggested: the interest in institutional aspects of labour – first propagated by those with a vested interest in such an approach (e.g. the Webbs) – was one such example. The way in which social history did, and does, bleed into other area, such as economic history, and, later, cultural history, should be apparent. The role which theory played should be clear insofar as historians deployed it. It must be remembered, however, that not every social historian is an historical sociologists, let alone a sociologist. British and American social history traditions have not been anything like as theoretically driven as those of, for example, German. In some respects, therefore, this has been a pragmatic overview of some of the authors who were social historians, or who deployed the term 'social', however untheoretically.

There does remain something of a shortfall in the provision of adequate definitions of social history. When pressed, historians tend to list things that might be included in a social history; while none who claimed to be a social historian would deny that the quest for the 'social', or the application of 'social' to our understanding of past 'society', was important. There is, however, a still conscious reference to canonical works when making such definitions. A major social history of Britain – the three-volume collection, edited by F.M.L. Thompson – contained a preface, which was diffident in the extreme when nodding to Trevelyan's dictum about history with the politics left out.[94] In one review, Dorothy Thompson criticised this collection for missing things out (notably lots about Britain in the broader [i.e. non-English] sense, and for lacking the theoretical shape that might be expected of what was supposed to be a major treatment of social history). She wrote: 'In these volumes we are back to Trevelyan – history with the politics left out – but with none of the master's breadth of knowledge and understanding ... behind it.' [95]

In the past 20 years, despite the rather conservative image displayed in the introduction to F.M.L. Thompson's *Cambridge Social History*, if not in the contributors' essays, social history has continued to develop in exciting ways. Class and gender still represent important elements of social history, though much of their ground has become occupied by **poststructuralist** interpretations from those interested in the **linguistic turn** and **postmodernist** perspectives. Moreover, since the 1970s, with the growing influence of the *Annales* School, and the expanding concern of historians with non-Marxist (sometimes anti-Marxist) perspectives on popular culture, social history has passed through 'new Social history' to become, in some fields, cultural history. The importance of these more recent movements is discussed in the following chapters, beginning with historical sociology.

2 Fruit of a 'special relationship'? Historical Sociology

▶ Introduction

At the heart of any discussion of the development of social history as a discreet field of enquiry must be an appreciation of the intersection of two disciplines: history and sociology. The marriage of the two has not always been easy and is of relatively recent vintage. No one today would question the mutual benefits of history and sociology operating in concert: but it was not always the case. The early rumours of a dalliance between the subjects gained credibility in the immediate post-war years. Richard Hofstadter, writing in 1956, emphasised the potential of such a union, even if he did not name the disciplines directly:

> The next generation may see the development of a somewhat new historical genre, which will be a mixture of traditional history and the social sciences. It will differ from the narrative history of the past in that its primary purpose will be analytical ... It will be informed by the insights of the social sciences and at some points will make use of methods they have originated.[1]

Hofstadter felt that, although the methods of the social sciences may be useful, the real value of such an enterprise would be that it prompted historians to ask new questions, and consider new problems. To a large extent, he has been proved right in his assertions, and a wave of historical works informed by the insights of the social sciences did follow. By the 1970s, a growing convergence between the two disciplines was apparent. As the historian Gareth Stedman Jones wrote in 1976:

> During the last fifteen years, the relationship between history and sociology, at least at a formal level, has been closer than at any time in the past. Not only have there been frequent discussions about the desirability of breaking down boundaries between the two subjects, but, at a practical level, a tendency towards convergence has been encouraged ...[2]

As Jones says, although there were still one or two conservative voices raised in objection, the consensus by this time was that it was 'desirable that history and sociology should achieve some painless form of symbiosis'.[3]

On the other side of the disciplinary divide, social scientists increasingly identified their own practice with that of history. One of the most prominent British sociologists, Anthony Giddens, went so far as to say: 'What history is, or should be, cannot be analysed in separation from what the social sciences are, or should be ... There simply are no logical or even methodological distinctions between the social sciences and history – appropriately conceived.'[4] Although the pioneers of social theory, such as Auguste Comte (1798–1857) and Herbert Spencer (1870–1903), were critical of the way that history was currently being practised, history and sociology, in particular, have always enjoyed a 'special relationship'. Marx, Durkheim and Weber, the founding fathers of sociology, were all concerned with historical problems and themes. Marx made frequent use of historical examples in his writing.[5] Durkheim had studied and written history, and he made it the policy of his journal, the *Année Sociologique*, to review history books, as long as they provided more than a mere narrative of events. Weber's historical knowledge was extensive. He never abandoned the study of the past and, although classed as a sociologist during his lifetime, he saw himself as a political economist or a comparative historian.[6] In Chapter 1, we saw something of how the relationship between history and sociology became such an area of controversy. In the present discussion, we will bring this story into the twentieth century, focusing particularly upon the interplay between sociology and history and the relationship between past and present in human knowledge.

▶ The temporary separation of history and sociology

The interest of Marx, Durkheim and Weber in historical questions was continued by subsequent sociologists and anthropologists. Then, around 1920, anthropologists (beginning with Franz Boas and Bronislaw Malinowski) and sociologists broke with the past. They started to carry out fieldwork in contemporary tribal societies or the city. This was the birth of **empirical** sociology.[7] This cultivation of the present at the expense of the past was due to a number of factors, not least the professionalisation of sociology as a discipline. As well as this, though, it must be pointed out that sociology in the first half of the twentieth century was largely dominated by work done in America. The first sociology department in the United States was formed at the University of Chicago in 1892.[8] The **Chicago School**, as shaped by Robert Park and his colleagues, was important in developing empirical field studies of urban society. The particular social problems of the United States, caught up in rapid industrial and urban growth, led to a concentration on social reform and maintaining order. The various members of the Chicago School produced studies such as: *The Hobo* (1923), *The Gang* (1927), *The Ghetto* (1928) and *The Gold Coast and Slum* (1929). These are valuable descriptions of urban life, but lacking in any real theoretical framework.[9]

Britain was slower to develop academic sociology and, although the Sociological Society was formed in 1903 by a variety of individuals with an interest in the discipline, the first sociology department was not opened until 1907 at the London School of Economics.[10] In his work on the history of British **empirical** sociology, Raymond A. Kent traces the origins of empirical sociology in this country back to the nineteenth-century concern with the condition of the working classes. This can be seen in the work of Frederick Engels, Henry Mayhew and Charles Booth and was continued into the twentieth century by Sidney and Beatrice Webb. Although only the latter two would have seen themselves as 'sociologists', Kent argues that they are all pioneers of empirical sociology.[11] We could argue about whether the studies produced by these authors should be categorised as 'sociology', but there was certainly a significant tradition of social investigation in this country that has fed into sociological research. The focus of this research has been on the living and working conditions of the contemporary urban poor. So the new empirical sociology, both in Britain and America, was very much a product of the social situations in which it was produced, which led many sociologists to become increasingly concerned with the present.

This is not to say that sociologists lost all interest in historical questions. One of the most notable examples of an attempt to combine history and sociology before 1945 came from the German scholar Norbert Elias. Elias's work has only recently been given the recognition it deserves. His major work was first published in German in 1939, and was largely neglected for decades. In addition, none of Elias's major works was available in English translation until the late 1970s.[12] As he was Jewish, his situation became untenable after Hitler came to power in 1933, and he went into exile. However, before he left Germany, he completed his thesis, which was not published until 36 years later as *The Court Society*.[13] This work begins with an interesting, and little-known, discussion of the relationship between history and sociology which, although it may seem somewhat dated to modern readers, touches on many of the issues, which were to subsequently dominate the debate. Elias wrote:

> The self-image of some historians makes it appear as if they are concerned in their work exclusively with individuals without **figurations**, with people wholly independent of others. The self-image of many sociologists makes it appear as if they are concerned exclusively with figurations without individuals, societies or 'systems' wholly independent of individual people. As we have seen, both approaches, and

the self-images underlying them, lead their practitioners astray. On closer examination we find that both disciplines are merely directing their attention to different
strata or levels of one and the same historical process.[14]

He goes on to say that he wants to see the creation of a unified theoretical framework, which will enable greater collaboration between the two disciplines. Elias is
now seen as a significant sociological thinker, as well as one who went to great pains
to combine 'theory' and 'research'.[15] He was also one of the first twentieth-century
sociologists to recognise the potential of historical sociology.

However, Elias's vision of a closer relationship between history and sociology was
not destined to be fulfilled for some years. Although historians and social theorists
never lost touch with the other completely during the twentieth century, there were
few examples of work that combined both until the late 1950s. As Dennis Smith
says, the first long wave of historical sociology, which began in the mid-eighteenth
century in Britain and France, and included in the work of the three 'founding
fathers' of sociology, crashed against the harsh realities of the dictatorships of the
Left and the Right.[16] The difficulties Norbert Elias encountered provide a graphic
illustration of the problems faced by individual scholars as a result of political
upheaval and war. Others, such as the distinguished *Annales* historian Marc Bloch,
did not survive the Second World War. By the end of the war there had been a partial
eclipse of historical sociology in America. Even though some individual scholars,
such as Robert Bellah, Reinhard Bendix, and Seymour Martin Lipset, continued the
historical tradition of the founders, the most prominent sociologists had broken
with the tradition.[17] It was against this background that C. Wright Mills wrote his
critique of current trends in American sociology: *The Sociological Imagination* (1959).

Mills identified three tendencies in 1950s American sociology. The first was historical, as exemplified in the work of Comte, Marx, Spencer and Weber. The second
was towards a systematic theory of 'the nature of man and society', or 'grand theory', as exemplified in the work of the **functionalist** sociologist, Talcott Parsons.
The third tendency was towards **empirical** studies of contemporary society.[18]
Talcott Parsons (1902–79) was the dominant figure in American sociology at the
time and his major concern was with how social order was maintained in
conditions of **modernity**. Along with Robert K. Merton, Parsons is credited with
bringing functionalism back into sociology. This is a concept that he took over from
Durkheim, which basically holds that any social practice that endures can be
explained in terms of the function it performs in maintaining a society. Parsons
sought to join functional analysis with action theory, a theory that emphasises the
intentional behaviour of individuals, and stems from the work of Weber. Parsons
himself is usually described as a structural functionalist. Mills directed his attack
against Parsons' *The Social System* (1951). In this work Parsons is concerned with
developing ways of categorising the social system as a whole. His argument is

highly complex, but is well summarised by Mills: 'We are asked: How is social order possible? The answer we are given seems to be: commonly accepted values.'[19] Such values, Parsons wrote, means 'the actors have common "sentiments" in support of the value patterns, which may be defined as meaning that conformity with the relevant expectations is treated as a "good thing" relatively independent of any specific instrumental "advantage" to be gained from such conformity'.[20]

Mills makes some very telling criticisms of Parsons (not least about his wordiness!) As he says, the model that Parsons develops does not seem to allow for dissent, conflict, coercion or the possibility of social change. His most significant criticism, though, is of Parsons' lack of contact with any specific **empirical** realities: 'The basic cause of grand theory is the initial choice of a level of thinking so general that its practitioners cannot logically get down to observation. They never, as grand theorists, get down from the higher generalities to problems in their historical and structural contexts.'[21] Mills is equally critical of abstracted empiricism for its accumulation of irrelevant detail, and its lack of theory.[22] This highlights the basic requirement of any social science identified in the work of the Enlightenment thinkers. Any version of historical sociology, or indeed any theory of society, must be based on both theory and observation. Mills calls for a reconnection of sociology with history, as 'All sociology worthy of the name is "historical sociology".'[23] Thus, for Mills, social science should deal with the relationship between biography, history and social structures. As we will see, in the years following the publication of his appeal, some historians and sociologists were to create a historical sociology that did take this prescription seriously.[24]

▶ Differing reactions to the growing convergence of history and sociology

As we will see, there is much disagreement amongst both historians and sociologists as to what the relationship between history and sociology actually is. While some welcome the coming together or 'convergence' of the two disciplines, others seek to keep them apart. There is also a continuing problem about how to categorise some of the work that has resulted from the combining of history and the social sciences. Should we think of it as 'historical sociology', 'sociological history' or 'scientific history'? In practice, it could be that the label we attach to this type of work may largely be the result of whether it is carried out in a department of 'history' or 'sociology', or even within another related discipline. One of the positive aspects of such difficulties is that it forces us to think afresh about what history is, how it should be practised, and whether some of the disciplinary boundaries we consider as 'natural' or 'fixed' are, in fact, artificial. In what ways can we combine history and sociology, though? What would (or should) 'historical sociology' look like?

Many history students tend to think that if we make history more 'scientific' or more 'sociological' then it must involve a greater degree of quantification. However, such an idea is based on a misguided notion of what sociology actually is, and the conception that, because it is a social science, it must employ a great deal of statistical data. In fact, the discipline is split between quantitative and qualitative sociologists, just as there are historians who employ traditional research methods, and those who employ quantitative methods. So if there is no hard and fast methodological divide between the two disciplines, what exactly is the difference between history and sociology?

Peter Burke provides a good starting point for a discussion of the relationship between history and sociology. 'Sociology may be defined as the study of human society, with an emphasis on generalizations about its structure and development. History is better defined as the study of human societies, with the emphasis on the differences between them and also on the changes which have taken place in each one over time.'[25] Instead of seeing the two disciplines as contradicting one another, Burke defended their complementarity, arguing: 'It is only by comparing it with others that we can discover in what respects a given society is unique. Change is structured, and structures change.'[26]

The most basic form of this disciplinary divide characterises historians as storytellers and sociologists as model builders. While history is concerned with the past, sociology is concerned with the present. History is seen as simply the investigation of past events through scholarly methods, while sociology is concerned with the construction of theory. However, we need to question whether there is such a straightforward division of labour between the two disciplines. There is a tension between narrative (storytelling) and structuring (explanation) in history that denies such a clear division of tasks. The traditional conception of the two disciplines has held that history should be concerned with events (i.e. with the particular) while sociology should be concerned with generalisation (i.e. theory). This was a distinction first made by Windelband in 1894. Thus history was seen as being **idiographic** (it sought to particularise) and sociology was characterised as **nomothetic** (it sought to generalise). The other distinction that is usually invoked in such discussions is that history is **diachronic** (it analyses change), while sociology is **synchronic** (it analyses societies in a static state). However, many scholars have questioned the validity of all these 'traditional' distinctions.

There have been a variety of responses by scholars to the notion of a closer relationship between history and sociology. The historian G.R. Elton argued for the autonomy of history and warned historians against listening too carefully to those outside the discipline. Even though he conceded there are things to be learned from other disciplines, he remained tied to the traditional notion that history is idiographic, and argued that historians should not seek to offer anything other than the most limited generalisations.[27] Gareth Stedman Jones has objected to the uncritical borrowing of theoretical concepts by historians, while still arguing for a closer relationship between the two disciplines in the construction of a historical science.[28] Peter Burke, on the other hand, unreservedly welcomed the convergence of history and sociology, maintaining that, 'Without the combination of history and theory we are unlikely to understand the past or the present.'[29] The difference between the historian Peter Burke and the sociologist Philip Abrams is partly a result of their different disciplinary perspectives, and also their slightly differing views of the relationship between history and the social sciences. Burke is a strong supporter of the 'convergence' of the two disciplines. Philip Abrams, on the other hand, like Anthony Giddens, holds the view that there is no effective distinction between the two subjects. As Philip Abrams put it: 'In my understanding of history and sociology there can be no relationship between them because in terms of their fundamental preoccupations, history and sociology are and always have been the same thing.'[30]

His argument is that, despite the apparent differences between historians and sociologists, they are united by a common project: 'It is the problem of finding a way of accounting for human experience which recognizes simultaneously and in equal measure that history and society are made by constant, more or less, purposeful, individual action and that individual action, however purposeful, is made by history and society.' Historians and sociologists share common purpose and an interest in the same question: 'How do we as active subjects make a world of social objects which then, as it were, become subjects making us their objects?'[31]

This is what sociologists call the problem of structure and **agency** or, more simply, the relationship between the individual and society, which will be considered at length in Chapter 4. According to Abrams, the central concern of historical sociology is to explain the relationship of social action and social structure as a genuinely two-sided phenomenon.[32] However, not all sociologists share Abrams' view of the inseparability of the two disciplines. The eminent British sociologist, John H. Goldthorpe has argued: 'attempts, such as that of Abrams and Giddens, to present history and sociology as being one and indistinguishable should be strongly resisted'.[33] Goldthorpe felt that the idiographic-nomothetic distinction was a valid description of the difference in *emphasis* of the two disciplines.[34] Many historians would now see the whole debate about the relationship between history and sociology as being somewhat dated, as the influence of sociology on historians has increasingly been supplanted by that of anthropology, literary criticism and other 'cultural' approaches, a development we will be considering at length in Chapter 5. However, the symbiosis of history and sociology has created a valuable body of work, demonstrating not only the value of a close association between history and the social sciences, but also the difficulty of drawing firm distinctions between the two disciplines.

▶ Historical sociology

Theda Skocpol, herself an important historical sociologist, offers four suggestive definitions of what historical sociologists do. First, and fundamentally, 'they ask questions about social structures or processes understood to be concretely situated in time and space'. Secondly, 'they address processes over time, and take temporal sequences seriously in accounting for outcomes'. Thirdly, they attempt to 'attend to the interplay of meaningful actions and structural contexts'. Fourthly, they seek to 'highlight the *particular* and *varying* features of specific kinds of social structures and patterns of change'.[35] This is clearly useful starting point; but it is also rather vague. We are still left with two difficult questions. How should we see the relationship between the two disciplines? What type of works should be seen as belonging within the category 'historical sociology'? What does each discipline contribute to Skocpol's four-point schema?

It is quite easy to identify an 'agreed core' of scholars who belong to this category, and are almost invariably cited in a survey of this approach. Green and Troup, for example, identify S.N. Eisenstadt, Barrington Moore, W.W. Rostow, Immanuel Wallerstein, Perry Anderson, Reinhard Bendix, R.J. Holton, Theda Skocpol and Michael Mann as some of the major figures.[36] These are scholars whose major works operate at the macro level of historical explanation, or in the tradition of 'grand historical sociology'. Thus, they offer explanations of the movement from antiquity to feudalism, feudalism to capitalism, or entire 'world systems'. So, is it possible to identify some more specific features that these scholars have in common?

The founding fathers of sociology were concerned with explaining the transition from an agrarian to an industrial society. Skocpol points out that historical sociology continues to explore the nature and consequences of the capitalist and democratic revolutions in Europe while also addressing new problems and offering fresh answers. In practice, the influence of the founding fathers of sociology is to be felt in both the questions asked, and the theoretical perspectives employed by contemporary historical sociologists.[37] This does not mean that historical sociology *must* be confined within one of the traditions established by the three 'founding fathers'. There are other sociological traditions to draw from, and one of the most notable, the micro-interactionist tradition, is American in origin and does not stem directly from the work of Marx, Durkheim or Weber.[38] There is also no reason why scholars should not employ a variety of theoretical perspectives in an 'eclectic' approach. As Skocpol goes on to say, the complexities of contemporary society requires new theories and new interpretations.[39] If the term 'historical sociology' is to mean anything at all, it must either employ or develop some type of theoretical explanation. However, there are many varieties of theory, and it can operate at different levels of generalisation, thus raising questions over what should qualify as 'theory'. In addition, theory by itself is also inadequate. As we have seen, it is not enough to present an abstract model of society if it is not closely related to **empir-ical** material that will support it. On the other hand, a 'purely empirical' historical study (if such a thing is possible) would lack the conceptual element that would define it as sociological history. Historical sociology is also strongly identified with the comparative method. Does this mean that it *must* employ this technique in order to qualify for the label?

There is also the possibility that some scholars, from both sides of the disciplinary divide, could be nominated as 'honorary' historical sociologists, even though they may not see themselves as such. E.P. Thompson, for example, is an obvious candidate for such a nomination, as his work combines Marxist theory with a rich and detailed historical narrative. In fact, Thompson has been included in previous surveys of this genre.[40] What of other scholars whose work may appear much more remote from the 'agreed core' though? An example would be Ian Kershaw, celebrated as Britain's leading historian of the Third Reich, and one whose work has examined the social and political structures in Nazi Germany. Although he is the author of a major biography of Hitler, he has also sought to go beyond 'biographical concern with the details of Hitler's life'.[41] In his work he has sought to understand the appeal of the 'Hitler Myth' to the German people, and the impact of Hitler's rule on rationally ordered government. The insights offered by the work of Max Weber are central to this project.

> Though Max Weber was writing before Hitler appeared on the political scene, his concept of charismatic rule has implications for both the sources and the exercise of Hitler's power. It is valuable in comprehending the character of Hitler's power base within the Nazi Movement and the corrosive impact of that power when superimposed upon a contradictory form of domination – the legal, bureaucratic framework of the German state apparatus.[42]

Kershaw revisited the broader theme of society and the individual, with Hitler as his focal point, in a celebrated two-volume life of the Führer. In the introduction to this study, Kershaw sought to defend the notion that an historian could understand the interplay between human **agency** and social forces through the medium of biography. Like Giddens, whose **structuration** theory seeks to explain phenomena in terms of the balance between agency and structure, Kershaw seeks inspiration in Marx's famous dictum: 'men *do* make their own history, but ... under given and imposed conditions'.[43] At all times, and at each step, Kershaw is anxious to balance biographical details of Hitler with analysis of the Nazi regime. The challenge was clear enough to the author: to see if the chasm between **structuralist** and biographical approaches to the Third Reich could be overcome by 'a "structuralist" historian' who was 'coming to biography with a critical eye, looking instinctively, perhaps, in the first instance to downplay rather than to exaggerate the part played by the individual, however powerful, in the complex historical processes'.[44] Kershaw's work directly addresses the challenge of setting a biography in social context, and attending to the interplay between the individual and social forces. Although Kershaw is considered to be a historian who has made use of sociological insights in his work, he is not usually considered to be a 'historical sociologist'. However, his integration of sensitive historical analysis with Weberian theory makes him an ideal candidate for the title of 'honorary' historical sociologist.

The inclusion of both Kershaw and Thompson in this category highlights the inclusive nature of historical sociology. It suggests that the category has obviously got to be enlarged beyond the type of 'grand historical sociology' that deals with large-scale transformations or 'world systems' to include theoretically informed studies of single societies or one social process within that society. In other words, studies do not have to be comparative, all-embracing, or international, in scope in order to qualify as 'historical sociology'. This is a point made by Philip Abrams:

> Historical sociology is not, then, a matter of imposing grand schemes of evolutionary development on the relationship of the past to the present. Nor is it merely a matter of recognising the historical background to the present. It is the attempt to understand the relationship of personal activity and experience on the one hand and social organisation on the other as something that is continuously structured in time.[45]

Abrams identifies three types of historical sociology. First, there was that practised by the three founding fathers of sociology (Marx, Weber and Durkheim), which was concerned with understanding the transition to industrialism and, through that understanding, the achievement of social process, or history in general.[46] Secondly, there was an attempt to model the social sciences on the natural sciences, which led to the search for 'social laws that could claim the force of natural laws'.[47] Such a view holds that society is moving, or evolving in a particular direction and that the actions of individuals have little relevance to this process. Thirdly, there is another type of sociology, which is genuinely historical, even though it does not concern itself with large-scale social transformations. This approach deals with individuals in small-scale social settings and can be described as micro-history.[48] As we noted earlier, Abrams argues that historians and sociologists are united by a common concern with what he calls the problematic of structuring, and this is a significant point. He concludes his work with a discussion of the work of, the *Annaliste* historian, Fernand Braudel, who was himself very much in favour of the union of history and sociology. He cites Braudel as a way of showing what a unified historical sociology would look like. Abrams approves of his distinction between levels or modes of historical time, and feels that this is realised with great skill in his study of the Mediterranean.[49]

While the *Annales* School does represent a significant attempt at combining history and the social sciences it has not been without its critics. Christopher Lloyd, for example, has pointed out that there is little room for human **agency** in Braudel's work. 'Structures are apparently remarkably stable and persistent across epochs and the surface pattern of events and actions disturbs them little.'[50] Lloyd feels that another representative of the *Annales* School, Emmanuel Le Roy Ladurie, has achieved a better synthesis of structure and agency. Lloyd's comment draws our attention to two theoretical problems. First, that historical explanation must always seek to deal with the reciprocal interaction between social structure and human agency. Secondly, that it must be able to cope with continuity as well as change.

Lloyd attempts to build on what he sees as some of the deficiencies in Abrams' work. His argument is complex and he employs a multitude of examples, which can make it difficult to follow in places. However, it represents an informed attempt to restate the need for a theoretical history in the face of postmodern scepticism, an issue that we will be returning to later. Lloyd asserts the need for 'a scientific history' based on the belief that there are structures of history (social forces), which have their own independent existence. By 'scientific' he does not mean that history should be based on quantification, but on a realist philosophy of explanation (one in which plausibility rather than truth is the aim, and not to be confused with **relativism**). He begins from the assumption that the old discussions about the differences between history and the social sciences are no longer relevant, as it is obvious that they should be part of the same enterprise, although they are not at the moment. Thus, economic history, social history, **political economy** and historical sociology should all be considered as, what he calls, social structural history. The distinction that should be maintained within the social sciences should be between the study of events and the study of structures.[51] He expands on this distinction as follows:

> If economies and societies can be understood as dynamic non-phenomenal yet real structures then all those who study the history of economies and societies (defined in a wide sense to include families, firms, markets, communities, political systems and **mentalities**) are, *ipso facto*, social structural historians. If social structures are not being directly studied then this label should not be used. If the objects of enquiry are primarily events, actions and the behaviour of groups, then that is not social structural history in the proper sense of the term but event history. However, structures and events are not somehow ontologically separate things, a mistake that tends to be made by some **structuralist** historians and sociologists.[52]

This poses a problem, for if we cannot separate structures and events in terms of explanation, how can we distinguish between historians who deal with either one or the other?

Lloyd talks at length about how structures have an independent existence of individuals and provide the context in which human action occurs. This is basically the same distinction as has always been made between structure and **agency**, although he tends to use the terms event/structure. It is necessary to recognise that he does wish to see the continuation of some type of division within the discipline: 'I emphasize that I am arguing against the complete collapse of all the socio-historical studies into each other. There needs to be a rational division of labour between the domains of event history and structural history within the single broad field of socio-historical enquiry.'[53] Lloyd sees the field of social studies as divided into four quadrants: events (dealt with by historical enquiry) and structures (dealt with by sociological enquiry). He proposes that the social sciences should be divided between those who would concentrate on the theoretical and the **empirical**, but without seeing these as separate processes. He gives examples of 'the best social scientists' (i.e. those who have combined the perspectives of all four quadrants). These include Clifford Geertz, Barrington Moore, Emmanuel Le Roy Ladurie, Alain Touraine, Charles Tilly, Allan Pred and Ernest Gellner. He then demonstrates his claim that **structurist** methodology (as he outlines it) informs the work of many structural historians. This includes examples of macro and micro **structuration**. The latter requires an insight into collective mentality, and includes many classic works of historical anthropology and cultural history.[54] There are, as he says, many examples of long-run structural studies, but he cites Barrington Moore and Hobsbawm's study of European society as good examples.[55]

Lloyd's analysis is highly nuanced, and has to be applauded for taking into account different levels of historical analysis, even though it is possibly overly elaborate. It might be simpler to see historical analysis in terms of 'adequacy at the level of theory', and sociological work in terms of 'adequacy at the level of historical context'. In other words, historians are successful if they employ a theoretical framework that is adequate for the level of explanation being attempted, and sociologists, if they supply a sufficient level of historical explanation for the studies they have undertaken. It is important to distinguish between different types of historical sociology, or structural history, in the way that Abrams and Lloyd do. Studies can be carried out at a number of levels to yield 'macro' or 'micro' historical sociology, or works that operate on some level in between. The basic requirement for a work to be considered as a work of historical sociology, or sociological history, has to be an awareness of the necessary historical and theoretical context in which a particular study is being carried out. This does not have to be a major restatement, or challenge, to classical sociological theory. Or even a new twist to the explanation of the transition from feudalism to industrialism, but the employment of a theoretical, or conceptual, framework that is adequate for the historical problem under consideration. This is obviously a highly inclusive definition of what would constitute historical sociology, and it would also bring in much of the work that may currently be categorised as 'social history'. Some, such as Christopher Lloyd, may want to object that there is nothing obviously 'theoretical' about much of the work that is carried out under this banner.[56] This is obviously true, and the intention here is not to defend all works of 'social history', just because they could be seen as belonging to that genre. The argument that is being made here is that social history 'works' if it employs an appropriate framework for the problem under discussion. So, for example, a study of Irish migrants in Britain should take into account all the social and economic factors that contributed towards migration from Ireland, and 'push' and 'pull' factors affecting migration. However, it would be unlikely to be located in a grand theoretical framework, dealing with the formation of 'world systems' or the rise and fall of empires, for example, as it simply would not be appropriate for the issue under discussion; yet, the issue of historical population movement more broadly conceived would indeed figure in such an analysis.[57]

We need to recognise that the boundaries of the genres have become blurred in recent years as sociologists have turned towards the study of the past, and historians have turned towards social history. So, the boundaries between social history, sociological history, and historical sociology are fluid, and this is something to be welcomed. Many of the sociologists who have turned to history have been concerned with explaining events at a lesser scale than world history. Such studies have been focused on the explanation of one aspect of the history of a single country, or even down to the level of a single community. Sociologists have become concerned with historical approaches to crime, collective action, power structures, occupational differentiation and a number of other topics. This does not necessarily mean that the sociologists engaged in such work have 'become' historians, or are engaged in archival research.[58] It means, as Charles Tilly puts it, that they are 'edging toward the adoption of genuinely historical arguments – arguments in which where and, especially, when something happens seriously affects its character and outcome'.[59]

There are a number of sociological studies that display sensitivity towards the historical process.[60] Two examples can be singled out for inclusion in the category of 'honorary' historical sociology: Goldthorpe et al.'s The Affluent Worker in the Class Structure (1969), and Richard Sennet and Jonathan Cobb's The Hidden Injuries of Class (1972). In The Affluent Worker in the Class Structure, Goldthorpe and his colleagues investigated the alleged changes that were said to have occurred within the British working class after the Second World War. They were particularly concerned with the extent to which *embourgeoisement* (the adoption of middle-class values and habits by the working class) had occurred amongst workers employed in the most advanced industries.[61] This is a celebrated example of British **empirical** sociology, but in what way is it historical? The study situates the contemporary empirical research within the theoretical framework of the debate on the working class stretching back to Marx and Engels, and the historical framework of the changes that have occurred in the living standards and working conditions of the working class since the nineteenth century.[62] Sennet and Cobb are also concerned with the impact of the improved material condition of the working class in the post-war period, in this case with regard to America. They are interested in the way the class system shapes an individual's sense of his or her own worth. Although the material conditions of American manual labourers had become markedly less precarious, this did not mean that class differences had disappeared.[63] The injuries of class that Sennet and Cobb are concerned with are hidden because they centre around the 'injured dignity' of individuals in a society where, on the surface, talent is rewarded, thus making individuals feel responsible for their own failure, and inadequate in relation to those 'above' them.[64] Their work is a well-known example of American **empirical** sociology. It is 'historical' in the sense that it begins with an account of the impact of immigration from Europe at the end of the nineteenth century on social and economic relationships in America, and makes reference throughout to ways in which workers' attitudes can be said to have altered over time.[65] In their use of interviews and the experience of individuals, both of these studies conform to C. Wright Mills' prescription that social science should deal 'with problems of biography, of history, and of their intersection within social structures'.[66]

Two examples of studies that combine elements of both 'historical' and 'sociological' method to create something that can be more readily identified as 'historical sociology' are Geoffrey Pearson's study of, and Avram Taylor's analysis of working-class credit networks. Pearson's work was an explicit response to a contemporary problem, the summer riots of 1981. It also has an explicit political purpose, to challenge the notion, propagated by tabloid newspapers and Conservative politicians, that the breakdown in law and order is the result of a massive historical shift. In other words, that there was a golden age of stability and decency in the past, which has been undermined by the advent of the 'permissive' society.[67] This prompts Pearson to go back in time to determine whether there was indeed a period when Britain was a society characterised by order and security. His starting point is to consider British society in the 1950s, where critics of the permissive revolution had located the 'golden age'. Of course, when he looks at this period he discovers a 'moral panic' about the unruly behaviour of Teddy Boys. Also, 'Before the emergence of the Teds there had been any number of alarms from the 1940s onwards about street violence, robbery attacks, "Blitz kids" and "cosh boys".'[68] In fact the word 'hooligan' can be traced back to 1898, and August Bank Holiday disturbances in London that gave rise to a moral panic that was to prefigure the later public concern over mods and rockers.[69] Pearson draws on newspaper reports and other contemporary sources to offer an account that employs historical methodology, but is informed by sociological insights.

Taylor's work is about those forms of credit that have historically been associated with the British working class. These included pawnshops, 'ticket' or tallymen, and various types of retail credit. Some of these went into decline during the post-war period, when they were challenged by newer developments, while others are still with us. Taylor looks at the effect of credit on working-class communities, and relates this to the debate about community. He is concerned with comparing the period before and after 1945. Taylor draws on archival research and oral history interviews. The work also employs an eclectic theoretical approach in order to offer an explanation that can function at both the macro and micro levels, drawing on the work of Marx, Weber, Ferdinand Tönnies, Anthony Giddens, Erving Goffman and others.[70]

▶ Historical sociology: the view from the air

It is clearly important to recognise that not all works of historical sociology can be classified as 'grand historical sociology', as the literature often leads us to believe that historical sociology is only concerned with large-scale transformations. Yet, a tendency towards systemic accounts, which marked the disciplines of sociology and history at their points of inception in the nineteenth century, have continued to carry some weight. Grand historical sociology has had many disciples and some classic works have been produced. By 1994, Randall Collins could confidently discuss a 'Golden Age' of historical sociology, which had begun 30 years previously, and had produced 'many of the finest and most ambitious projects in historical sociology ever attempted'.[71] The sheer scale of the works produced by 'grand historical sociologists' is impressive, but also carries with it certain methodological difficulties. Due to the broad canvas on which these researchers work, the only practical means of writing studies on this scale is to draw together the existing secondary material. However, the fact that these studies are produced by scholars who have not themselves had first-hand contact with the primary research materials has led to criticism of this approach.[72] The comparative method is also fundamental to the creation of much of the work in this genre, and this is an approach that will be considered at length in the subsequent chapter. Good examples of the comparative method in action can be found in Barrington Moore's *Social Origins of Dictatorship and Democracy* and Skocpol's *States and Social Revolutions*. Again, we will be discussing the former work in the next chapter, but we should now turn to Skocpol's study in order to gain an appreciation of how this approach works in practice.

A good example of historical sociology in the grand style is Theda Skocpol's study of revolutions, a comparative study of the French, Russian and Chinese revolutions, which claims to present a new theoretical model of social revolution.[73] Social revolutions involve a change in both the political and the social structure. The old-regime states come into crisis when they become subject to military pressures from more economically developed nations abroad. Their responses to this were constrained by domestic class structures and the agrarian economy. This resulted in revolution from below. As Skocpol says, 'in each case, social revolution was a conjuncture of three developments: (1) the collapse or incapacitation of central administrative and military machineries; (2) widespread peasant rebellions; and (3) marginal elite political movements'.[74]

The approach Skocpol adopted had three characteristics. First, the adoption of a 'nonvoluntarist, structural perspective' as opposed to a voluntarist approach, which emphasises the role of the key groups that launch a revolution. As she says, 'Revolutions are not made; they come'.[75] It is more important to analyse the relations between groups and societies. Secondly, the inter-societal and world-historical contexts were highly significant. Depending on when they occurred, there may or may not be other examples of social revolution to serve as a model. This also influences the technological or organisational innovations the revolutionary regime can take advantage of. Modern social revolutions only took place in countries 'in disadvantaged positions within international arenas'. Military backwardness and political dependency have been crucially important, 'especially defeats in wars or threats of invasion and struggles over colonial controls', which have been instrumental in most outbreaks of revolutionary activity.[76] These international pressures were transmitted to national politics through the political regime. This leads to the third characteristic: 'the potential autonomy of the state'. As she says, 'The state properly conceived is no mere arena in which socio-economic struggles are fought out. It is, rather, a set of administrative policing, and military organizations headed and more or less well coordinated by, an executive authority.'[77] These state organisations obviously exist within the context of a class society, but they 'are at least potentially autonomous from direct dominant-class control'.[78] Although the state and the dominant class both share an interest in keeping the subordinate classes in place, the state might also pursue its own interests ('in maintaining sheer physical order and political peace') in opposition to those of the dominant class.[79] Skocpol applies these core assumptions to the analysis of social revolutions. So, what types of 'grand historical sociology' can we identify?

Skocpol explicitly draws on Marxism, but also on the ideas of political-conflict theorists. This is because, as she argues, Marxism explains class tensions, but not how and when class members find themselves able to engage in struggle. This highlights the complexity of the problems that historical sociologists have set themselves, the debt they owe to the 'founding fathers' of sociology, and the need to expand, modify or reconsider the assumptions of those approaches. It also raises the issue of whether the best solution to the complex web of social circumstances contained within any given historical conjuncture is to adopt an open-minded approach, and be theoretically eclectic, drawing on several traditions, as opposed to dogmatically 'Marxist' or 'Weberian'. Most recent attempts at constructing a 'grand historical sociology' tend to draw upon the work of either Marx or Weber (or both). Weber saw causation as 'multivocal' or 'polymorphous' and rejected the primacy of economics that Marx put forward.[80] Weber's model of social action has produced several types of Weberian historical sociology. Those influenced by Weber include: Reinhard Bendix, S.N. Eisenstadt, Clifford Geertz, Ernest Gellner, John A. Hall and Michael Mann. Practitioners of Marxist historical sociology include: Barrington Moore, Rodney Hilton, Perry Anderson, Theda Skocpol, Robert Brenner and Immanuel Wallerstein. We now consider the work of the latter as an example of historical sociology on a global scale.

In an incisive essay outlining his own approach to the social sciences, Wallerstein discussed not only his belief in the artificial nature of some established disciplinary boundaries, but also his concern to connect 'historical social science' with politics, as well as the seeming ambiguity of labelling particular types of scholarship according to disciplinary boundaries. Wallerstein was intrigued by the fact that though he himself is a PhD and professor in sociology, one of his major works, *The Modern World System*, is regarded by many as 'work of history, more specifically of economic history'. He also made a useful point about the objectivity of the author by expressing his 'committed and active' approach to politics and regard his acknowledgement of the importance of polemic in scholarship. Summing up, he contended: 'Some might feel I am caught in a set of contradictions. I myself feel that I am being thoroughly consistent and that my concern with history, with social science, and with politics is not a matter of engaging in three separate, even if related, activities, but is a *single* concern, informed by the belief that the strands cannot be separated, nor should they if they could.'[81] An honest assessment, Wallerstein's view strikes at the heart of core concerns in the traditionalist assumptions about historical knowledge and production.

Wallerstein's perspective is, as we have deduced, heavily informed by Marxism. But it is not dogmatic. Randall Collins suggests: 'Even though Wallerstein is the most "orthodox Marxian" of the major historical/comparative sociologists of today, I would still maintain that the logic of his world system leans in a Weberian direction.'[82] Charles Tilly has criticised Wallerstein for his emphasis on relations of exchange rather than production, which contradicts traditional Marxism.[83] Wallerstein's major work, *The Modern World System*, deals with the development of the global economy from about 1450 to the present day and he intends to develop his argument over four volumes, three of which have already been published.[84] His starting point is the notion that a global economy emerged, in the fifteenth and sixteenth centuries, with the development of overseas trade and colonial expansion among the European powers. This was something of a turning point: not an empire in the way they would emerge, but 'a kind of social system the world had not really known before and which is the distinctive feature of the modern world-system. It is an economic but not a political entity, unlike empires, city-states, and the emerging nation-states. It is a "world" system, not because it encompasses the whole world, but because it is larger than any juridically-defined political unit'.[85] Wallerstein thus distinguishes between a world economy and a world empire, both of which are types of world system, which embrace several cultures. By contrast, mini-systems, such as hunting and gathering, are small and only contain a single culture. Wallerstein's argument is that, the global quest for economic resources that began in the fifteenth century was precipitated by the economic, ecological and demographic crisis of feudalism within Europe. In the mid-fifteenth century, Europe was only slightly more advanced than elsewhere, but over a period of centuries, and certainly by the present day, Europe has been able to advance through exploitation of non-Western, countries through the means of an economic system organised on a global scale. He divided the world system into three geographical areas, the capitalist core, the semi-periphery and the peripheral areas. The core states have relatively strong state machineries, and state structures are relatively weak in the periphery.

It is difficult to summarise Wallerstein's argument in full here, but we can briefly consider how his work has addressed several major historical problems, and how his work has pointed to a new direction in historical sociology.[86] To begin with, he addresses one of the central issues of both historical and social science inquiry: why did the West progress faster than the rest of the world after about 1500? Here Wallerstein returns to Weber's discussion of why development did not occur in China, and considers the differences between the conditions in that country and the West.[87] His argument is that, in Europe, the development of the capitalist system was actually aided by the lack of political unity, this kept profits in the hands of merchants and manufacturers, and away from imperial rulers. The Chinese Empire, by contrast, sought internal peace and stability at the expense of extending economic activity. It was also more concerned with expanding rice production within its frontiers, than it was with expansion overseas.

Wallerstein also addresses the issue of how and when economic backwardness originated. He argues that the peripheral nations do not merely stagnate once they are incorporated into the world economy, they undergo a process of active retardation. He makes a comparison between Russia and Poland to illustrate this point. The significance of this comparison, for Wallerstein, lies in its demonstration of the role of outside forces, on the economies of those countries, caused by the differences in their interaction with world capitalism. The essence of his argument is that the core countries exploit the peripheral countries. The introduction of capitalist markets coerces the local peasantry into forced labour to extract primary products for the world system, with devastating social consequences and, as the core became richer, it was able to extend its control over non-core regions.

The concept of 'crisis' is central to Marxist history, as each **mode of production** arises out of the crisis of the preceding one. The notion that capitalism undergoes periodic crises, or regular long cycles of expansion and contraction, has been challenged by a number of economic historians.[88] Wallerstein retains the Marxist conception of the importance of economic crises, and justifies this through the argument that a crisis may be precipitated by a relative shift in the way a key product is traded.[89] In order to appreciate this, it is necessary to consider the manner in which a crisis is experienced in the system as a whole. In this sense, the notion of a world system is not merely a metaphor, but is intended as a means of comprehending the interaction of the various elements of the global economy. Wallerstein creates a scheme that can not only account for nations at all levels of economic development, but also give a sense of the process by which countries can rise from the periphery or the semi-periphery. Although it has been extensively criticised, Wallerstein's analysis has also attracted much praise. Ragin and Chirot argue: 'Wallerstein's history of the world system ... has demonstrated its ability to handle both old and new problems and set them in a new, overarching theoretical framework.'[90] As they go on to point out, Wallerstein's influence can be seen in the numerous studies that followed which took as their subject, smaller but still macroscopic parts of the world system, and employed Wallerstein's core-periphery model to explain the relationships between different societies.[91]

▶ Historical sociology on the ground: an example

Neither Wallerstein nor Skocpol are historians in the classic sense of the word: their canvases are expansive; their sources are not those associated with narrow monographs written in History departments; their approach is systemic, seeking to tease out broad conclusions about grand issues. There are, however, many examples of historians utilising sociological theory to deepen the meaning of their findings. The historical sociologist's aim must be to build a bridge between theory and evidence, and then to develop an interpretative framework that will support analyses of society and the individual. This is most acutely noticeable in a superlative study of suicide in nineteenth-century England. Having discovered a near-complete run of coroners' reports detailing suicides in the east-coast port town of Hull during the nineteenth century, the historian in question, Victor Bailey, chose to move beyond the methodologically simple, if still time-consuming, reportage of case after case, until each of his more than 700 individuals had been logged and reported. Instead, Bailey sought consciously to intermix his evidence with the structuring potentialities of the sociology of suicide; his aim was to gain deeper meaning and broader understanding – both within cases and across time – by working at the interface of theory and history.

Drawing upon the work on suicide by the noted sociologist Emile Durkheim,[92] which was later developed by Durkheim's followers and opponents,[93] Bailey began with a clear hypothesis: to test his evidence against conflicting theoretical positions. This might then result in, on the one hand, greater appreciation of those theories, and, on the other, deeper insights, and more structure, to the evidence in question. Bailey saw the challenge of applying the theory to his work quite clearly. To him, the compelling importance of broader social reasons for suicide, and failure of **ethnomethodological** perspectives to acknowledge 'statistical patterns', juxtaposed with the apparently overly impersonal approaches of Durkheimian accounts, meant the challenge was clear: 'I wish to offer a modified Durkheimian approach, one that, in the attempt to explain suicide, incorporates both social structural factors and the ways in which social factors manifested themselves in the realm of experience.'[94] He responded to this challenge by adopting an approach that sought to outline the pressures experienced by individuals during the various stages of their life cycle, or in his preferred terminology, life course, in the particular social setting of a Victorian city. As he puts it: 'The chief merit of the life-course perspective ... is that it centers upon the complex relationship between individual choices and strategies, social interaction within the family and workplace, and the constraints and possibilities of the socioeconomic environment.'[95]

Bailey is extremely careful to position his reconfigured Durkheimianism in such a way as to recognise the combination of factors, which Halbwachs described variously as the 'psychiatric thesis', the 'social' and 'psychopathological' dimensions. For Halbwachs, as for Bailey, there is a balance to be struck between 'social **determinism**', with its echoes of a social history still redolent of Marxism, and the 'organic determinism' of the person at the centre of the life choice.[96] There is a clear appreciation here of the need to balance the approach. Bailey himself quotes Giddens on the necessity of avoiding replacing 'an imperialism of the social object' with 'an imperialism of the subject'.[97] Neither the crudest social determinism, nor the harshest **ethnomethodology** can alone take us to a new level of understanding of suicide – both approaches have their sponsors and yet Bailey still felt able to retrace the well-worn path with the intention of finding a new, complementary position within the historiography. Bailey demonstrated sensitivity to the problems of official statistics on suicide, and the difficulty of pronouncing upon an open verdict. This is particularly important in view of the fact that many criticisms of Durkheim have centred on his uncritical acceptance of suicide statistics.[98] This might lead us, in turn, to question theorists' use of historical evidence in a way that is unacceptable to historians.

Bailey recognised the need to draw upon many different approaches to the past, social forces, culture and individual choice. Recognising the importance of a variety of perspectives, including anthropological concerns to understand phenomena such as suicide as a mass of symbols and signs, a ritual to be deconstructed according to a variety of concerns and perspectives. Bailey is thus an historian availing himself of tools in which he taught himself to be skilled; but the social theory is not some appendage to **empiricism** of the documentary sources; it is instead positioned at genuine, vibrant and dynamic interstices where the dead, the coroner, the historian and the sociologist meet.

He points out that historical work on suicide has too readily dismissed 'the role of loneliness and isolation in the aetiology of suicide'.[99] Durkheim said suicide was an indication of the weakness of social bonds in an urban industrial setting, and Halbwachs supported this conclusion. Bailey concludes that the social isolation of the individual is a key factor in the decision to commit suicide, but that there are a number of identifiable social causes, such as unemployment, that can precipitate this situation. He contends that although 'suicide can be meaningfully related to the subjective experience of urban life on the different stages of the life course', Durkheimian approaches, developed in Halbwachs' work, 'may yet have some merit'. For, Bailey suggested, 'Social isolation remains an essential explanatory concept for the interpretation of the incidence of suicide and the meaning of those men and women who willed and accomplished "this rash act".'[100]

Thus Bailey seeks an accommodation within the theory and evidence available in order to write what is, not only a major work of history, but also a significant contribution to a long-running debate within sociology. Chapters on the coroners' system, the town at the heart of the study – Kingston upon Hull – and the analyses of patterns of suicide can each be read purely through the lens of the historian. But it is in tying the material together that Bailey's theoretical acuity becomes clear: the sense that Bailey knows the answers derives not from his ability to instance every type of suicide among sundry social categories of people – this is not history by myriad examples (even if the author does, indeed, have hundreds of cases). It is history which informs and explains because of the author's clarity of purpose in arriving at a model of study, which aligns with Anthony Giddens' **'structuration** theory'.[101] As a dialectical position between **structuralist** concerns with wider social forces and the need to understand social action, structuration theory acknowledges the 'duality of structure', or, as Bailey writes, 'that structure is simultaneously the unintended "outcome" of human activity and the "medium" of that activity'.[102] This recognition of a dialectical energy between the setting of human action and the action itself is a major move forward from structuralist accounts – often but not exclusively associated with materialist accounts found in certain forms of Marxism. Bailey's marriage of detailed empirical study, the creation of historical context and sophisticated statistical patterning with anthropological or psychological insights certainly moves towards the type of explanatory mode that Giddens favours. Bailey thus meets the requirement to bring theory and evidence together in a way redolent of Christopher Lloyd's sophisticated and intelligent appeal. For Lloyd, the challenge is to move away from an arid materialism in which 'history ... has been seen as taking place "behind the backs" of ordinary people as a largely alien, incomprehensible, and usually oppressive process, determining their actions but not being produced by them'.[103]

▶ Conclusions

Historical sociology can be seen to provide tools, theories and apparatus to tackle history in new ways. As an approach, it does not seek to replace the careful consideration of **empirical** evidence with unsubstantiated theoretical assumptions. Historical sociology does not mean sociology alone; where it works best, historical sociology is a genuine meeting of the core assumptions of each discipline: from history, the desire to interpret and understand the past; from sociology the ability to structure variables, test hypotheses and grant wider meaning to disparate phenomena. The true intention of historical sociology must be to bring deeper meaning to our evaluations of past phenomena, and to provide a tier of evaluation which otherwise would be absent.

The examples we have considered illustrate the excitement and the challenge of 'doing' historical sociology. They return us time and again to problems of structure and **agency**, and the primacy of causes in historical explanation. These are questions that both historians and sociologists (or historical sociologists) are centrally concerned with, they are questions that need to be addressed if we are to try and understand the world we live in, how it came to be the way it is, why it is not otherwise and the forces that made it so. Dennis Smith's viewpoint provides a fitting, intelligent, finale to this discussion. For him, 'historical sociology is rational, critical and imaginative', searching out 'mechanisms through which societies change or reproduce themselves', and seeking 'the hidden structures which frustrate some human aspirations while making others realizable, whether we appreciate it or not'. Smith suggested it was useful to determine 'whether you are pushing against an open door or beating your head against a brick wall. One of historical sociology's objectives should be to distinguish between open doors and brick walls and discover whether, how, and with what consequences, walls may be removed.'[104] Thus, historical sociology can show us that, as Smith again recognises, 'some walls, at least, are temporary – as in Berlin'.[105] Even though the walls seem permanent to those who have lived with them, they can eventually come crashing down; not everything, perhaps nothing, has permanency of place. Historical sociology, or historical studies in any of its manifestations, may not enable us to predict the future, so as to anticipate events before they happen. What historical sociology can do is perhaps more modest than that. However, distinguishing between open doors and brick walls is (at least) a start, and even though it is a difficult task to make sense of the past and to imagine where society is headed, historical sociology – in its broadest conception – offers us the best existing means of achieving such a goal.

3 'A mass of factors and influences?' Systemic, 'Total' and 'Comparative' Histories

'The more aspects you study, the more specialization there is, the more life becomes a mass of "factors" and "influences" with no unifying theme.'[1] So wrote Theodore Zeldin when describing the problems of trying to encapsulate long periods of history, covering large, general questions of historical importance, over large areas of study: much as he himself had done in his own most famous work.[2] Despite the problems associated with large-scale long-run histories, philosophers, theorists and historians have sought at various times to capture human society on a vast canvas. This chapter focuses on two such approaches. The first, the vogue for 'systemic' or 'total story', most closely associated with Fernand Braudel, offers an opportunity to consider the interplay between history and social sciences at its grandest level. The second, the emphasis upon comparative methodologies, allows us to focus upon one of the most important examples of the interconnection between social science and history. In both instances, we will be discussing some important theories and methods which help to explain the structures of history and enhance the study of social phenomena by providing a systemic, scientific account of past society as a whole.

▶ The intellectual context of large-scale thinking in social history

The desire to describe or explain the totality of human society is not new. Since the Greeks, philosophers have sought to encapsulate the entirety of human development, or its essential features, through an understanding of the historical process. The Enlightenment was something of a high point for the exposition of totalising visions of the development of human society.[3] The concern of the scholars of this period was with civilisations and cultures, and with the importance of man's ideas in shaping social development. In the nineteenth century, a different form of writing emerged which, like its predecessors, took an interest in the systemic nature of societal change, but which, unlike the writings that went before, stressed the importance of the material world in shaping all other configurations, social, political and cultural. The rise of **positivism**, most plainly in its Marxist form – but by no means exclusively so – led to an interest in the organic nature of society, and in the historical development of society, that had been unnoticed previously. Moreover, the key factor in this relationship between men, Marx argued, was the material requirement of human beings for the functional aspects of life: clothing, food and shelter. Social organisation provided for these needs and thus shaped human society. As material factors changed, so history seemed to move on through different stages, each one distinguished by the conditions of material life. By such a formulation, Marx was suggesting a pattern of economic and then social change, which could be modelled systematically. Marx explained his position in 1859, thus:

> In the social production of their existence, men inevitably enter into definite relationships, which are independent of their will, namely relations of production. The totality of the relations of production constitutes the economic structure of society, the real foundation, on which arises a legal and political **superstructure** and to which correspond definite forms of social consciousness. The **mode of production** of material life conditions the process of social, political and intellectual life. It is not the consciousness of men that determines their existence but their social existence that determines their consciousness.[4]

Here, Marx and his collaborator Friedrich Engels periodised history according to the material circumstances of any given time. In so doing, they determined that history was divided into three essential epochs: the Ancient (Greek and Roman), the Feudal and the Bourgeois. The latter, the bourgeois epoch – the modern world of Marx's own time – was defined by capitalist relations. Each of these epochs grew from the chaos of the last, through a process of **dialectical** development, and each was characterised, in material terms, as more modern than the last. The epochal approach of Marx was similar to that of previous writers, like Giambattista Vico and G.W.F. Hegel, except that Marx saw the rise and fall of each stage progressing in linear, rather than circular, fashion. The idea of modernisation and the development of increasingly antagonistic relations with successive epochs, was central to Marx's conception of historical change. The term that we use to describe Marx's notion of change over time, **historical materialism**, captures the essence of the systemic view outlined in the *Contribution to the Critique of Political Economy* (1859), which is also known as the **material conception of history** or **dialectical materialism**. Whichever term we use, the essential feature of Marx's history, conceived of as it was across the entire history of human civilisation, was the progress of material – that is, economic – change over time, which provided a foundation for the study of Marx and Engels' central concern: the relationship between the economy (**base**) and social, cultural and political formations (**superstructure**) and the necessary linkage between the two.[5]

We can see that Marxist thought in its original formulation focused on three epochs, each of which was different. In any attempt to understand what this might contribute to total history or long-run systemic analysis, the critical element is the sense that each of Marx's stages of development was characterised by the nature of the economic base – the **mode of production**. The mode of production was governed by the level of technological-economic development at a given time and the nature of social relations at the point of production (i.e. within the economic sphere). For this economic reality, according to Marx, determined the superstructure of society: ideas, institutions, politics and government, and social life. Marx asserted that in each epoch the nature of the base threw up class antagonisms, which were rooted in the relations of production. This referred to the nature of economic exploitation, and centred on questions of labour value: what did workers produce, how much was it worth, how much of that was paid in wages, and what proportion went in profits to the owners of the means of production (i.e. capitalist employers)? In the Ancient epoch, where slave labour was a norm, profit was affected by the cost of maintaining, buying and reproducing slaves, and by the relative inefficiencies (or otherwise) of bonded, as opposed to free, labour. Marx viewed each epoch as riddled with contradictions. Slavery was evil and inefficient and doomed to collapse. Wage slavery, whilst more efficient and morally more acceptable, was still hamstrung by the failure of workers to achieve the full value of their labour. For Marx, false consciousness prevented workers from realising their exploitation; class consciousness would see them seize the means of production. In other words, revolution would occur. At root, for Marx, each societal system was marked by conflicts that developed between old modes of production and the new. The consequence of these class antagonisms was social revolution.

Marx's model of historical progress had the advantage of providing a clear pathway through complex social and economic processes. Its **dialectical** dimension had the advantage of focusing on change as the essence of history. Thus, Marxism was considered useful to historians whose desire was to 'totalise' historical experience. Marxism threw up many instances of scholarship where a vision of total history was quested after like the Holy Grail. Other nineteenth-century positivists, such as Auguste Comte, also expressed a desire to understand societal change in long and large terms. An essential feature of such works was to understand not just social change, but the essence of social change. To achieve such a thing would enable forecasts about the future. This hinged upon the discovery of the laws of historical and human development; if this were known, then predictive tools could be deployed. The character of the Marxist approach to the past, however, with its attempts to reduce complex and multitudinous phenomena to a series of tests or hypotheses was in keeping with other experimental sciences. Even critics of Marx, among them the totalising historians such as Fernand Braudel, whom we will discuss later on, genuflected to Marx, if only by seeking an alternative view of the process of historical change.

Many critics have argued that Marx was an economic **determinist** that everything was explained in terms of the economic system at any given time. Marx and Engels, however, never intended a **unilinear** and **monocausal** conception of history to be their pitaph. Their conception of the forces of production, for example, included much more than just the economic system or that produced by the sweat of workers. Science, technology and other aspects of creative output were also included. In 1890, Engels defended himself and Marx in a letter to Joseph Bloch: 'Marx and I are ourselves partly to blame for the fact that the younger writers sometimes lay more stress on the economic side than is due to it. We had to emphasise this main principle in opposition to our adversaries.' Their philosophy was in fact much more complicated, as Engels went on to tell Bloch: 'According to the materialist conception of history the determining element in history is ultimately the production and reproduction in real life. More than that neither Marx nor I have ever asserted.'[6]

While the notion of **base-superstructure** and the emphasis upon economic **determinism** clearly had a utility for Marx and Engels, they also argued that no economic system was completely without the vestiges of the previous one. How else could the hugely powerful landowning aristocracy in 1850 be reconciled with the emergent, powerful but ultimately immature bourgeoisie? In other words, Marx and Engels were accepting the notion of historical change at different paces. Marx saw economic structures as placing limitations upon the superstructure rather than simply defining it without possible variation. Furthermore, both men wrote works that allowed for variations within his notion of the materialist conception of history. Marx's essay 'Eighteenth Brumaire of Louis [Napoleon] Bonaparte'[7] is a classic example of the role of opportunism and individual action in shaping the course of history: but only within the constraints of structural forces. The intrigues of the Bonaparte dynasty did not stop France developing class antagonisms, nor could these individual actions shape the material conditions of French life over, say, a century.

▶ *'Histoire Totale'*: the world of Braudel

Marx was to be hugely influential in modern social history in the twentieth century. Even those who stood against his material conception for its rigidities or limitations still had to deal with the ghost of the man and his ideas. Among those who stood in contradistinction to Marx and who offered an alternative social history to one favoured by Marxist or marxisant historians, the *Annales* historians stand out. The *Annales*, often called a 'school', but more of a philosophical and methodological 'mood', was founded in 1929 by two young scholars, Marc Bloch and Lucien Febvre. They, and their disciples, would offer a kind of social history, which sat next to Marxist social history in several important ways. One, which was alluded to earlier, offered a new perspective on ordinary people. The other, which we will discuss now, sought a grand vision of history over the long term (*la longue durée*) competed with Marxist **dialectical materialism** to explain the 'total' picture. In some senses, at the outset, Bloch and Febvre's mission was part of a worldwide trend among young scholars to achieve what the Americans dubbed a 'New History'. These two young men were 'problem-orientated' historians who eschewed traditional narrative forms. They also attempted to answer big questions by thematic examination of structural change: in other words, a move towards the total history most clearly envisaged by Braudel, began with the first generation.

This was certainly recognised by Hugh Trevor-Roper, who posited three central features of their paradigm. First, they, the *Annales* historians, tried to 'grasp totality' and 'the vital cohesion of any historical period' by delineating its structures, whether social, economic, mental or physical. Secondly, their approach is '**deterministic**', in that it espouses a belief that 'history is at least partially determined by forces which are external to men'. Thirdly, that the *Annales* constructed an 'intricate web of method, theory and philosophy [which] give coherence to French social history'.[8] The *Annales* group represented the first systematic attempt to theorise a new way of understanding the past. In the early years, Bloch and Febvre tackled history with fresh methodologies, building in new conceptual models, and borrowing freely from other disciplines. At the same time, Bloch and Febvre demanded that other historians should follow their example and work out the ways in which the traditional bastions of history could be broken down. Such new approaches were to emerge into something of a philosophical system.

In post-war France, where an interest in regions has also traditionally been strong, *Annales* torch was passed to Fernand Braudel, a protégé of Lucien Febvre. Braudel's classic book, *The Mediterranean and the Mediterranean World in the Age of Philip II* (1949), came closer than any other to total history. Indeed, one writer described Braudel's efforts as 'a new kind of history, total history'.[9] Perhaps more than any other French book, even Bloch's *Royal Touch*, it be regarded as the greatest historical work of the twentieth century. It is an enormous study, crammed with masses of material, which Braudel assiduously pieced together over twenty years. *The Mediterranean* was Braudel's attempt to reverse the increasing fragmentation of history – which had been a feature of the 1920s and 1930s outside the *Annales* School – and to halt 'thematic specialisation': that is, to depart from 'prefix' (social, economic, political, etc.) history and to look at whole problems or society as a whole. Braudel's vision was to write an all-embracing history: *'histoire totale'* ('**total history**'). Bloch and Febvre had done this for parts of the past – but never for whole ages; and never to the extent that Braudel did. Bloch's *Feudal Society*, for example, was concerned not with the whole medieval world, but with the key aspects of its social and mental structure.

In the work of Febvre and Bloch, however, we can detect two different totalising impulses. The first, associated with Febvre, and drawing upon Emile Durkheim (1858–1917), focused upon *mentalités* the mental structures that linked people. The second, an ecological–geographic **structuralism**, noticed in Bloch's work (influenced by Francois Simiand and developed by Henri Pirenne and Braudel), sought out vast socio-economic structures over lengthy periods of time, theorising them 'as multi-layered and multi-temporal'.[10] Such a concern with geographical and environmental approaches has been influential elsewhere, not least outside France: notably in the historical geography of writers such as W.G. Hoskins and N.J.K. Pounds.[11]

Braudel reached out across time and space, seeking to knit discrete layers of society into a composite whole. Whilst his most obvious relationship, in terms of intellectual approach, was with Bloch's long-run analyses of social structure, the whole *Annales* canon bleeds at the edges, and both Bloch and Braudel demonstrated more than a passing interested in collective psychology, the intellectual ties that bound individuals, groups and societies. Braudel, however, took the structural approaches of the *Annales* to a new level, examining layers of society, the environmental elements that underscored human society, the material aspects of life, 'collective destinies and general trends', 'modes of feeling and thought', intellectual life and the political aspects of *histoire événementielle*. Braudel seemingly ran the whole gamut. Whether we accept that he was successful or nor; whether we criticise his megalomania and sigh at the impossibility of it all, there can be no doubt that total history was his aim. As one scholar has noted, 'The effect produced by reading Braudel is one of travelling through layer and, in each layer, feeling the seismographic waves recorded there.'[12] James A. Henretta, described the *Mediterranean* and its multitude of vistas succinctly as 'a comprehensive, multi-dimensional cubist portrait of the society'.[13] The key problem with 'total history', Braudel argued, was that time was many-layered, that the history of different aspects of the world changed at different paces. In wrestling with the immense problem of writing the history of Philip II's empire, Braudel organised his book, and with it his overarching conception of history, into three phases. The first, la *longue durée* (the long run), spanned the seemingly timeless phase of human interaction with the natural world. At this level, the effects of the passage of time, Braudel argued, were slowest. In the second phase, Braudel framed the quicker-moving medium term in which political, social and economic structures – states, nations and economic systems, for example – were formed. Finally, the third part of the *Mediterranean* tackled the fast-flowing short term (***histoire événementielle***): people's actions; the narratives of events; political and diplomatic history.[14]

Braudel's Mediterranean has been likened to Gibbon's *Decline and Fall of the Roman Empire*: both authors display a vast historical knowledge to conclude that the empires they studied, Spanish and Roman respectively, were limited by their own scale. In writing his masterpiece, Braudel captured a variety of **interdisciplinary** procedures. Braudel was more than just an innovative methodologist; his work, like Gibbon's, has style as a literary force expressing the author's eye for detailed observation. In any age, Braudel would have been a great historian. He shared the 'totalist' vision of sociologists, but did not write in that dry, social science language: he had the turn of phrase of a Macaulay, a Ranke or an Acton.

Criticisms of Braudel's schema began to develop. He was, for example, accused of **determinism**, of reducing men to inevitable defeat in their natural world. Moreover, it is not always apparent that there is a link between his three-tiered conception of time. Others argued that 'total history' was impossible beyond the local level (something which influenced later *Annales* writers) and claimed that something as big as the Mediterranean world cannot be treated inclusively. In trying to offer an alternative conception of historical change to Marx, Braudel was accused of failing to integrate political history with the environment and demography.[15] Marxists also argue that Braudel's work lacks the dynamism of Marx's **base-superstructure** philosophy. Otherwise, scholars, whether Marxists or not, alighted on the schematic nature of Braudel's threefold vision, and the strong sense the reader gains of parts of past society being deemed more important than others: 'One receives the strong impression that the slowest pulses, those of the longue durée, are the most "real". Unfortunately, this produces the effect of travelling through the book from important and portentous towards the relatively insignificant and trivial.'[16]

Here, then, Braudel's environmentalism becomes substituted for Marx's **material conception of history**. In other words, one determinism (that of ecology, of the natural world) replaced another (that of the material conditions of life and the nature of production). But there remained one vital weakness, when Braudel is compared to Marxism. As Henretta argued, splicing his own argument with that of Hexter: 'the three dimensions of existence – geographic, social and political – are not interrelated but simply stand one beside the other, each...itself an essay in general explanation'.[17] Whilst Braudel was consciously seeking an alternative to Marx, we can still see very clearly the influence of the type of nineteenth-century **positivism**, which underpinned Marx's own thinking. The combination of methodology and interpretation were thus responsible for Braudel making the same mistakes he saw in Marx. Again, Henretta's words, are illuminating: 'To interpret the world in **structuralist** terms is to contest the philosophical primacy of nineteenth-century notions of **unilineal** causation.' The essence, then, is to comprehend events within wider contexts. In order to achieve this, '**Structuralists** adopt a "'holistic" perspective, stressing the internal relationship among elements of a self-contained institution or world-view.'[18] Moreover, by focusing on long-run structural factors in historical development, Braudel was considered to have under-played the role of human **agency**. The people in Braudel's work are seen as buffeted by environmental and structural factors: they certainly lack agency in their own lives. As Eugene and Elizabeth Genovese suggested, 'For the basic human community in his work', they wrote, 'figure more as part of nature – as an ecological feature – than as a collectivity acting upon nature'.[19] as told by Braudel. As Marxists, the Genoveses also have a view of Braudel's contrast to Marx, stating that the *Mediterranean*, with 'its structural … [and] anthropological, ecological and archaeological predilections, implicitly negates the historical process itself'.[20] In addition, Braudel, despite his concern with ideas and *mentalités*, had little to say about ordinary people. Lloyd considers this a failure adequately to conceptualise 'the agency/action/structure interrelationship'[21] in Braudelian-type *Annales* histories. Despite the vehemence of some of Braudel's critics, his major works are magisterial and provide a crucial stepping-stone between the first generation of *Annales* scholars, Bloch and Febvre, and those, like Emmanuel Le Roy Ladurie, who came later.

▶ Braudel's influence

Braudel's grand vision clearly had a significant influence on later scholars. Le Roy Ladurie, for example, one of Braudel's own students, demonstrated ambitious plans for long-run historical analysis, which though showing the Braudelian influence, were more modest and less positivistic in temperament and methodology. Le Roy Ladurie took many of Braudel's ideas and shared his totalising vision. However, Ladurie is most clearly associated with two developments, one linking to, and influenced by, the Braudelian approach. Equally, in the other, he showed great skill in developing the Durkheim/Febvre analysis of *mentalités*. Ladurie's earliest work, a vast, quantitative analysis of the socio-economic lives of peasants in medieval southern France,[22] demonstrated a clear connection to the full Braudelian range – the totality of the past. His aim was 'To observe, at various levels, the long-term movements of an economy and of a society – **base** and **superstructure**, material life and cultural life, sociological evolution and collective psychology, the whole framework of a rural world which remained very largely traditional in nature.'[23]

Ladurie developed *histoire sérielle*, the notion of examining long-run trends in historical analysis, using computers to systematically interrogate far greater quantities of data than was previously possible. In this sense, Ladurie was part of the 'cliometric' revolution associated with Robert Fogel and other 1960s scholars who were themselves bringing a technological **determinism** – and zealotry for the

utility of computers – to bear upon their own totalising vision of historical reconstruction. In Fogel's case, the philosophy went further with a belief that through
long-run quantification it was possible to ask **counterfactual** (what if) questions
to strengthen the historian's ability to explain the past.[24] As well as examining long-
run phenomena, and the changing of worlds in which traditionalism nevertheless
remained dominant, Le Roy Ladurie also developed an appreciation of the importance of caesura – ruptures and changes – in the historical continuum. In discussing
features alighted on more focused regions and localities when developing a total
history (what we might call 'focused total' history). In his important micro-study,
Carnival in Romans and Montaillou, Ladurie mixed the two **structuralisms** of the
earlier *Annales* – ecological **determinism** and **mentalités**. Though these works
did not frame the gargantuan vista of Braudel, Ladurie's aim was still to understand
the world of the peasants of the Pyrenees.

Braudel's vast project to study the early modern Mediterranean world was published at a time when, with the Cold War setting in fast, scholars were searching for
interpretative matrices to link past and present in their explanations of the world
they lived in. Braudel, though determinedly historical in his approach, was
matched, in some respects, by other scholars who sought to explain the interlink-
ages between the past and the present. W.W. Rostow undertook his study of industrial modernisation[25] not simply to provide better explanations of Britain's or
America's Industrial Revolutions, but to offer what he called a 'non-Communist
manifesto', which the Third World might use to model its own pathway to **modernity**. Rostow saw a possibility to turn emerging powers away from the Soviet bloc
as much as to explain the progress of Man.[26] Historians have, however, dismissed
Rostow's work – both as economic history and as a contribution to societal theory.
Few have been more tart than Hobsbawm who noted that 'though there are now a
few social scientists from other disciplines who have made themselves sufficiently
expert in our field to command respect, there are more who have merely applied a
few crude mechanical concepts and models. For every *Vendée* by a Tilly, there are,
alas, several dozen equivalents of Rostow's *Stages* [*of Economic Growth*].'[27]

Others, less portentous in their aims and more adept in their theory and practice
than Rostow, also developed the grand, thematic approach to historical writing,
drawing inspiration from social theory where it enabled broad-run comparisons
and multi-territorial studies to be initiated. Ideas and concepts also provided a spur
to large-scale works. One notable example will suffice, a work dating from a little
after Braudel's time: R.R. Palmer's notion of 'democratic revolution'. For Palmer,
there was a natural connection between Europe and America, drawing upon the
way in which levelling tendencies and revolutions, on the one hand, and lofty ideas
of democracy and popular sovereignty, on the other, spread systematically between
America, France, Ireland and Britain. Palmer noted types of government, types of
social structure, notions of governance, and the domination of one system of ideas

or another. In so doing, he likened together the nations that nurtured first the idea and then the practice of democracy. The United Irishmen, the grouping behind Ireland's Rising of 1798, captured the sort of linkage that Palmer was interested in:

Question: What have you got in your hand?
Answer: A green bough
Question: Where did it first grow?
Answer: In America
Question: Where did it bud?
Answer: In France
Question: Where are you going to plant it?
Answer: In the crown of Great Britain[28]

In the same way, though, Palmer's work might be seen providing useful context for his own time. For then, the Atlantic world was shaping around the idea of a military alliance, North Atlantic Treaty Organisation (NATO) to stand against the sorts of powers which failed to enjoy the types of political change (either reformist or revolutionary) in the age of democratic revolutions about which he wrote.

Such systemic accounts as either Rostow's or Palmer's were in vogue at that time of almost unparalleled international uncertainty: the nuclear age was a time for reflection and alliance-building. But later studies also demonstrate a seduction with Braudel's master-sweep: none more so than a major study by the sociologist Giovanni Arrighi. His aim was to develop a major study of what Charles Tilly has called 'the two interdependent master processes of the [modern] era: the creation of a system of national states and the formation of a worldwide capitalist system'.[29] Arrighi admitted immediately his indebtedness to Braudel, particularly the vast trilogy *Capitalism and Civilisation*, which provides the 'interpretative schema' for Arrighi's own book.[30] Arrighi seeks to further Braudel's own work by finding a way of tackling the issues, which Tilly claims Braudel shied away from. Tilly, as with others, saw serious flaws in Braudel's 'world historical analysis':[31] 'If consistency be a hobgoblin of little minds, Braudel has no trouble escaping the demon. When Braudel is not bedevilling us with our demands for consistency, he parades ... indecision. Through the second volume of Civilisation matérielle, he repeatedly begins to treat the relationship between capitalists and statemakers, then veers away.'[32]

Both Tilly and Arrighi have problems with such evasion. Tilly's aim was to bite off more manageable chunks: to find more workable modules of analysis than 'entire world systems'.[33] Arrighi, whilst acknowledging the sheer range and density of Braudel's **empirical** knowledge, made a case for mapping the terrain of the 'captain' (Braudel), choosing for himself 'the smaller task of processing his overabundant supply of conjectures and interpretations into an economical, consistent, and plausible explanation of the rise and full expansion of the capitalist world system'.[34]

In so doing, Arrighi touches upon central issues in Marx's writings: the progress of capital and money supply; the nature of economies and their development; the emergence of modern capitalism and all that this implied. Instead of focusing upon the rise and fall of modes of capital accumulation and economic life, Arrighi instead rejected linear assertions of the epochs of types of economic behaviour.

Central to Arrighi's model is the belief that finance capitalism is not a stage in the development of world economic systems, but a recurring, cyclical event (or series of events). He takes three crises as defining his long twentieth century: the depression of the 1873–96, the 30 years crisis, 1914–45, and the economic crisis of the 1970s, when the concept of 'stagflation' came into common currency.[35] As with any exponent of systemic analysis, Arrighi found it difficult to separate one epoch from another – especially when, by rejecting a simple Marxist framework, the rhythmic and cyclical, and repetitive dimensions of world capital evolution take precedence. Arrighi himself noted how, as one system was in demise, another was rising, the two of them coexisting simultaneously for a while. The schema and time frame outlined by Arrighi was not so abstracted from the historical moment as to be meaningless: far from it. He saw, in alignment with his three core crises (1873–96, 1914–45 and the 1970s), real historical cycles at work. The first phase was associated with the emergence of the British capitalist–imperial hegemony; the second with Britain's decline and the rise to prominence of the United States; and the third with the globalisation of American hegemony and the beginning of its demise.[36] With the model in place, however, Arrighi found himself needing to explain the rise of these finance-capital systems of the long twentieth century. British capitalism did not begin from nothing, or grow from a text such as Adam Smith's *The Wealth of Nations* (1776). Smith's enunciation of **mercantilism** could only be written once something like the system he described was in existence, lacking only a name. Thus, in order to explain his own moment of study, Arrighi had to go back to the origins of finance capitalism (what he called 'the genesis of high finance'), before leading his reader through the first (Genoese) and second (Dutch) 'systemic cycle of accumulation'.[37]

For our purposes, then, we can see immediately how the challenge facing Giovanni Arrighi is also the one facing any scholar who seeks to comprehend any systemic-level occurrence over a significant period: where to start. Where does one epoch begin and another end? Clearly, it is possible to go so far back that clear differences between system-level organisations can be seen quite easily. A world before gas or electricity clearly has different capabilities in the productive sphere than one that enjoys these, and other, sources of power and light. Electricity was, for many years, inferior to gas as a source of light (factoring in cost, safety, necessary infrastructural investment). But as technologies developed, and new ways of generating electricity came about, this was no longer the case. Here, transition is crucial. And it is the very same problem faced by grand-scale historians and sociologists, such as

Tilly and Arrighi. Probing for the point upon which one system or society hinged inevitably leads to an examination of very long trails of past societies and the ways in which they were organised. This is why more than one-third of Arrighi's study is dedicated to earlier systems that were precursors to, or overlapped with, his spheres of interest.

Recent, more **empirical** and less theoretical, scholarship also resonates with the echoes of Braudel. Not that today's historians very often claim to be able to conceptualise the totality of society, as once Braudel did. Instead, Braudel's influence can be seen in two ways. First, as a platform upon which to build further studies of the Mediterranean world which he had made his own. Secondly, as an inspiration to those seeking to mix economies, cultures and politics with an appreciation of the natural world and its influence upon human society. A recent study which perhaps illustrates both elements of the Braudelian legacy is Linda Colley's important book on the early British Empire and those who fell into captivity during its making and endless renegotiations.[38] The first part of Colley's study owes much to Braudel. Her acute appreciation of the difficulty of terrain and travel, of the much greater equality of power between old empires, such as the Ottoman, and the newer, western European ones, is predicated upon an understanding of how distance, climate and weather might level the playing field of imperial competitors. But Colley also seeks to draw us back to the Meditteranean Sea, even though Braudel ended his epic saga at the threshold of the seventeenth century. Braudel's decision, based upon his view that the Mediterranean declined in importance thereafter, is used by Colley to explain why so many historians thereafter turned their attentions to the Atlantic.[39] Seeing the rise of the Americas, particularly of the United States, following the revolution (1776–83), as important, is one thing; but ignoring the ongoing interaction of multinational, multi-ethnic, multi-faith empires and encounters in the Mediterranean, is quite another.

Colley's book demonstrates a desire to explain how the British imperial project did not follow some kind of inevitable and preordained pathway, and that the triumph of the British imperial will, whilst obvious by 1880, was nowhere near so accepted even a century prior to this. Colley shows, using a complex and beguiling interweaving of stories of the captivities endured by ordinary Britons and Irish, how the great British Empire, which made slaves of countless thousands, exacted a cost: the enslavement of its own peoples. Until naval vessels could truly outgun their corsair foe, or could out-fight the military might of the Ottomans or African potentates of that great empire, then nothing much was guaranteed except a fairly equal struggle, especially in the theatre of Braudel's Mediterranean, where thousands of white European were captured into Islamic bondage. The experiences of these peoples, the military reversals for British naval power, and the changing of tactics of North Africans, are woven together by Colley in a way which reflects a very Braudelian appreciation of time and space, as well as of culture, society and politics. But she also shares his appreciation of the complexity of cultures in a waterway in which the water itself, quite naturally, has no physically markers of territory or tradition. Colley wrote: 'As Braudel chronicled with such magnificent sweep and arresting detail, the early modern Mediterranean was above all a region where the different states of Western Christendom confronted and sometimes co-operated with the Ottoman empire and with Islam.'[40] In explaining this process of cooperation as well as conflict, Colley strikes to the heart of the matter: never one-sided, never a teleological forward march of western ideas and institutions, the imperialisms of the period, notably in the Mediterranean, were complex and multilayered.

▶ Comparative history

It is perhaps a short step from 'total' to comparative history. For example, Colley's work, outlined earlier, is consciously comparative: aligning cultures and peoples, experiences and episodes, from more than one angle. Both total history and comparative history are based, in some respects, upon the concept of distance: whether **synchronically** (as in Braudel's *Mediterranean*), across vast periods of time (or else **diachronically**, that is, in the same time frame but across more than one geographical space).[41] Jürgen Kocka, for example, sought to develop theories of comparison that allowed analysis that compared phenomena across time and space in this way.[42] Indeed, along with the French *Annalistes* and the British Marxists, the West German 'New Social History' (*Gessellshaft-geschichte*) approach has been important in developing comparative history, particular with respect to a structural societal history, strongly influenced by Max Weber (1864–1920), and other sociologists. Where 'total history' obtained its energy from the encapsulation of the essential character of societal change over time, comparison seeks methodological and philosophical utility from its theoretical ability to throw sharper light on to one case-study area by noting similarities and differences in one place and the other. It is also possible to argue that, as David Englander remarked: 'All history is comparative history; for without the drawing of comparisons the relationship between the unique and the general could never be known and history, as a discipline, would be impossible.'[43]

Comparative history enjoyed early intellectual exposure among the historians of the *Annales* School. Indeed, Marc Bloch wrote an important contribution on the importance of comparative history, one that stands the test of time today.[44] Driven by a desire to understand society in almost a macro-sociological way, Bloch pointed to comparison as a way forward, not least because it provided an 'important heuristic means for tracking down new research problems'.[45] His notion of what constituted comparative history was as much commonsensical as it was profound. For him, it was 'a parallel study of societies that are at once neighbouring and contemporary, exercising a constant mutual influence, exposed throughout their development to the action of the same broad causes just because they are close and contemporaneous, and owing their existence in part at least to a common origin'.[46]

Bloch, on discovering the importance of enclosures in English agricultural history between the mid-1500s and1800, found similar processes in French agrarian experiences.[47] Thus, Bloch's own substantive work was also evidence of comparison in action. His major work, *The Royal Touch*, was a classic early example of comparative history.[48] This study of culture, superstition and belief was in early modern France and Britain, where it was believed that the monarch's touch could cure the skin disease scrofula. Another of Bloch's works, a study of feudal societies, was also consciously comparative, drawing material from across national boundaries.[49] This book was not confined to an examination of land tenure and social relations under feudalism, but looked at the whole of feudal society. Moreover, although Bloch's focus was primarily upon European feudalism, it also considers Japanese Samurai culture.

The pursuit of comparison in history is dogged by challenges of methodology and sources. Traditional historians might argue, for example, that any comparison of, say, politics in Germany, France and Britain should involve research in the national archives of all the countries involved; and that this would, in turn, require significant language skills. It would also be an expensive process to undertake. For this reason, many of the great comparative works of this century are based predominantly on secondary reading. In the case of Braudel's *Civilisation and Capitalism* (1979), for example, that secondary reading is prodigiously wide. Originally intended to complement volumes by Febvre (who died before they could be written), *Civilisation and Capitalism* bears a striking structural resemblance to a Marxist conception of society. Its three volumes were principally concerned with modes and impacts of consumption, distribution and production in the old regime (1400–1800). Braudel attempted systematically to unite, by comparison, the major civilisations of the Eastern and Western worlds – India, China, Japan and Indonesia, the Americas and Europe. In so doing, he combined the 'history of everyday life' with greater social and economic developments.[50]

The key feature of the comparative method, according to W.H. Sewell, is hypothesis testing.[51] This means that by engaging with problems and issues comparatively, historians are seeking to add an explanatory dimension to their knowledge of what really interests them. An analysis of class formation and Chartism in Victorian Britain might be said to be enhanced by appreciation of examples from France or America, where such examples of class formation were either different or absent. Van Den Braembussche offers an interesting reading of Sewell, adding further analytical edge to the latter's notion of comparison. For Sewell, he argues, the method is 'a means for systematically testing the validity of our explanations'. Thus, 'where an historian ascribes the appearance of phenomenon A in one society to the existence of condition B, he can test this hypothesis by looking for other societies in which A appears without B and vice versa'.[52]

Whilst this might enforce the specificity of particular countries' histories, and lead to a stress on the uniqueness of historical conditions in given places, it would at least add confidence to any hypotheses offered. We can see from Sewell's model why concepts such as revolution have commonly been subjected to such comparative analysis, not least in the works of sociologists, such as Theda Skocpol and Barrington Moore Jr, as well as historians such as Eric Hobsbawm.[53] However, Hobsbawm, for one, is sceptical about the extent to which comparative history – such hypothesis testing – is useful at all. For him, it is 'actual history ... we must explain'. Thus, he continued, 'The possible development or nondevelopment of capitalism in imperial China is relevant to us only insofar as it helps to explain the fact that this type of economy developed fully, at least to begin with, in one and only one region of the world.'[54] Hobsbawm's thus points towards the utility of the method only in proving the uniqueness of capitalism's origins in western Europe. The examination of less peculiar phenomena would, we imagine, make a less clear-cut case than that of capitalism. Moreover, broad-ranging issues, such as the nature of social relations, bear out the usefulness of comparison: indeed Hobsbawm goes on to make much of this point in relation to feudalism.[55]

Classic examples of the way in which the comparative method allows large-scale systemic analysis of phenomena, can be found in important works by Barrington Moore and Theda Skocpol. These works adopt approaches in which various secondary studies are assembled to create a grand design by a researcher who has not themselves had first-hand contact with the primary research materials. Because the comparative method requires some distance to be placed between the author and the usual, or traditional, **empirical** approach to original documents. 'The comparative historian's task – and potentially distinctive scholarly contribution – lies not in revealing data about particular aspects of the large time periods and diverse places surveyed in the comparative study, but rather in establishing the interest and prima facie validity of an overall argument about causal regularities across the various historical cases.'[56]

Barrington Moore also discusses the advantages of a comparative approach, arguing that the method leads inevitably to interesting questions, some of them novel. Moore also saw in comparison a 'rough negative check on accepted historical explanations' as well as the possibility of 'new historical generalizations'. Developing this theme, he argued that the search for connections across time and space unified comparative history as a 'single intellectual process'. Thus, for example, 'after noticing that Indian peasants have suffered in a material way just about as much as Chinese peasants during the nineteenth and twentieth centuries without generating a massive revolutionary movement, one begins to wonder about traditional explanations of what took place in both societies and becomes alert to factors affecting peasant outbreaks in other countries, in the hope of discerning general causes'.[57] It also has to be recognised, therefore, that there are several ways of approaching comparative history. Skocpol and Somers identify 'three distinct logics-in-use of comparative history', and show how, although it is possible to combine them, individual works tend to rely primarily upon a single logic.[58] One approach, the parallel type of comparative history, uses a number of historical examples to persuade the reader that a particular hypothesis or theory is applicable to a wide range of historical contexts.[59] Another is the contrast-oriented approach that seeks to bring out the unique features of each particular case included in their discussions. 'In short, contrast-oriented comparativists aim to place historical limits on overly-generalized theories, but they do not aspire to generate new explanatory generalizations through comparative historical analysis.'[60] Finally, there is a group of scholars, including Barrington Moore and Theda Skocpol, who use comparative historical analysis by selecting or referring to historical examples to test the validity of existing theoretical hypotheses, and generate new ones. Such works tend to move back and forward between alternative explanations and historical examples.[61] Barrington Moore provides a good description of this approach in the earlier quote.[62]

Barrington Moore attempts to provide an analysis that is structured by comparison of one socio-political system with another, and by cross-referencing epochs, periods and key moments in the history of social organisation and political systems. Insofar as historical sociology is concerned, the approach is important because it operates consciously within an historical framework: history and historical change are used to inform contemporary sociological conditions as he saw them at the time of writing. In this respect, Barrington Moore's systemic analysis represents a return to the earlier traditions of historical sociology represented by Max Weber's monumental study of the landowner–peasant relations in a bewildering array of countries: England, France, America, China, Japan and India.[63] Moore's aim was to show how varying material and cultural circumstances gave rise to parliamentary demo-cracy, fascism or communism. Barrington Moore was concerned with a very fundamental question in the history of societies: namely, how countries change from an agrarian to an industrial state, and how the relationship between lord and peasant can produce parliamentary democracy, fascism or communism.

The focus was thus upon account for the differing political trajectories account for by specific economic and social conditions. In this work Barrington Moore identified three alternative political routes to the modern world: (1) through 'bourgeois revolution' to liberal democracy; (2) through 'revolution from above' to fascism; and (3) through 'peasant revolutions' to communism. By discussing the differences in the strengths of the bourgeoisie in relation to landlords, to modes of agricultural commercialisation, and to types of peasant communities and peasant–landlord relations, Moore asked why specified sets of countries travelled one route rather than the others. Whilst Moore's study was conceived on a massive scale, drawing upon sustained examples from many nations, it was not total-global history, but, rather, what we might term comparative-systemic. Rather than seeking, perhaps fancifully, to write a history of the world, organising all known nations, Moore defined the extent of his study by drawing upon a series of case studies. Thus, the democratic route, from bourgeois emergence to liberal democracy, was discussed in relation to England, France and the United States (the English Civil War, the French Revolution and the American Civil War being the necessary bourgeois revolutions in question). Contrastingly, Japan was settled upon as the instance where 'revolution from above' was thought to have provided the driver for fascism. The third route, the progress through peasant revolution to communism, was exemplified by Russia and China, especially the latter, which was discussed in detail by Moore. To provide a further testing ground for his tripartite system of analysis, he discussed India, which according to his model, had seen neither a capitalist-bourgeois revolution from above nor a peasant revolution from below. Yet, as Moore shows, despite its similarities with other peasant societies that turned to communism, India has developed a parliamentary democracy. The case of India, then, provides a theoretical check on the other cases discussed; and in each series of discussions by Moore, we can see the application of a scientific method of experimentation, remodelling and further experimentation. It is a breathtaking book when read as one complex whole. However, historians of different countries or different subjects tend to atomise such studies, so that while the *Origins of Dictatorship and Democracy* is compelling in general, its component parts are criticised. This reflects both the problems of comparative history as well as the tendencies of historians themselves. At the same time, comparison remains something that historians – especially those with a strong theoretical grounding (for this enables the ordering of complex materials) – try to achieve. Scholarship in this area of 'total', 'comparative' and 'societal' history has not been restricted to historians. Far from it: Moore's account is a work of historical sociology, as much theoretical modelling as **empiricism**.

Whether scholars approach such issues as comparative social and political systems from the historian's perspective or not, they will inevitably rely heavily upon the scholarship of sociologists and philosophers – for historians, evidence-based empiricists in particular, might be said not to have the tools to model interpretation over *la longue durée* or in an explanatory way. Since Marx, and noticeably through the work of Max Weber, totalising historical approaches have owed more to theorists than to historians. Thus, a classic example of comparative history on a grand scale is Weber's 'Social Psychology of the World Religions'.[64] This essay, the introduction to more detailed works, is a grand tour of five major beliefs – Confucianism, Hinduism, Buddhism, Christianity and Islam – in 50 pages of text. In this study, Weber identified what he believed were the salient comparisons and contrasts between the various religions, in terms of their rise, leadership, support-base and charisma, etc. Weber's study effectively covered thousands of years and ranged across the Orient and Occident. It was not, however, a study primarily in the historian's mode, and was not based upon primary research. Instead it was an attempt to draw out comparative trends. It was based fundamentally upon Weber's conception of the social psychological role of religion, which was, for him (as for Marx), underpinned by key factors, which existed irrespective of time, location or denomination. This, it might be argued, is the key feature of comparison in social theory, although most historians would balk at claiming such work as 'history proper'.

A prime exponent of the important Weberian approach is Michael Mann, who conceives of societies as 'multiple overlapping and intersecting power networks'. He argued: 'A general account of societies, their structure, and their history can best be given in terms of the interrelations of what I will call the four sources of social power: ideological, economic, military and political (IEMP) relationships.'[65] The key issue of sociological theory has been that of ultimate primacy or determinacy. Is there one, or are there more decisive and ultimately determining elements, or keystones of society? Mann explicitly acknowledges his debt to Weber's vision of the relationship between society, history and social action. His theory is that the four sources of social power fundamentally determine the structure of societies. Mann's central question was: what are the relations between these four power sources? For him, none of the four has ultimate primacy. The predominant source of power has varied according to the world-historical context. This is why Mann viewed society as a 'patterned mess'.[66]

Mann uses this model in the first two of four projected volumes where he covers world history up to 1914 and also in the second volume, which goes from 1760–1914. So he is working on a vast historical canvas. All of world history is covered, and he is attempting to describe the rise and fall of whole civilizations in Volume One (5,000 years of the history of civilization, worldwide). How valid is this attempt though? Well, one point we could make is that Mann is simply doing what historians have done all along (i.e. looking at all the factors that contribute to the making of history to construct a multi-casual explanation of events). But he is doing it in a more conscious and 'theorised' manner than a 'conventional' historian. In the second volume, the most general argument is that eighteenth-century society was ultimately shaped by economic and military power and nineteenth-century society by economic and political power. He says: 'as military power was subsumed into the "modern state" and as capitalism continued to revolutionize the economy, economic and political power sources began to dominate. Capitalism and its classes, and states and nations, became the decisive power actors of modern times.'[67]

Because the sources of social power are entwined thus, they cannot be given a singular ultimate primacy. Does such a statement tell us anything at all novel about the nineteenth century? He is right to emphasise the complexity of social relations, and to says that this complexity often exceeded the understanding of contemporaries so that 'their actions thus involved many mistakes, apparent accidents and unintended consequences'.[68] Here we find ourselves confronting, again, that classic of Marx historical configuration. Whilst men's actions could shape daily life and political circumstances, the structural forces at play would have the ultimate say in the shape of the future: 'Men make their own history, but they do not make it just as they please; they do not make it under circumstances chosen by themselves, but under circumstances directly encountered, given and transmitted from the past.'[69]

If human society is a 'patterned mess', rather like Zeldin's 'mass of factors and influences', did Mann evolve the best way of explaining it? In fact, he faces two difficulties. First, there is the problem of the sheer scale of the enterprise Mann has attempted. He has to cover a vast time period, and deal with an enormous amount of secondary literature, synthesize it, and incorporate it into his argument. On the other hand, just because a task is difficult, does not mean that it should not be attempted but, in Mann's case, this does seem to lead to a restatement of the major historical literature. Secondly, the approach he adopts seems to involve a repetition of his opening statement in every single context he encounters: to identify the four sources of social power, and then rank their relative causal weights.[70] In a sense, this tells us everything and nothing. At any one time, we are told particular power sources overtake others and dominate a period. In many ways this does not seem to answer many of the specific problems of historical explanation, as they are eventually subsumed within this broad explanatory framework. This is not to say that Mann's work is not stimulating and valuable and that it does not contain many useful insights into the development of state power.[71] Whether it delivers in terms of an overall explanatory framework is another question though.

Comparative history premises the notion of extending knowledge, or of locating historical phenomena in comparative context, and this, itself, provides reason enough for students and scholars to come to grips with the implications of comparative approaches. But we also have equally pressing personal reasons for so doing. While professional historians usually specialise during research, they have to teach much broader aspects of history to be of any use to students. The latter are often faced with courses that are at least subconsciously comparative. The texts and monographs that support such courses usually are not comparative, requiring the teacher and student to draw the comparisons out in discussions and essay-writing. Equally, many studies, while focused upon single themes, are inherently comparative. The development of an interest in the Atlantic world, particularly within American scholarship, bears a strong weight of comparison. The British Atlantic, for example, involves conscious intellectual interactions between British, Irish, African and American spheres: in some ways, these replicate the migratory patterns and flows of goods and ideas that made the Atlantic world in the first place.[72] Similarly, themes such as 'class' also lend themselves to comparative reflection. Again, we can see this in the context of the Atlantic world, where an important recent work by Peter Linebaugh and Marcus Rediker has demonstrated how class, struggle, protest and brutality were part of the economic, social and migratory forces than held together the British and American North Atlantic.[73] This is brilliantly captured in words, which have comparison very much in mind: 'The circular transmission of human experiences from Europe to Africa to the Americas and back again correspond to the same cosmic forces that set the Atlantic currents in motion.'[74]

Regional history has already begun to show the potential richness of comparison in historical enquiry. It is arguable, indeed, that the history of particular regions, or aspects of such a region's history, is limited in utility if it is not done with comparative reflection at heart. One of the definitions of nationally or internationally important regional history must surely be that it is only by comparing, by thinking about other regions, that firm statements about a given locale can actually be made. At the same time, pitfalls are present. As Stefan Berger recently noted: 'interregional comparisons will have to take account of the fact that regions ... can neither be seen as a synthesis of individual localities nor as part and parcel of a wider whole'.[75] In other words, regions themselves, the notion of regionality, become the first point of discussion. From there, an ability to work in two languages allows scholars to compare not only intra-state regional factors, but also interstate regions. Such approaches, allied to such skills, have led to innovative work in, for example, the area of comparative deindustrialisation and urban regeneration in Britain and Scandinavia. Scholarship in the field of comparative regional studies draws upon twin sources of sustenance. Drawing upon contemporary notions of the shape of Europe – in this case the 'Europe of the Regions', designed by the European Community – such works are shaped by critical thinking in the current context; by extending the hypothesis testing from a single theatre of research to two or more, those same works meet exacting standards of scholarship.[76]

The case for comparison is made compelling, too, in the case of migration studies. The history of Irish migration, for example – like that of any migration – lends itself to comparative consideration. The essence is to try to engage with the Orange Order and its migrant constituents through notions of 'linear', 'divergent' and 'convergent' models of migrant experience, as described by Nancy L. Green.[77] Green has offered an interesting insight into the way in which comparative methods should be applied to the study of migration. She suggests three levels on which the comparative method might be employed. The first, 'the linear model' involves the comparison of sending and receiving nations. This is an approach governed by contrasts as well as similarities. 'The convergent model' involves the study of different migrant groups in particular locales to plot their comparative performance, economically, socially, politically and so on. Analysing, say, Irish and German migrants in New York provides an opportunity to see if one group adjusts more readily than another; and if so, to ask why this is the case. Her third approach, 'the divergent' model – and the one most applicable to this chapter – involves the comparison of the same groups in different locales, in this case Irish and other Orangemen in Britain and elsewhere.[78] This very approach has been usefully applied in Green's own widely acclaimed collection on Jewish workers.[79] This third model offers us a way to understand both relative group success in different geographical locations, but also uncovers important findings on the countries in which the migrant group settled. In discussing these models, Green attempts to make explicit what she believes already to be implicit in migration studies.

Comparison enhances our understanding of phenomenon A or B (or A and B together) by allowing us to understand both the essential and the particular. The essential factors are those things that apply beyond rigid boundaries. Essential factors are what we might term general factors. These phenomena have some kernel of meaning across religious, cultural, national and historical boundaries: class, kinship, feudalism or democracy might be examples. Each should be sensitive in terms of national/local practice, but their core assumptions are applicable on a comparative level. For example, while the term 'working class' might mean something different in France and Scotland, scholars and students can use agreed indices of measurement in comparing this difference. We might talk about economic influences or cultural influences; we might chart different events in the history of class; but certain statements will provide the bedrock of the comparison. On the other hand, particular factors are things with which comparative historians are less concerned. The particular is usually confined to surface occurrences: remember, for example, Braudel's comment, in his *Mediterranean*, that events are 'surface disturbances, crests of foam that the tides of history carry on their strong backs'.[80]

Comparative dimensions to historical inquiry also provide a crucial check on explanatory models, leading, for example, to the conclusion that explanation in case x may not be applicable in case y. For this reason comparison occupies a special place in social theory and was vital in the formative years of the development of sociology. The nineteenth-century French sociologist Emile Durkheim claimed: 'comparative sociology is not a special branch of sociology. It is sociology itself.' Durkheim offers two principal areas of comparison. First, societies which were/are apparently similar: Greek and Roman; German and French; British and American. Secondly (and here we might use 'contrast'), those societies and civilisations which were different: for example, British and Indian, Chinese and European. Max Weber, the German social theorist, supported the principle of comparison as central to understanding the past: 'We are absolutely in accord that history should establish what is specific, say, to the medieval city; but this is possible only if we first find what is missing in other cities.'[81]

▶ The postmodern challenge

Attempts at offering large-scale explanations of historical processes, a **'total' history**, or systemic accounts of the past have become increasingly unfashionable of late for a number of reasons. The main cause of this turn away from the attempt to comprehend the broader structures of history is the influence of **postmodernism**, an approach that we now need to briefly consider, before concluding this chapter. It is extraordinarily difficult to offer a definition of the term 'postmodern', because it has been used in so many ways. Although the word has a number of uses, we can usefully distinguish between '**postmodernity**' and 'postmodernism'. The first is a concept that describes the particular age in which we live, in terms of its socio-economic, political and cultural condition. This is to do with the increasingly post-industrial nature of western society, involving the growth of service industries, and an 'information society'. 'Postmodernism', on the other hand, describes the broad aesthetic and intellectual concerns in our society at the level of theory. This is concerned with particular artistic styles, claims about the ability of language to describe the world, and the nature of 'truth'.[82]

The sociologist Anthony Giddens reckoned the term 'postmodernism' 'is best kept to refer to styles or movements within literature, painting the plastic arts, and architecture'.[83] Thus postmodernism can be seen as an identifiable trend within the cultural sphere, distinct from (or a progression from) **modernism**, which means that it may be appropriate to talk about a particular building or novel as being 'post-modern'. As Giddens says, though, to speak of 'postmodernity' implies that we are moving into an era of postmodernity. This suggests that this is a distinct phase of social order that takes us away from the institutions of modernity in a manner that would entail a fundamental break with those institutions. Giddens not only argues that such a break has not yet occurred, but also offers an alternative position to postmodernity, which he calls 'radicalised modernity'.[84] So, this calls into question, the more dramatic pronouncements of some postmodernists. Keith Jenkins, for example, has asserted, with a degree of confident closure, that 'today we live within the general condition of postmodernity. We do not have a choice about this.'[85] Even if we do accept that present-day society is essentially 'postmodern', this still does not inevitably mean that we have to accept postmodernism as what Trevor Noble called 'the relativist theory of an incoherent era'.[86] We should now consider 'post-modernism' as a challenge to existing academic disciplines and ways of thought, in other words at the level of theory.[87]

Postmodern theory abandons explanatory goals, and argues that there is no way to describe, analyse or explain reality in an objective or scientific way. This is often described as the challenge to the 'Enlightenment Project'. It emphasises hetero-geneity, multiplicity and marginality, and the production of knowledge as opposed to truth. Rather than a general, universal theory it is concerned with the local and the specific. Rather than seeking to establish a singular, unitary reality it stresses the existence of multiple realities.[88] The other main plank of postmodern theory is that it questions the ability of language to represent anything outside itself. So words are no longer seen as the straightforward reflection of an external world, but are implicated in the construction of that world. These are just the broad outlines of what amount to a number of complex overlapping ideas. So let us now try and unpack the various components of **'postmodernism'**, which we shall be returning to in subsequent chapters.

Although it is obviously much easier to identify the 'essential' characteristics of, for example, Marxism than those of postmodern thought, a number of thinkers are usually cited as significant in relation to the development of this approach. Although the word 'postmodernism' has a long and complicated history, its contemporary usage is associated with **poststructuralist** and deconstructionist ideas.[89] The key elements of this are: Jacques Derrida's theories of deconstruction and grammatology, and Roland Barthes's 1960s essay 'The Death of the Author'. To this we can add Jacques Laccan's notions of desire, Michel Foucault's 'genealogical' theory of history, Jean-François Lyotard's rejection of **'metanarratives'** and Jean Baudrillard's discussion of the way electronic media has created a supposed state of 'hyperreality'.[90] The key feature of the postmodern critique of conventional academic practice that needs to be emphasised within the context of a discussion of history written on a grand scale is Lyotard's scepticism towards all general theory.

Lyotard's *The Postmodern Condition: A Report on Knowledge* (1979) has become one of the key statements of postmodern thought. Its significance stems from the way it weaves together a number of strands: postmodern art, poststructuralist philosophy and the theory of post-industrial society into something approaching a coherent whole.[91] Lyotard defines the postmodern in contrast to the modern. For him, the word postmodern, 'designates the state of our culture following the transformations which, since the end of the nineteenth century, have altered the game rules for science, literature, and the arts'. From this position, he argued, his own work would 'place these transformations in the context of the crisis of narratives ... Simplifying to the extreme, I define *postmodern* as incredulity toward metanarratives'.[92] These grand stories have always involved some notion of progress. The Enlightenment notion of progress, the emancipation of the proletariat in Marxism, or the release from unconscious trauma invoked in Freudian theory are all examples of metanarratives.[93] Let us now explore Lyotard's argument in a little more depth.

Lyotard opens with something of a proclamation. 'Our working hypotheses is that the status of knowledge is altered as societies enter what is known as the post-industrial age and cultures enter what is known as the postmodern age.'[94] The start of this postmodern age was the end of the 1950s, and it is characterised by the demise of the aforementioned *grandes histoires* or 'incredulity toward metanarratives', and the emergence of what he calls *petites histoires* or micronarratives in their place. So there is disillusionment with grand large-scale explanations of reality, such as are offered by science, religion and Marxism. This is replaced by a concern with single-issue campaigns. Put crudely, this leads people to concentrate on saving the whale rather than saving the working class. Lyotard says that, in the **postmodern** era, knowledge can no longer be legitimated by the great narratives that have shaped western knowledge so far. **Metanarratives** are seen as tyrannical in their imposition of a 'totalising' pattern to events, and Lyotard declares 'a war on totality'. Instead, he asserts the need for local narratives to explain things, which means that knowledge can only be partial. Such an approach is intended to liberate us from the tyranny of grand designs. This 'anti-foundationalism' rejects all the existing norms of academic scholarship. The individual postmodern scholar would thus be able to work without rules.[95] In essence, Lyotard's position, which is also representative of the postmodern position in general, is that it is impossible to determine any order in the world, therefore it is impossible to theorise about it.

Such a position is obviously a fundamental challenge to existing academic practice in general, not just that of historians, and has prompted a great deal of debate within a number of disciplines. As the sociologist Nicos Mouzelis says, as well as rejecting 'holistic theories', postmodernism also 'is equally opposed to the notions of representation and **empirical** reference'. It thus 'scorns the idea that social theory could or should, directly or indirectly, represent a social reality existing "out there", a reality that is constituted and continues in time separately from, or irrespective of, theory'.[96] Mouzelis espouses a social realist position, which maintains that theory must be grounded in empirical reality, but also attempts to steer a delicate course between the universalising generalisations of the modernists and the extreme **relativism** of the postmodernists.[97] This raises the issue of how an accommodation with postmodernism could be reached, and whether in fact such a 'compromise position' is either possible or desirable. These issues cannot be resolved here, but we will be returning to some of the implications of the postmodern position in subsequent chapters.

▶ Conclusion

The central aim of this chapter has been to consider some important scholarship, which has gone beyond the local, specific historical issue or problem, looking out towards the broadest vista possible. Attempts to conceptualise and understand the entirety of human society did not begin and end with Fernand Braudel: even within his own *Annales* School he had mentors. Besides, the Braudelian vision was one that bore uncanny resemblance to the aims of nineteenth-century thinkers such as Marx, but others too. Braudel, like the nineteenth-century **positivists**, sought answers to big questions. More recently, Barrington Moore, Charles Tilly and Giovanni Arrighi, have similarly sought to interpret historical change over Braudel's *longue durée*. All these works are implicitly comparative: some compare epochs and others compare systemic factors (as in Arrighi, with his focus on economic-fiscal dimensions of life). But all of them deal with more than one location or territory. Braudel's *Mediterranean* was a meeting point for dozens of territories, cultures, customs and histories – even one part of that territory, the Ottoman Empire, was, in Braudel's own words, a 'jig-saw'.[98]

The comparative method does not claim to offer totalising systemic accounts such as these. But it does share with **histoire totale** an appreciation of the need to get beyond the minute empirical case studies that comprise much historical scholarship. Both approaches also have at their heart a desire to push on from a fact-based, observation-led position, in which the sanctity of the documents is above all else, to one where the theoretical apparatus is bolder and the modelling of systems, concepts and ideas becomes more apparent. Not that comparative historians entirely eschew the rigorous, archival researches that have been central to the discipline since the Rankean revolution of the nineteenth century. Many of the examples offered here are based on at least double the archive work involved in a non-comparative study, simply because the theatres of analysis are at least twice as numerous.

In both cases, an emboldened spirit and a methodological rigour has been developed because of engagement with other disciplines. Without geography, there would be no *Annales*. Macro-sociological approaches, such as Barrington Moore's or Theda Skocpol's, can offer us a better understanding of large-scale structures and processes of social change, through the use of both the comparative method, and a conceptual framework drawn from the social sciences. The influence of classical sociology continues to be felt in such work. Charles Tilly noted: 'Anyone who surveys the recent big studies of large-scale structural change employing small numbers of cases notices the remarkable staying power of the classics. In one form or another, Durkheim, Tocqueville, Weber, and especially, Marx, continue to set the problems – even for those investigators who intend to leave the grandfathers behind.'[99] Both approaches – total and comparative history – demonstrate, in the most fundamental and impressive way, how subjects fuse and theory aids the explanation and understanding of social phenomena, past or present.

4 Social Structure and Human Agency in Historical Explanation

▶ Introduction

In Britain before the Second World War higher education was largely the preserve of a privileged minority. It was extremely unusual for anyone from a working-class background to attend university. The main reason for this was that there was very little free educational provision after the age of 14 until the 1944 Education Act.[1] Thus, those from poorer backgrounds were usually prevented from attending university for financial reasons. However, the existence of such structural factors did not prevent some, particularly determined, individuals from underprivileged backgrounds from gaining a place at a university. One such person was Ralph Glasser, who was born to Jewish immigrant parents, and grew up in the Gorbals, a slum district of Glasgow. Due to the family's straitened financial circumstances, Glasser had to leave school at 14 and began work as a soap-boy in a barber's and then as a presser in a clothes factory. Determined not to neglect his education, he continued to study both by himself and in extramural classes at Glasgow University. His hard work finally paid off when he was awarded a scholarship to Oxford after submitting an essay in the vague hope that something might come of it. Glasser made the journey from Glasgow to Oxford on a bicycle, because he was too poor to afford rail travel. Although his studies were interrupted by the Second World War, he returned after the war to complete his degree. After leaving Oxford, he went on to work for the British Council, became involved in development projects in the Third World, and also had several of his own works published. Thus that one action of submitting an essay transformed his whole life.[2]

As Glasser says in his autobiography, he was highly aware of the exceptional nature of his achievement in gaining a place at Oxford at this time: 'In pre-war days, for a Gorbals man to come up to Oxford was as unthinkable as to meet a raw bushman in a St James club...'. This almost anthropological divide was determined partly by a lack of familiarity: 'for a member of the boss class, someone from the Gorbals *was* in effect a bushman, the Gorbals itself as distant as unknowable, as the Kalahari Desert'.[3] The exceptional achievement of Ralph Glasser, demonstrated that self-improvement was always possible, but this is not the key point. Glasser's experience highlights the existence of the structural factors that prevented most people from his sort of background from ever going to an institute of higher education. While movement across the structural division was not impossible, Glasser was the exception that proves the rule in this case. Thus, it is important to bear in mind the way that broader social forces influence the lives of individuals, as well as the ways in which individuals can transcend their circumstances through their actions while we consider the way that historians and sociologists have approached the problem of structure and **agency**.

▶ Structure and agency in history and sociology

There are a number of 'social' factors that can prevent individuals from fulfilling their full potential, and social class is only one of them. People can be discriminated against on the grounds of their gender, ethnicity or sexuality. So, for example, racial discrimination may be the explanation for why an individual may not be offered a particular job. The existence of such discrimination may serve to limit the options (or 'life chances') of particular social groups in some circumstances, but this does not mean it cannot be overcome, on either an individual or a societal level. Social structures do not have to operate at such an explicit level either. They can also function at the level of ideology or mental structures. So, for example, lack of confidence as a result of social background may serve to limit an individual's freedom of action. This could prevent him or her from even attempting to pursue educational attainment, or applying for particular jobs that they feel to be out of their reach. These are all ways in which social structures can be seen to operate at an individual level.

Marx said: 'Men make history, but they do not make it just as they please; they do not make it under circumstances chosen by themselves, but under circumstances directly encountered, given, and transmitted from the past.'[4] This elegantly expresses the relationship between social structure and human agency, which is central to both history and sociology. Philip Abrams has argued that historians and sociologists are united by the common project of understanding this 'problematic of structuring'.[5] The central theoretical questions in understanding the operation of society lie in the nature of what should be accorded primacy:

> Is the community which is a society a collection of individuals who, as individuals, actively forge their relationships with one another and create society in the process of doing so? Or do the social relationships which make up society achieve an autonomous identity that establishes them as external conditions which determines the activities of the members of society as they enter into them?[6]

The first position is often referred to as individualistic, voluntaristic or action sociology, and considers society to be formed from the actions of individual members. The second position is often labelled holistic, deterministic or **structuralist** sociology, and it sees society as a system of relationships that determines the actions of its individual members.[7]

Social theorists tend to align themselves within these broad categories, although there is always a tendency to lean, if only slightly, towards the opposite position within their work. Karl Marx and structuralist Marxists, such as Louis Althusser, Emile Durkheim and **functionalists**, such as Talcott Parsons, can be classified as structuralists. Max Weber, Georg Simmel, and symbolic interactionists such as George Herbert Mead, and Erving Goffman can all be classified as action theorists.[8] However, such a distinction ignores some of the subtleties in the arguments of these major sociological thinkers, and it is also not an exhaustive list of social theorists. It merely represents a convenient starting point in this discussion. For example, it leaves out the problem of where to place various important contemporary sociological thinkers, such as Anthony Giddens, who have explicitly attempted to resolve the difficulties of these two approaches to sociology. In this sense, Giddens can be said to have created a sociology of both structure and **agency**, a theory of **structuration**, which is often held to have resolved many of the theoretical problems of the dichotomy of structure and agency in the social sciences.[9] The work of the sociologist Norbert Elias, can also be said to have offered a resolution to this theoretical dilemma, and we will return to both of these thinkers later.

Although historians are equally concerned with the relationship between social structure and human agency, they do not always discuss it in such explicit terms. History has traditionally been seen as driven by the actions of 'great men' rather than vast impersonal forces, and historians have always written biographies of important historical figures. Carlyle expresses this, nineteenth-century, view of history in his assertion: 'universal History, the history of what men have accomplished in this world, is at bottom the History of the Great Men who have worked here'.[10] Although most contemporary historians would be critical of the 'great man' theory of history, this has not led to the death of either this perspective or of historical biography.[11] However, the nature of historical biographies has changed. While some Victorian biographies could degenerate into hagiography, biographies by contemporary historians are more likely to pay attention to the historical context of the individual, thus not ignoring structure.[12]

In English-speaking countries the dominant approach to history until recently was what is often referred to as the '**empiricist**', 'common-sense', or 'traditional' approach, captured in the works of historians such as Hugh Trevor-Roper and Geoffrey Elton. As Christopher Lloyd says, 'Concepts of society as an independent structure with causal power play no part in their work but they do usually have a vaguely holistic concept of the *Zeitgeist* or character of an epoch.'[13] Alun Munslow characterises such historians as **'reconstructionist'**, while those historians who take the structures of history seriously would fall into his broad category of **'constructionist'**.[14] This latter term applies to all historians who employ some sort of explanatory framework to explain the past. **Structuralism** in history appears in various forms, but it is primarily associated with those historians who favour some sort of theoretical explanation of the past. The most prominent among such approaches are the Annales and Marxist schools of history, and those scholars who are usually classed as 'historical sociologists'. To use the label 'structuralist' in this context does not imply that these approaches invariably ignore the role of the individual in history, but that their heightened awareness of historical structures means that this is always a potential danger.

Munslow's third category of historical writing is **'deconstructionist'**, a term used to describe those historians influenced by the various **postmodern** approaches to the past.[15] As we saw in the previous chapter, this is a complicated critique of conventional academic practice, which cannot be easily summarised here, but essentially asserts that, since language is unable to represent the real world accurately, and knowledge about the world is intrinsically linked with power, we can never attain objective knowledge about the past. The authors most closely associated with this approach in terms of historical writing are Hayden White, Keith Jenkins and F.R. Ankersmit. It is worth emphasising, though, that this type of history forms a special category in itself, and stands outside of 'normal' historical practice in order to challenge it. So we need to be wary of treating it as merely another theoretical perspective to be applied to the study of the past.[16] Many commentators have noted the absence of a theory of **agency** in postmodern theory in general.[17]

Regardless of differences of approach, and the terminology employed, the best works of both history and sociology treat the relationship between structure and agency in a sensitive manner. Such works depict human beings as serious social actors who play a part in shaping the course of events, but do not ignore the genuine constraints placed upon the actions of both individuals and groups by social circumstances. Society is not just a collection of individuals, so we need to think in terms of social structure, but in so doing we also have to consider the extent to which this structure determines the actions of the members of society. There are a number of levels on which we can discern the operation of structure and agency in the historical process, although obviously the extent to which individuals have an influence on the course of events varies. For example, politicians, statesmen and military leaders exert a much greater degree of influence than 'ordinary' people. However, this does not mean that such significant individuals can act totally without restraint. They also have to consider the wishes and feelings of the rest of the population of a country, and in this way, all members of a given society are part of the historical process. This raises the issue of the effect that unequal access to social, political and economic resources has on individual action. Two questions are worth considering in this respect. Have there ever been individual rulers whose power was so great that they enjoyed completely unrestricted freedom of action? Have there ever been individuals whose oppression was so great that they could exercise no freedom of choice in their actions? In addition, even those who are in a position to shape events cannot always foresee what consequences their actions will have. So both historians and sociologists have to be aware of the importance of the unintended consequences of any action. This chapter will explore the way in which notions of structure and agency are employed within the work of both historians and sociologists. We shall begin by considering the work of a number of key social theorists on this question, many of whom we have already come across in the course of this discussion.

▶ Society and the individual: structure and agency in social theory

A good starting point in a consideration of the relationship between social structure and human **agency** is the difference between human and animal societies, a distinction that is clarified by Norbert Elias: 'The relationships, the interdependences between ants, bees, termites and other social insects, the structure of their societies can, as long as the species stays the same, be repeated over many thousands of years without any change.' We can account for this because, in these instances, social structures rely upon biological factors. Yet this is not so, Elias has argued, with humans whose societies 'can change without a change in the biological organization of human beings'.[18]

The specific transformation that Elias mentions in this connection is the transition from the *ancien régime* to the early industrial regime of the nineteenth century, involving a change from a rural society to a more urbanised one. Such an alteration of society is obviously not a result of biological changes in the human race. (Although some nineteenth-century commentators may have thought they perceived some in the urban proletariat.) The transition to a different type of society is the result of human action, and is specifically related to the process of the continuous social accumulation of knowledge, as Elias points out.[19] However, this still does not tell us why European society underwent such a transformation at that particular time. A number of different, and competing explanations have been offered for this major social transformation. As we saw in an earlier chapter, the founding fathers of sociology, Marx Durkheim and Weber, were concerned with explaining the transition from an agrarian to an industrial society. We should go on to consider how this transformation has been described by social theorists, beginning with Marx.

In the preceding discussion, we categorised Marxism as a **structuralist** theory. Structuralist theories offer differing explanations of social structures and institutions.

As David F. Walsh points out, culturalist theorists, such as Durkheim and Parsons 'argue that there are certain basic and environmentally determined conditions to which society has to adapt in order for social life to be possible' and this is achieved 'through the cultural creation of institutions and structures that provide solutions to the problems that these conditions create'.[20]

Marxist theorists, on the other hand, see the structural organisation of social relationships as the result of the collective organisation of the processes of production. The first principle of Marx's theory of history, which is usually known as **historical materialism**, and has already been briefly outlined in Chapter 3, is that human action is circumscribed by the material conditions within which it takes place. As Marx puts it in *The German Ideology* (1845–46):

> The first premise of all human history is, of course, the existence of living human individuals. Thus the first fact to be established is the physical organisation of these individuals and their consequent relation to the rest of nature. Of course, we cannot here go either into the actual physical nature of man, or into the natural conditions in which man finds himself – geological, oro-hydrographical, climatic and so on. The writing of history must always set out from these natural bases and their modification in the course of history through the action of men. Men can be distinguished from animals by consciousness, by religion or anything else you like. They themselves begin to distinguish themselves from animals as soon as they begin to *produce* their means of subsistence, a step which is conditioned by their physical organisation. By producing their means of subsistence men are indirectly producing their actual material life.[21]

Thus Marx is saying that people define themselves through the process of reproducing their material conditions of existence. However, this productive activity does not take place in conditions of complete freedom, it is conditioned by the economic system of production of a given age. In a capitalist society, this activity is primarily governed by the need of the employer to produce a profit. The demands of a capitalist economy are such that neither the worker nor the capitalist is free to act exactly as they wish.[22] Such an approach obviously prioritises the structuring role of economic factors, but to what extent does this mean that economics structures every aspect of human life?

There is a common conception that Marx's theory of history offers a crude form of economic reductionism or economic **determinism** in which material circumstances are the only cause of historical development. However, we need to ask whether such an interpretation does justice to the subtlety of Marx's theoretical writings? A simplified version of the ideas of historical materialism appears in *The Communist Manifesto* (1848) where Marx states: 'The ruling ideas of each age have ever been the ideas of its ruling class.'[23] Statements such as this do seem to indicate that Marx held a **determinist** view of history. The most celebrated exposition of Marx's theory of history, the Preface to his *Contribution to the Critique of Political Economy*(1859), also highlights the primacy of material factors:

> In the social production of their existence, men inevitably enter into definite relations, which are independent of their will, namely relations of production appropriate to a given stage in the development of their material forces of production. The totality of these relations of production constitutes the economic structure of society, the real foundation on which arises a legal and political **superstructure** and to which correspond definite forms of social consciousness. The **mode of production** of material life conditions the general process of social, political and intellectual life. It is not the consciousness of men that determines their existence, but their social existence that determines their consciousness.[24]

This passage is the classic formulation of the **base/superstructure** metaphor in Marx's thought. Base and superstructure was an architectural metaphor used by Marx and Engels in order to convey their conception of society. The base is the economic structure of society and the superstructure is the State and social consciousness. The key question is: what is the relationship between base and superstructure in Marxist theory? There is, in fact, an element of reciprocity in classical Marxist thought, and this is made explicit in Engels' claim that the base determined the superstructure only 'in the last instance', thus leaving some space for individuals and groups to act independently of its requirements.[25]

Marx's account of historical change starts from his assertion of the importance of material factors in the development of society:

> At a certain stage of their development, the material productive forces of society come into conflict with the existing relations of production, or – what is but a legal expression for the same thing – with the property relations within which they have been at work hitherto. From forms of development of the productive forces these relations turn into their fetters. Then begins an epoch of social revolution.[26]

Thus, in certain periods, the existing social relations of production can hinder the development of the productive forces, resulting in a crisis of the existing social system, which, in turn, will lead to a revolution. This raises the question of whether or not Marx saw revolution as the inevitable result of the workings of the laws of historical development. In fact, Marx emphasises the role of human **agency** in changing social relationships, as a particular mode of production can only be changed once those who are subject to it recognise their subjugation: 'Of all the instruments of production, the greatest productive force is the revolutionary class itself. The organisation of the revolutionary elements as a class presupposes the existence of all the productive forces that could be engendered in the womb of the old society.'[27] In a capitalist society, the revolution would be accomplished by a class-conscious proletariat who would collectively act as agents of social change. In the process of making the revolution, the proletariat would also remake themselves. Thus there is a coming together of the historical situation with purposive social action that results in the remaking of society. As Marx and Engels said, 'The materialist doctrine concerning the changing of circumstances and upbringing forgets that circumstances are changed by men and that it is essential to educate the educator himself. This doctrine must, therefore, divide society into two parts, one of which is superior to society.' Furthermore, they suggested, 'The coincidence of the changing of circumstances and of human activity or self-changing can be conceived and rationally understood only as revolutionary practice.'[28]

Marx went to great lengths to spell out his position on the role of human **agency** in history. First, he rejected the decisive role of the individual will in history, seen as independent of social forces.

> Man is in the most literal sense of the word a *zoon politikon*, not only a social animal, but an animal which can develop into an individual only in society. Production by isolated individuals outside society – something which might happen as an exception to a civilised man who by accident got into the wilderness and already possessed within himself the forces of society – is as great an absurdity as the idea of the development of language without individuals living together and talking to one another.[29]

Marx thus rejected the 'great men' view of history, as he did not see history as the result of the actions of isolated individuals. At the same time, he also disagreed with those who saw 'society as a person, as a subject'.[30] Marx argued that people produce society, as much as they are produced by it. So we should avoid drawing a rigid distinction between the individual and 'society', as we are all social beings. As Marx says, 'all history is nothing but a continuous transformation of human nature'.[31] However, history does not have an existence independent on the actions of real, living individuals: 'it does not possess immense riches, it does not fight battles. It is men, real, living men, who do all this, who possess things and fight battles. It is not "history" which uses men as a means of achieving – as if it were an individual person – its own ends. History is nothing but the activity of men in pursuit of their ends'.[32] We have seen that the notion of structure and agency within classical Marxist thought, far from being deterministic, offers an extremely useful view of the relationship between the individual and society for both historians and sociologists alike.[33]

In direct contrast to Marx, Durkheim argued: 'Undoubtedly a society is a being, a person.'[34] Thus Durkheim's theory of society is more **structuralist** than that of Marx. His starting point is that human association creates a separate reality with its own properties, which consists of social facts external to the individual. Human societies are thus different from those of animals. Among animals, individual instinct is key; for humans, 'certain ways of acting are imposed, or at least suggested *from outside* the individual and are added on to his own nature: such is the character of the 'institutions' (in the broad sense of the word) which the existence of language makes possible, and of which language itself is an example'.[35]

Durkheim saw 'social facts' as the proper domain of sociology: but what is a social fact? For Durkheim, 'it consists of ways of acting, thinking and feeling external to the individual, and endowed with a power of coercion, by reason of which they must control him'.[36] They are distinct from biological phenomena and psychological phenomena: 'When I fulfil my obligations as a brother, husband or citizen, when I execute my contracts, I perform duties which are defined, externally to myself and my acts, in law and in custom.'[37] For Durkheim, social facts have three characteristics: they are external to individuals, coercive and objective, not merely a product of subjective definitions. Law is the best example of a social fact. However, Durkheim did not see individuals as mainly governed by fear of the consequences of failing to conform to social norms and expectations, but that their behaviour was primarily a result of their own acceptance of the moral authority of society. The example he uses, fatherhood, is not just a biological relation, but a social phenomenon. Fatherhood carries with it a set of social obligations that require individuals to act in particular ways. They are not just the product of the individual, nor are they usually enforced by law. Fathers accept that becoming a father carries with it a set of social obligations, and they accept these as natural, they do not usually have to be coerced into accepting those obligations.[38] Commentators have pointed out that his emphasis on constraint devalues the importance of individual free will.[39] After all, society is made up of the actions of the individuals within it. It has been argued that social phenomena are not like things but they are dependent on the meanings that we attach to them. This is a difficult debate to resolve as it brings us to the central paradox of social structure and human **agency**. On the one hand it is true that social institutions do precede us as individuals. On the other hand it is also true that we can still make our own choices. Social structure may constrain what we do, but it does not determine it. We are not simply governed by the society we live in, we also help create it.

The central concern for Durkheim is social solidarity or cohesion, those elements that bind a society together. In older, pre-industrial, forms of society individual consciousness was not highly developed so that, 'Individual minds, forming groups by mingling and fusing, give birth to a being, psychological if you will, but constituting psychic individuality of a new sort.'[40] This new sort of **mentality** is a collective consciousness – a collective body of ideas, values and norms – which joins the members of a society into a community.[41] The *conscience collective* thus stands outside the consciousness of individuals, but also dominates it. The type of social solidarity produced by the *conscience collective* is called mechanical solidarity. This type of solidarity is only possible in a society in which there is very little division of labour. There is no individuality in such a society, thus there is also no **agency** and action is communal.

As society grows and develops, though, the nature of social solidarity also changes. Durkheim concluded that in industrial societies, social solidarity is transformed as a result of the greater division of labour within such societies. He argued that the division of labour in industrial society creates the basis for a new type of solidarity: organic solidarity. He said that mechanical solidarity is increasingly eroded by social progress, and that the division of labour itself comes to form the basis of social cohesion. As Philip Abrams puts it, 'The division of labour differentiates people but it does so in a way that impels them powerfully to cooperate with one another.'[42] The role of the collective consciousness is reduced in this society. The new basis for social solidarity, identified by Durkheim, is the recognition of interdependence between specialised occupations. Although individuals are defined by the roles they have to adopt within modern society, the greater differentiation of roles also produces greater individuality. This does not mean that society becomes a collection of individuals pursuing their own interests though. In order for society to be maintained, the freedom of the individual must be limited by the community, which exercises a controlling function over the behaviour of individuals within it.[43]

In contrast to Durkheim, and other **structuralist** theorists, Max Weber rejects the notion that society is a reality *sui generis*, existing independently in its own right. For Weber social groups are seen as tendencies towards action. He sees society as a collection of individuals whose interactions with each other create social life. Weber's very definition of sociology is the study of social action and its meaning for individual actors. This leads Weber to make the important distinction between the social and the natural sciences: that the former are about people. Moreover, whereas in natural science 'the molecules in a chemical reaction do not care about one another ... the objects social scientists study involve people's conscious or unconscious feelings and ideas'. Social sciences thus differ from natural sciences in that the subjects of enquiry are of 'meaningful to the actors involved' and their explanations 'cannot be solely in terms of *causes* and effects', but must also embrace people's motivations. In other words, 'to be convincing ... they have to be adequate at the level of meaning'.[44]

Weber's sociology stands in stark contrast to Durkheim's because for Weber 'there is no such thing as a collective personality which "acts"'.[45] Weber chooses to start from a consideration of individual actors, their agency and their motivation. In the course of considering the actions of individuals, certain **empirical** patterns will be detected in 'courses of action that are repeated by the actor or (simultaneously) occur among numerous actors since the subjective meaning is meant to be the same'.

This enables sociology to move beyond the study of individual actions to 'typical modes of action'. Thus sociology becomes a discipline that 'searches for **empirical** regularities and types' of social action.[46]

Weber's view that social groups merely represent tendencies towards action, rather than forces compelling people to act, can be seen in his view of collective action flowing from class interest (i.e. class struggle.) Weber does not deny the importance of class struggle in history but, unlike Marx, he does not see it as inevitable. Like Marx, he sees class as resulting from common economic interests. However, for Weber, 'classes are not communities; they merely represent possible, and frequent, bases for communal action'.[47] It is clear from what Weber says about the possibility of class struggle, that the extent to which workers will pursue their interest is dependent on individual characteristics, the social situation they find themselves in, and so on. His analysis of class struggle carries with it a warning of the dangers of Marxist notions of 'false consciousness':[48]

> Thus every class may be the carrier of any one of the possibly innumerable forms of 'class action' but this is not necessarily so. In any case, a class does not in itself constitute a community. To treat 'class' conceptually as having the same value as 'community' leads to distortion. That men in the same class situation regularly react in mass actions to such tangible situations as economic ones in the direction of those interests that are most adequate to their average number is an important and after all simple fact for the understanding of historical events. Above all, this fact must not lead to that kind of pseudo-scientific operation with the concepts of 'class' and 'class interests' so frequently found these days, and which has found its most classic expression in the statement of a talented author, that the individual may be in error concerning his interests but that the 'class' is 'infallible' about its interests.[49]

It is difficult to deny that history consists of periods of both class struggle and relative stability, and that this must be considered in any analysis of social relations. Weber's analysis is thus quite useful in first drawing our attention to the importance of class relations in structuring people's actions, and also pointing out that the existence of such social formations do not, in themselves determine people's actions. It is also apparent from this that Weber does not ultimately sees society as a collection of separate individuals, although it can appear this way if we take some of his statements at face value.

After taking one of the first German chairs in sociology at the University of Munich, Weber wrote to an economist who had attacked sociology:

> I do understand your battle against sociology. But let me tell you: If I now happen to be a sociologist according to my appointment papers, then I become one in order to put an end to the mischievous enterprise which still operates with collectivist notions (*Kollektivbegriffe*). In other words, sociology, too, can only be practised

by proceeding from the action of one or more, few or many, individuals, that means by employing a strictly 'individualist' method.[50]

However, Weber's emphasis on the individual as the point of departure for the social sciences, does not mean that he saw people as isolated individuals unconnected with wider society. Gerth and Mills point out that, if we were to accept what Weber says about his own methodology at face value, then we would not expect him to treat structural factors, such as class, seriously. In his own work, though, he does provide structural explanations of events.[51] Likewise his conception of the importance of the 'charismatic authority' of individual leaders would lead us to suppose that he would see history as the result of the actions of great men. In practice, though, he does not so much focus on 'the great figures of history', as their wider influence: 'Napoleon, Calvin and Cromwell, Washington and Lincoln appear in his texts only in passing. He tries to grasp what is retained of their work in the institutional orders and continuities of history. Not Julius Caesar, but Caesarism; not Calvin, but Calvinism is Weber's concern.'[52] Weber also makes us aware of the unintended consequences of the actions of such significant historical figures.

As individuals we are born into a society, which has been produced over centuries by the multiplicity of choices and decisions made by our ancestors, and we have to live with this inheritance. In addition to this, we have to contend with the fact that the intentions which were embodied in the actions of our ancestors have necessarily had unintended consequences which they could not and did not envisage. As David F. Walsh says, 'History does weigh on the present and human **agency** does not necessarily entail control over the future.'[53] For Walsh, Weber's Protestant ethic helped to shape attitudes that blended spiritual or religious values with economic considerations, thus impacting upon subsequent structures of belief and action in a manner not envisaged by ascetic Protestant ministers. Thus, a further significant point that emerges from a discussion of Weber's view of history is that the actions of those that went before us has unforeseen consequences that we still have to live with today. We should now move on to consider how the work of these founders of sociology has been developed by subsequent theorists, beginning with Marx.

As we noted earlier, non-Marxists often criticise Marxists for adhering to a crude economic **determinism** in which the base determines everything else within society. However, many contemporary Marxists view Marx's work as offering a non-determinist view of history, and we have seen that this is consistent with the portrayal of structure and agency within Marx's own writings. The work of the Italian Marxist, Antonio Gramsci (1891–1937) is particularly important in this respect. Marxist thinkers and historians influenced by the Gramscian concept of hegemony, cannot be said to take a determinist view of history, and we need to consider his ideas, alongside those of the French Marxist, Louis Althusser (1918–90), in order to appreciate the development of Marx's ideas after his death.

The central concept in Gramsci's political thought is **hegemony**. Robert Bocock points out that, for Gramsci, hegemony denoted the interrelationship of three factors: the economic, the state and civil society.[54] Hegemony is centred on the nation-state, and means 'leadership of the people of all classes in a given nation-state'.[55] The concept of hegemony originated in Russian Marxism as a strategy for overthrowing Tsarism. Lenin was concerned with how to seize state power in Russia, and this was obviously realised in the Russian Revolution of 1917. Gramsci described this as a 'war of movement' a tactic suitable for a society where civil society was almost non-existent. It was possible to capture the Russian state by a direct attack upon the capital (Saint Petersburg), which represented a direct assault on the state. This was not possible in the West. Gramsci developed a strategy for use within West European societies, this was his 'war of position'. In this case the aim is to try to achieve hegemony for the proletariat in civil society before the capture of state power by the Communist Party. It is important to bear in mind that Gramsci developed the idea of a war of position in response to the specific historical conditions that existed in Italy at the time, and the rise of fascism in particular.[56] Gramsci's conception of how hegemony would work in Italy is expressed this way:

> The Turin communists posed concretely the question of the 'hegemony of the proletariat': i.e. of the social basis of the proletarian dictatorship and of the workers' state. The proletariat can only become the leading [*dirigente*] and the dominant class to the extent that it succeeds in creating a system of class alliances which allows it to mobilize the majority of the working population against capitalism and the bourgeois state. In Italy, in the real class relations which exist here, this means the extent that it succeeds in gaining the consent of the broad peasant masses.[57]

Gramsci, more than any other writer on the subject, clarified the **base/superstructure** relationship and, in the process, freed Marxist historians from crude economic **determinism**. Gramsci attempted to answer the question, how is political power exercised and social stability maintained? He answered this by first drawing a distinction between 'rule' (*dominio*) and 'hegemony'. 'Rule' is the maintenance of order by coercion in times of crisis, and 'hegemony' is the means by which society coheres in normal times.[58] Gramsci said that hegemony is a system of class alliances that gives the dominant class 'cultural moral and ideological' leadership over allied and subordinate groups.[59]

In a capitalist society the bourgeoisie are the economically and ideologically dominant class, and in Liberal-Democratic states the bourgeoisie maintain hegemony through the superstructure of society. Gramsci refined the concepts of base and superstructure by distinguishing two superstructural levels, which had different, complementary functions. The first was civil society, which consisted of 'private' organisations such as the political parties and the church. The second level on which the **superstructure** operated was through the State, which exercised direct political power. As we will see, the French Marxist Althusser derived his ideas about the state from those of Gramsci. It has been argued that the major difference between the two is that Gramsci's ideas are not as **deterministic** as Althusser's. An important part of Gramsci's theory of **hegemony** is that it does not assume that the dominant social group has complete control over the subordinate groups. Gramsci said: 'the fact of hegemony presupposes that account be taken of the interests and the tendencies of the groups over which hegemony is to be exercised, and that a certain compromise equilibrium should be formed'.[60] Gramsci describes the idea of negotiation as follows:

> Thus it is incongruous that the concrete posing of the problem of hegemony should be interpreted as a fact subordinating the hegemonic group. Undoubtedly the fact of hegemony presupposes that account be taken of the interests and the tendencies of the groups over which hegemony is to be exercised, and that a certain compromise equilibrium should be formed – in other words, that the leading group should make sacrifices of an economic – corporate kind. But there is also no doubt that such sacrifices and such a compromise cannot touch the essential; for though hegemony is ethico-political it must also be economic, must necessarily be based on the decisive function exercised by the leading group in the decisive nucleus of economic activity.[61]

Althusser's main project is a rereading of Marx, through which he attempts to theorize the concept of ideology. Thus, works such as *Reading Capital* or *For Marx* attempt to present and interpret Marx's ideas in a new way, and use Marxist classics as a reference point for the construction of a theory of society. For example, in his theory of **overdetermination**, which we shall consider shortly, Althusser attributes special importance to Engels' later remarks about determination in the last instance. He makes particular use of Engels' letter to Joseph Bloch in which he denies that either he or Marx had ever claimed that 'the economic element is the only determining one'.[62] Althusser attempted to reformulate the **base** and superstructure model because he objected to economic determinism. The superstructure does not just reflect the base, but rather the superstructure is seen as necessary to the existence of the base. This model allows for the relative autonomy of the superstructure. There is still determination, but determination in the last instance. The economic is always dominant, but not necessarily at a particular point in history (e.g. under Feudalism the political was the dominant level), and it is the economy that determines which level should be dominant.[63] Althusser sees the relationship of the base to the superstructure in terms of a tension between, 'on the one hand determination in the last instance by the [economic] **mode of production** on the other, the relative autonomy of the superstructure'.[64] Chris Rojek points out that there are obvious difficulties with this statement. It is contradictory as the **superstructure** cannot have 'relative autonomy' if it is determined in the last instance by the economic **base**. To further complicate the issue, Althusser also says, 'the last instance never comes'.[65]

> The economic dialectic is never active in *the pure state*; in History, these instances, the superstructures etc., are never seen to step respectfully aside when their work is done, or when the time comes, as his pure phenomena, to scatter before His Majesty the Economy as he strides along the royal road to the Dialectic. From the first moment to the last, the lonely hour of the 'last instance' never comes.[66]

The concept of **overdetermination** is one that Althusser takes over from Freudian psychoanalytic theory, where it is used to show how several factors can simultaneously work together to contribute to the formation of symptoms. Thus, a dream can be overdetermined if it has multiple sources of determination, which make it susceptible to several possibly contradictory interpretations. The term has also been used by to describe the Herodotean view of history, which suggests that multiple sources of determination can converge on a single result in history.[67] Paul Ricoeur's discussion of Althusser's notion of overdetermination points first to the theorist's use of Lenin's question 'how was it possible that socialist revolution occurred in Russia, when Russia was not the most advanced industrial country?' Ricoeur then continued:

> Lenin's response is that to claim that revolution should occur in the most industrial country implies that the economic base is not only determinant in the last instance but the sole determinant factor. What we must realize, then, is that the economic base never works alone; it always acts in combination with other elements.[68]

Althusser uses this term to question how a single determinant – the state of economic technology – can possibly explain such a great variety of political and intellectual practices. The point that he makes here is that if, for example, Greek political life was determined by the slave economy, then how do we explain the fact that slavery existed elsewhere without the politics of the city-state? If Catholicism is the product of the feudal **mode of production**, how do we explain the existence of feudalism without Catholicism, in Japan, for example? As Steven B. Smith says, 'At most it appears that the economic mode of production is a necessary but by no means sufficient condition for the emergence of various superstructural properties.'[69] This raises some interesting questions about the relationship between base and superstructure. However, Althusser himself admits 'that the theory of the specific effectivity of the superstructure and other "circumstances" largely remains to be elaborated'.[70] Such fundamental problems have led some to ask whether the base-superstructure metaphor should not be rejected altogether.

The problem with Althusser's Marxism is that, although he claims that he has found a way out of **determinism**, the way that he describes the role of the state in capitalist society suggests that he sees economic factors as the sole determinant of social relations. He starts from the existing Marxist theory of the state, as a repressive agent of the ruling class, and then adds to this in a way that would seem to allow very little room for human **agency**. Althusser makes a distinction between Repressive State Apparatuses (RSAs) and Ideological State Apparatuses (ISAs). The concept of ISAs is what Althusser claims to add to the Marxist theory of the state. The RSAs are, 'the Army, the Police, the courts, the Prisons etc.' and the 'ISAs include religion, education, the media, and, most significantly, "the cultural ISA" (Literature, the Arts, sports etc.).'[71] As the function of the ISAs, according to Althusser, is to reproduce the relations of production, the working class are continually subordinate to a repressive ideological **superstructure**. This has the effect of reducing the individual to an unthinking cog in the wheel of the capitalist machine, as several commentators have observed.[72]

▶ Looking for an exit from the structuralist maze: post-structuralism, figuration and structuration

We should now move on to consider the work of more recent thinkers who have attempted to find their own resolution to the problem of structure and agency, either through an original restatement of the problem, or through a determined repositioning of themselves outside of any existing theoretical traditions. The latter stance is that adopted by the French **poststructuralist**, Michel Foucault. Although much of his work deals with either the past itself, or how to approach the study of the past, he is not a 'historian' in any conventional sense of the word. Similarly, his work does not belong to any of the dominant '**structuralist**' approaches to history mentioned earlier. Thus, his work stands outside both Marxist and *Annaliste* paradigms, and cannot easily be assimilated into any of the 'classical' theoretical traditions.[73] As we noted earlier, Foucault's work falls into the third category identified by Alun Munslow: **deconstructionism**. Thus, it forms part of the **postmodern** critique of conventional academic practices and historical studies. His central principles are well captured by Christopher Lloyd, who says that Foucault's post-structuralism effectively denies the existence of history as a process. Foucault thus does not see societies evolving from one to another, Lloyd argued, but instead suggests that 'there are complete ruptures of one [society and period] into another, without continuity or progress'. Instead of focusing on the nature and cause of change, as historians principally do, Foucault (according to Lloyd) placed pre-eminence in uncovering 'archaeologically' and reconstructing 'the essential structure of these particular discourses and epochs and to show the power relations that exist within them'. Foucault sought to avoid 'preconceptions, especially of a historical kind', in order to 'grasp each system of knowledge in its own terms, there being no external criteria of truth or progress'. For Lloyd, therefore, Foucault seemed 'to advocate a radical **relativism** while adopting a transcendent position for himself'.[74] If Lloyd's analysis is correct, then Foucault seemed to be allotting to himself the position of ultimate objectivity, while also denying the possibility of absolute truth. For Foucault the state, the body, society, sexuality, the soul, the economy are not stable objects, they are fashioned through **discourses**. As he said: 'My general theme is not society, it is true/false discourse: let me say it is the cor-relative formation of domains, of objects, and of discourses verifiable and falsifiable which are assignable to them; it is not simply this formation which interests me but the effects of reality which are linked to it.'[75]

This reveals the centrality of discourse to Foucault's study of power. Foucault says that we must free ourselves from an image of power as law and sovereignty if we are to understand how power actually operates in our technologically advanced societies. Power is to be understood as 'the multiplicity of power relations' at work in a particular area, and these power relations are the site of an unceasing struggle in which they are transformed, strengthened and, sometimes, reversed. Power does not radiate out from a single, central point, it is everywhere. Foucault puts it like this: 'Power is everywhere: not because it embraces everything, but because it comes from everywhere .... One should probably be a nominalist in this matter: power is not an institution, nor a structure, nor a possession. It is the name we give to a com-plex strategic situation in a particular society.'[76] According to Foucault, where there is power, there is resistance, but just as there is no centre of power, there is no cen-tre of revolt, no unified class that is the seat of rebellion. While there is something to be said for the wider definition of the operation of power in society that Foucault offers, the actual workings of real manifestations of resistance do suggest otherwise. If we consider the French or the Russian Revolutions, for example, the significance of the seizure of centres of power (however symbolic) during these revolts does sug-gest that there are, in fact, easily identifiable centres of power in societies that can be targeted by those seeking to overthrow a particular social order.

By comparison with Marx, it is much harder to identify a 'centre' to Foucault's work. However, if Marx was concerned with the development of the modes of pro-duction, it can be argued that Foucault's history of Western civilization is centred around, what we could term, a 'mode of normalisation'. Or, as he puts it, his aim had not been 'to analyze the phenomena of power, nor to elaborate the founda-tions of such an analysis. My objective instead has been to create a history of the different modes by which, in our culture, human beings are made subjects.'[77] In other words, Foucault is concerned with the way in which discipline and power in modern society aims to segregate, differentiate, hierarchalize, marginalise and exclude people in it. This power is exercised through supervision and surveillance, and is accompanied by the right to punish those who do not conform to the dominant definition of normality.[78] Foucault sees Jeremy Bentham's plan for the **panopticon** as a metaphor for the operation of power in our society. Foucault says, 'There is no need for weapons, physical violence or material constraints, only a gaze. A gaze which watches attentively and which each person feeling its weight, ends up by interiorising to the point of watching himself.'[79] Along with 'surveillance', 'normalisation' also became 'one of the great instruments of power'. The object was that every individual should conform to a certain 'norm' or idea of normality so that people can become uniform and more malleable for those in positions of power. The judges of normality are everywhere in this system: in schools, prisons, hospitals, for instance. So the controlling strategies are discipline, surveillance and normalisation. At the centre of these disciplinary procedures is the 'examination'. So does this mean that society eventually becomes an extension of the prison for Foucault? Does Foucault allow for the role of human **agency** within this system?

Lawrence Barth argues: 'It would be a mistake to understand Foucault as suggesting that western society is governed like a prison. Because of the power of discipline, our society is precisely unlike the prison.'[80] What Barth means is that panopticism creates a society in which every individual is self-regulating, rather than being visibly subject to an external authority. So Foucault does not see society as resembling a prison in a literal sense. However, the way in which Foucault describes the operation of power within society does seem to suggest that the individual can never free himself or herself from its constraints. In fact, Foucault is unclear on this point. His discussion of 'the formation of a disciplinary society', certainly seem to emphasise the all-embracing operation of a system of power with the apparent aim of eradicating individuality. Society seems to be dominated by mechanisms of surveillance and normalisation that perpetually control the way in which individuals act.[81] At the same time, as we noted earlier, according to Foucault, where there is power, there is resistance. This is because the very nature of power, the activity of one party trying to dominate another, creates resistances to itself. This resistance is conceived primarily in terms of marginal groups challenging the imposition of normal identities, which does reintroduce the role of human agency into this web of control, but without really addressing the question of how resistance is possible within such an all-embracing system of control.[82] The root of the problem is identified by Giddens, who points out that Foucault's argument is based on the premise that prisons and asylums allow us to see the nature of disciplinary power in our society more clearly than other institutions. However, certain institution, for example, factories and schools, are not like this. Indeed, 'It is an observation of some significance ... because complete and austere institutions are the exception rather than the rule within the main institutional sectors of modern societies.'[83] The value of

Foucault's work lies in the way in which he draws our attention to the varied ways in which power operates within our society. The central problem with his depiction of society is that, although he stresses the fact of resistance, and the fact that power should not be seen solely in terms of repression and domination, it inevitably leaves individuals trapped in the 'fine meshes of the web of power', he describes.[84]

As was stated earlier, both Norbert Elias and Anthony Giddens are held to have offered a resolution to the theoretical dilemma of structure and **agency** but, unlike Foucault, they operate within the confines of conventional academic practice. In his major work, *The Civilising Process* (1939), Elias offers both a detailed account of the development of manners, etiquette and social behaviour from the early Middle Ages to the nineteenth century, and also the development of the European state during the same period. He seeks to link changes in the individual with changes in the structure of society.[85] Norbert Elias emphasises the interdependence of human beings, and that out of 'the interweaving of innumerable individual interests and intentions – be they compatible, or opposed and inimical – something eventually emerges that, as it turns out, has neither been planned nor intended by any single individual. And yet it has been brought about by the intentions and actions of many individuals ... this is the secret of sociogenesis and social dynamics.'[86] Although Elias emphasises the unintended consequences of human action, and the difficulty of controlling events, he also makes it clear that certain individuals within these interdependencies have a greater influence on the course of events than others. This brings us to his contribution to the problem of structure and agency: the concept of **figurations**. Elias uses this term to describe the way that individuals are shaped by the social networks they create. This returns us to the point that Marx made about the impossibility of studying individual human beings in isolation from each other. This term could be applied at any social level, from a class in a school, to a village, a city, or a nation.[87] Elias made use of different metaphors to help convey the dynamic nature of social figurations. In the following passage, he uses the metaphor of a dance to describe society: 'The image of the mobile figurations of interdependent people on a dance floor perhaps makes it easier to imagine states, cities, families, and also capitalist, communist and feudal systems as figurations.' The concept of the dance thus allows us to 'eliminate the antithesis, resting finally on different values and ideals, immanent today in the use of the words "individual" and "society" '.[88] In some ways, it is still difficult to assess the significance of Elias, as he has yet to be fully assimilated by English-speaking academics, particularly historians. However, as has been indicated previously, his work does provide an interesting synthesis of history and sociology, and a useful contribution to the debate over structure and agency.

By contrast, the work of the British sociologist, Anthony Giddens, is both widely known and extensively discussed. In some ways his contribution to the structure and agency debate, at least on the surface, resembles that of Elias.[89] Giddens explicitly set out to combine **structuralist** sociology with the sociology of action. As Edgar and Sedgwick point out, 'Giddens recognises a partial truth in both extremes, for society is patterned, so that the isolated and self-interested actions of its individual members do take on the appearance of having been planned or co-ordinated.'[90] Giddens is critical of social theories that fail to recognise the knowledgeability of actors and the duality of structure. He posits an alternative to such theories in the theory of **structuration**.[91] The central tenet of this theory is: 'The constitution of agents and structures are not two independently given sets of phenomena, a dualism, but represent a duality.' In this concept of duality, moreover, 'the structural properties of social systems are both medium and outcome of the practices they recursively organise'. In this sense, 'structure is not "external" to individuals: as memory traces, and as instantiated in social practices, it is in a certain sense more "internal" than exterior to their activities in a Durkheimian sense'.[92] Structure thus creates an interaction between 'constraining' and 'enabling' elements. For Giddens, social structure exists mainly as a way of enabling individuals to organise their lives. He begins with the assumption that people find routine (whatever is done habitually) as desirable. The repetition of various activities is the basic grounding of social life. The routinization of social life is primarily carried out by that part of our consciousness, which Giddens calls 'practical consciousness' (that part of our consciousness which allows us to function in everyday life).[93] Giddens argues that, in order to enact a social practice, participants must necessarily draw on a set of rules; these rules can be seen to structure, to give shape to the practices that they help to organise. This does not mean that every situation is dominated by rules, but that there are sets of rules that we can 'try out' to see if they fit a particular situation. Thus, skilled social actors are needed in order to make social interaction work, but these actors are in turn dependent on the structuring properties of rules.[94] Social rules are not necessarily like the rules of games (in this example, chess) because such rules are not usually questioned by the players of a game in the way social rules may be.[95]

Giddens' notion of structuration involves a conception of 'structure' that includes 'the rules and resources recursively implicated in social reproduction'.[96] He identifies two kinds of resources, 'authoritative resources, which derive from the co-ordination of the activity of human agents, and allocative resources, which stem from control of material products or of aspects of the material world'.[97] Resources make the exercise of power possible, because in order to make things happen in the world, one must possess the appropriate resources. For Giddens, structure has both a positive and a negative aspect, as rules and resources both create opportunities for action and place limits upon our actions. An important difference between structural sociology, and structuration theory is: 'structuration theory is both enabling and constraining'.[98] In essence, our actions are influenced by the structural features of the society we inhabit, while at the same time we reproduce and transform those structural features through our daily activity.[99] Thus, 'to study the **structuration** of a social system is to study the ways in which that system, via the application of generative rules and resources, and in the context of unintended outcomes, is produced and reproduced in interaction'.[100]

Few scholars would quarrel with the fundamental principles of structuration.[101] This does not preclude the possibility of disagreement with some aspects of the way that Giddens depicts the 'duality of structure'. One particular weakness would appear to be the question of structural constraint. Giddens' definition of 'structure', as rules and resources, does seem to emphasise its enabling aspects at the expense of its constraining ability, as Giddens and others have noted.[102] We have to recognise that **agency** is quite often severely limited by structure. This is not to say that structure predetermines action, but that it sets limits upon action, which Giddens also acknowledges. However, the extent to which structure limits action is usually dependent upon an individual's position within the social structure. Those at the lower levels of society have less choice than those in the higher reaches of the social structure. This brings us to the significance of class within the structuring of social relations. While Giddens recognises the 'asymmetrical' nature of the relationship between capitalist and worker, he also says that Marx exaggerated the significance of class struggle and class relations in history. Instead, power, for Giddens, 'is generated in and through the reproduction of structures of domination'.[103] However, many structural constraints are, indeed, based on class, although not exclusively so, for we also have to acknowledge the unequal power relations created by other factors, primarily: gender, ethnicity and sexuality. Here we confront an explanatory problem that is difficult to resolve: the need to recognise the importance of numerous forms of domination within the historical process, while not losing sight of the centrality of material factors, and the role of class struggle within that process.

▶ Class, gender and ethnicity in the historical process

To what extent does social structure act as a constraint on the actions of individuals in past societies? In order to consider this question, the final section of this chapter is concerned with the different sources of social division and group identity created by divisions of class, gender, race and ethnicity and how an awareness of these divisions can aid our understanding of the historical process. These divisions will be considered in two ways. First, in the ways in which they structure social action, which should be seen in terms of both providing opportunities and limitations on the way particular individuals and groups can act. Secondly, we will consider the ways in which individual historians and social theorists have dealt with these divisions within their writing. This will be considered primarily from the perspective of social history, placing at the centre of the discussion the question of how different sources of social identities interact with each other, and whether one should be seen as having primacy over others.

There are a number of problems involved in a discussion of these different sources of social identity, not least problems of definition, as the meaning of each of these terms has been the subject of considerable controversy. However, our central concern is the importance of these social divisions within the historical process. There are a number of issues that tend to recur in both historical and contemporary discussions of class, gender and ethnicity. To begin with, there is the question of whether a particular social group has an identity of interest, or is fragmented by internal subdivisions. This is particularly apparent if we consider 'women' as a social category, as the experience of individual women differs according to their class, sexuality, ethnicity and age. It is thus important to consider whether individuals can have multiple sources of identity, and what the implications of this might be for our understanding of past societies. Following on from this, there is the question of whether social disadvantage is additive, entailing a compounding of different sources of oppression. So, for example, this would mean that working-class women were oppressed more than working-class men, and working-class women who also belonged to an ethnic minority were even further disadvantaged. While there is something to be said for such a calculus of disadvantage, as we will see later, the reality of the interaction of different forms of social division is not always so simple. Another issue that confronts us in such discussions is whether some social structures, such as patriarchy or racism, are historically constant, and manifest themselves in all societies. The problem for historians is they need to avoid an ahistorical analysis of social structures, but it can sometimes seem as if certain sources of social structuring are transhistorical, in that they have remained essentially the same over centuries.

One of the central issues for feminists has been the relationship between class and gender. Zillah Eisenstein has argued that the fact of women's shared oppression cuts across all other social divisions. 'What better proof can there be that women are a sexual class', Eisenstein asks, 'than women organizing across political orientations to build a unified feminist movement?' and this, she adds 'is the real proof of feminism that no Marxist will be able to explain away'.[104] However, the problem with such an assertion is that the feminist movement is not totally unified, as differences of class, ethnicity and sexuality cut across women's gender identity.

The relationship between class and gender has been extensively discussed by those feminist historians who emerged directly from the Second Wave of the women's movement such as Sheila Rowbotham and Gerda Lerner. Gerda Lerner wrote: 'patriarchy as a system is historical: it has a beginning in history. If that is so, it can be ended by historical process'.[105] She also drew attention to the sexual exploitation of women: 'from the earliest period of class development to the present, sexual dominance of higher class males over lower class women has been the very mark of women's oppression. Clearly, class oppression cannot ever be considered the same condition for men and women.'[106] She is thus arguing for a consideration of the difference between male and female experiences of class subordination. Ralph Miliband counters this argument from a Marxist perspective. He concedes that men of all classes have engaged in sexual exploitation, but that higher-class males have a greater potential to oppress and exploit women than working-class men. He somewhat undermines this point by also drawing attention to the ways in which working-class men have abused their power in the home, but still maintains that the notion of 'patriarchy' and concomitant oppression of women by men ignores the differential in power relations created by class.

As well as disagreeing about the relationship between class and gender, feminists also disagree as to the relationship between ethnicity and gender and how these two forms of subordination interact. Black women have pointed to the false universality of mainstream feminism, which has tended to ignore, or negate, black women's experience. Imelda Whelehan points out: 'Patriarchy and imperialism caught black women in a tenacious double-bind. Whether they chose to opt for racial or sexual solidarity, either allegiance would only address half of the problem.' Whelehan went on to note than black women's experiences captured the dichotomy of race and gender, with allies in either camp subsuming 'the black female voice'. For this reason, 'feminism seemed to refer only to the needs of white women, and civil rights only addressed the oppression of black males'.[107] Despite the fact that one of the slogans of the women's movement is 'Sisterhood is powerful!' black women have often felt excluded and marginalised by the white women's movement. So, many black women have felt that some of the divisions of society as a whole have been carried over into the women's movement. Alice Walker has gone so far as to say it was, 'apparently inconvenient, if not downright mind straining for white women scholars to think of black women as women'.[108] Thus the problem that non-white women face within the women's movement is a result of the fact that they feel oppressed both in terms of their gender and their ethnicity. This means that they often see white women as relatively privileged, although white women themselves may not see it that way.

Historians need to be sensitive to the sub-divisions that can exist within any apparently homogenous group, be it 'the working class', 'the Jews', or women. For example, during the nineteenth century, the working class in Britain was divided in a number of ways, not least according to region and occupation. At the extremes, there was an obvious difference between the representatives of the London poor eking out a living on the margins of society described by Henry Mayhew, and the Victorian 'labour aristocracy', who represented the most affluent and 'respectable' members of the labouring classes of the time. Even within a single industry, such as shipbuilding, there is usually a separation between skilled and unskilled workers.[109]

Working class communities have usually been perceived as either 'rough' or 'respectable' by contemporaries, and this contributes to the status of the individuals who inhabit them. In addition to these sources of identification, further divisions are created by differences of ethnicity and gender, which often serve to undermine any sense of working class unity. Thus historians of the working class need to be aware of the divisions that can exist within it, just as women's historians need an awareness of what divides women as well as what unites them, and historians of different ethnic groups to consider the ways in which these groups are themselves divided by differences of wealth, class belonging, gender, religion and so on.[110]

The most recent developments in the way that historians view social division in history is based on a linguistic approach to the past, and is a result of the influence of the various thinkers associated with **postmodern** or **deconstructionist** approaches to history. This is concerned with the fracturing of identity, and the way that identity cannot just be reduced to the dichotomy of male and female, for example, but is also based on sexuality, ethnicity and age. The work of Joan Scott has been central in introducing this approach into gender history, as we will see in the following chapter. Postmodernists have also questioned the explanatory power of the concept of class, and some commentators have gone so far as to proclaim the 'death' of class analysis. This notion has arisen both in response to a number of social changes that have taken place within contemporary western society, and the influence of postmodern theory. Historians, such as Patrick Joyce, have set out to incorporate some of the insights of **poststructuralist** theory into the writing of social history. He describes the impact of postmodern thought upon social history as a series of challenges, chief amongst these is the challenge to the 'founding categories of social history, above all class and the social'.[111] Joyce argues that historians should reject the modernist grand narrative of class that provided the foundation for the new social history. Instead they should take their cue from Foucault and concern themselves with 'the discursivities of the social, including the ways in which they are produced by, and produce, power'.[112] At the same time there are also many historians, such as E.J. Hobsbawm, who would maintain that class has lost none of its usefulness, and that 'Marx remains the essential base of any adequate study of history ...'[113]

For postmodernists, identities are not constructed around an essential core, but fractured and dispersed, thus they emphasise the notion that individuals have multiple sources of identities. Both Patrick Joyce and James Vernon have argued that the linguistic turn (as the postmodern influence is usually called) has been particularly fruitful for the analysis of gender and racial identities, and investigating the ways in which gender, class and race historically intermesh. Joan Scott has also emphasised the idea of 'difference within difference' asking: 'If there are so many differences of class, race, ethnicity and sexuality, what constitutes the common ground on which feminists can organize collective action?'[114] Craig Calhoun points out that recent **postmodernist** approaches 'stressed the incompleteness, fragmentation and contradictions of both collective and personal existence'. In order to indicate the complexity of 'the relationship among projects of identity, social demands and personal possibilities ... they have commonly started with the deconstruction of "essentialist" categories and rhetorics'.[115] Although postmodern theorists and historians have constantly drawn attention to the notion of difference, the existence of multiple identities, and divided loyalties, it has to be remembered that historians' concern with the significance of class, gender and ethnicity in the historical process predates the influence of postmodernism, and that there are ways of dealing with the interaction of these identities that do not involve 'the deconstruction of "essentialist" categories and rhetorics'. As a means of illustrating this point I would like to move from a consideration of these issues in abstract terms and consider their operation in the specific historical periods mentioned earlier: the Ancient, the feudal, and the capitalist **mode of production**.

Although both Ancient Greece and Rome made use of slave labour, they were distinct societies, and the institution of slavery was of greater significance in Greece than it was in Rome. Historians have also questioned the economic significance of servile labour in both societies.[116] Slavery was a state of absolute subjection, and the rights of slaves were severely limited by law.

> Both Greeks and Romans assigned their slaves a legal position which clearly separated them from other, 'free', members of the community. Although chattel slaves were human beings, and thus had certain moral rights ..., legally they were property in the absolute control of an owner – even to the extent that an owner could transfer his rights to someone else by gift or sale.[117]

Classical texts give the impression that slavery was an essential division of the household, and that other divisions were comparatively insignificant. In Rome, slaves had to accept the religion of their new owner's household, had no kin, were technically not permitted to marry and thus could not produce legally recognisable families, and were even named by their owner.[118] Athenian slaves were similarly named by their owner, had no rights to property of their own, their families were not legally recognised, and their names appeared on no official register except for inventories of possessions.[119] One Classical source summed up the life of the slave as consisting of three elements: work, punishment and food.[120] Since one could be a slave by birth, slavery is an extreme example of a social institution that restricted an individual's freedom of action. Both Greek and Roman slaves could become free, but the freed slave often still maintained a relationship of dependence with his or her former master.[121] Regardless of their religion, sex or ethnicity, slaves were always at the mercy of their master. Thus, for slaves, slavery outweighed all other forms of social division in Ancient society.

Both women and slaves were seen as the natural and biological inferiors of the patriarchal male citizen within Greek culture. Neither women nor slaves were entitled to vote in Classical Greece. Marriage was, therefore, based on a fundamentally unequal relationship.[122] Roman culture was also patriarchal, giving all power to the head of the family in a manner that paralleled the authority granted to the Kings and later the Caesars under the Empire. However, there were differences between Greek and Roman society in this respect, and the situation within Rome was also subject to alteration, as Judith P. Hallett makes clear: 'scholars are quick to point out that, by the first century BC, Roman women enjoyed considerable power and freedom, particularly when one compares them to their counterparts in fifth century Athens and in the early Roman Republic'.[123] This greater degree of freedom must itself be placed in context. Only a limited number of women could take advantage of it, and even the most 'liberated' of women in Roman society lived in a state of subjection compared with Roman males. Despite these qualifications, this difference between the early and late Republics draws our attention to the fact that societies are never static, and we need to consider both continuity and change in any discussion of social relationships.

An interesting investigation of the relationship between class and gender for the period under discussion here is provided by a collection edited by Sandra R. Joshel and Sheila Murnaghan. They preface this volume with a discussion of the interrelationship of the institution of slavery and that of patriarchy: 'Women and slaves were similarly distinguished from free men by their social subordination and their imagined otherness.' They also shared exclusion from participation in political life and were 'viewed as morally deficient and potentially dangerous'.[124] The editors stress that gender and slavery are not independent phenomena, and must be considered together, as they 'come into existence *in and through* relation to each other'.[125] For example, the master–slave metaphor was applied to marriage by Roman authors, and good wives were meant to placate their husbands just as slaves were to placate their masters.[126] However, wives were not the same as slave women as, to take one significant difference, women could administer corporal punishment to both slaves and children. Richard P. Saller makes the point that, 'categories of free and slave were more important than hierarchies of gender or generation in determining who whipped whom'.[127] Perhaps the most direct attempt at addressing the interrelationship of these two forms of subordination is offered in William G. Thalmann's discussion of the position of female slaves within Classical Greek culture. Thalmann asks whether they should simply be perceived as 'doubly disadvantaged' because of their class and gender. He stresses that this is not simply an additive process as, 'In some ways, women slaves might be better treated than male slaves, and they were free of some of the restrictions placed on the behaviour of elite women.'[128] He goes on to describe the problem in terms that can be applied to any period of history: 'The challenge is to understand class and gender in their reciprocal influence on one another and so as parts of a system that is not static but is constantly being recreated, without ignoring the distinctions between them.'[129]

The second historical epoch identified by Marx is the feudal one. In *Feudal Society* (1940), the *Annales* scholar Marc Bloch offers an analysis of the main features of this society that is not incompatible with a materialist approach. Bloch considers: the environment, the structure of feudal society and people's mental outlook ('modes of feeling and thought') to provide a **'total history'** of feudal society. This work also includes his famous definition of feudalism:

> A subject peasantry; widespread use of the service tenement (i.e. the fief) instead of a salary…; supremacy of a class of specialized warriors; ties of obedience and protection which bind man to man and, within the warrior class, assume the distinctive form called vassalage; fragmentation of authority – leading inevitably to disorder; and, in the midst of all this, the survival of other forms of association family and State.[130]

Medieval society saw itself in terms of three estates: priests, knights and labourers, and this characterisation has been adopted by a number of historians, although there is continued debate as to whether medieval society should be seen in terms of social orders rather than social classes.[131] We also need to consider the differences between the early and the late Middle Ages in our understanding of medieval society. Maurice Keen makes the point that, between 1300 and 1500, English society developed a more complex social structure, in which successful merchants or lawyers, and other representatives of an urban elite, enjoyed a greater degree of social mobility, and older, feudal, relations were modified in the form of 'bastard feudalism'.[132]

For Marx, the peasantry were the 'directly producing' class in medieval society, and this notion has been defended by the British Marxist historian, Rodney Hilton.[133] He begins by criticising the generalised concepts of 'peasant economy' and 'traditional' societies that merge all pre-industrial societies together. Such interpretations risk losing the specific features of ancient, medieval and early modern societies, as well as the distinct class character of the peasantry. As he said,

> But it is not only by minimizing the role of the other classes that the position of the peasantry and in particular the medieval peasantry is falsified. This is also achieved in a reverse sense by reducing the peasantry to a subordinate position in society, with no independent role to play. We find this in some currently fashionable theories about medieval and early modern societies whose stratification, it is said, was by 'order' or 'estates' not by 'class'.[134]

Against those who wish to see pre-capitalist society in Europe in terms of estates, orders or status groups determined by attributed esteem, dignity or honour, Hilton defines the peasantry as a class, 'determined by its place in the production of society's material needs'.[135]

S.H. Rigby's study of English society in the later medieval period discusses divisions of class, status and gender within a theoretical framework drawn from sociology. The main aim of this work is to test the usefulness of the theories it employs for historians through a consideration of the available evidence on the period. As the work is a survey of late medieval society, rather than being based on primary sources, it makes use of the work of other historians on medieval social stratification in order to assess the usefulness of 'closure theory' in particular.[136] Rigby favours closure theory as he feels that in synthesising elements from Marxist social theory and 'liberal' stratification theory it manages to overcome some of the problems associated with both approaches individually. Closure theory starts from Weber's remarks about the manner in which one social group uses the characteristics of another group as a pretext for monopolizing resources and achieving 'the closure of social and economic opportunities to outsiders'.[137] These ideas have been developed in the work of a number of writers, but Rigby singles out the work of Frank Parkin on closure theory as a particularly good example of this theory as it encompasses divisions both *between* and *within* particular classes, as well as offering an analysis that takes account of divisions of race, religion and gender.[138] Additionally, Rigby suggests that, due to its level of generality, Parkin's closure theory be combined with Runciman's social theory which distinguishes three modes of power: the economic, the coercive and the ideological, and in order to refer to the entire spectrum of social groups defined by their allocation of power, coins the term 'systacts', 'groups or categories of persons sharing a common endowment (or lack) of power by virtue of their roles' and who also share a common interest, such as classes.[139]

The main group discriminated against because of their ethnicity during the Middle Ages was: the Jews. Rigby provides a concise description of their position in England, and the deterioration of attitudes of both Church and Crown towards them in the thirteenth century. Having included some of the kingdom's wealthiest subjects in 1200, religious change, persecution and popular ill-will meant 'the Jews were ruined by the end of Henry II's reign and were expelled by Edward I in 1290, an action which was to provide a model for other European rulers. Their fate provides a dramatic illustration of the ways in which political and ideological power could determine economic power.'[140] Indeed, a consideration of the restrictions placed on Jews within Europe as whole raises the question of whether ethnic divisions are not, at least, as significant as class differences. At the most fundamental levels of existence, being granted the right to life by fellow human beings, and also to residence within a particular territory, Jews were discriminated against. The papacy's official line was that Jews should not be persecuted, or subject to forcible conversion. However, the Church also sought to avoid excessive contact, particularly of a sexual nature, between Jews and Christians, and to this end it stipulated that Jews should wear a distinctive badge on their clothing, a measure enacted into law by the monarchs of England and France in the early thirteenth century. Although there are many examples of Christians and Jews peacefully coexisting, Christian society was generally ill at ease with the Jewish presence, and this unease periodically manifested itself in violence.

Rigby shows that attitudes to gender in the Middle Ages display considerable continuity with those of the classical world discussed earlier. The idea of women as physically, mentally and socially inferior was inherited from Greek and Roman thought, and strengthened by the account of the Creation and Fall in the book of Genesis.[141] An understanding of the relationship between class and gender is also important for the medieval period. Attitudes towards gender meant that wives were primarily responsible for the management of the household and childcare, and domestic labour, precisely because it was women's labour, was not as highly valued as work carried out by men. Whatever their social class, women had fewer opportunities in both education and employment than men. However, aristocratic women had greater access to education, property and political power than peasant women, as well as a greater standard of material comfort. At different stages in the life cycle, women had different degrees of restriction. Wives were subjected to their husbands, and daughters to their father. However, widows could achieve a certain degree of independence. The daughters of labourers and artisans often left home at twelve or thirteen, and this could offer them a freer choice of husband than a young aristocratic girl, whose parents would tend to see her marriage as a way of either expanding their influence or consolidating their property.[142]

Rigby emphasises the economic significance of the sexual division of labour and of women's domestic role in the peasant household, where women were also involved in commodity production, such as brewing. Some historians of the period have even argued that peasant women experienced a relative economic equality with their husbands, compared to the classes above them. Rigby asks whether women's crucial role within the peasant economy minimised the social exclusion experienced by women within peasant society? He argues that medieval peasant women did encounter gender-specific forms of social exclusion, but that these cannot solely be explained in terms of the benefits they offered to the ruling landlord class. For Rigby, the persistence of female subordination during the medieval period is result of the fact that it did not have a disruptive effect on social relations. 'What we *can* say is that the fact that patriarchal social relations were not dysfunctional for feudalism was certainly a factor for the maintenance of such relations.'[143] Rigby also discusses the position of noblewomen, who, although still subject to patriarchal authority, also acquired authority and status from their families and landownership, and could enjoy a certain amount of authority in the domestic sphere. He concludes: 'gender inequalities cannot simply be seen as contingent or derivative from contemporary class relations but need to be seen as a form of social exclusion in their own right'.[144]

We now turn to Marx's third historical epoch: capitalism, and the creation of the first capitalist society in Britain. Despite debates about whether industrialisation was a revolution or a process, the creation of industrial capitalism in Britain is usually held to have taken place between about 1700 and 1850. Although it sometimes appears that Marx's view of industrial society consisted of a simple 'two-class' model (capitalists and workers, or the bourgeoisie and the proletariat) he recognised that class structure was more complex. Historians have also offered a number of accounts of the class structure of early nineteenth-century Britain. Perkin argued that a class society emerged sometime between 1789 and 1833, or, to be more exact, between 1815 and 1820. This society was characterised by 'class feeling', that is by vertical antagonism between a small number of horizontal groups, each based on a common source of income.[145] By the mid-nineteenth century, Perkin reckoned, there were three major classes (each with its own mobilising ideal): the entrepeneurial, the working class and the aristocratic. However, there was also a fourth forgotten class, the middle class. This was composed of professional men virtually 'above the economic battle'.[146] Doctors, lawyers, writers and even the clergy found a greater demand for their services after the industrial revolution and, consequently, greater self-respect. New middle-class professions also arose as a result of industrialisation. However, most significant 'was the general rise in the status of the professional intellectual in society.'[147] For Perkin, this fourth class is outside the prevailing economic system, and thus has a special status. The members of this class were able to choose their ideal from the available options. One of the distinctive features of Perkin's analysis is the notion that each class had its own ideal and that: 'The class ideal thus sublimated the crude material self-interest of the competition for income, sanctified the role of class members by the contribution they made to society and its well-being.' This, in turn, 'justified the class and its claim to a special place and special treatment within the social framework'.[148] R.S. Neale argues: 'as Perkin's argument progresses the class ideals appear increasingly separated from their basis in conflict over income'.[149] Thus, the mid-nineteenth century is made to look as if it was merely a struggle between different class 'ideals', and the material aspect of the conflict is obscured. Such a struggle might better be expressed (in Gramscian terms) as a struggle for hegemony, without losing sight of different class interests.

Neale explained utility of the application of the tripartite division of classes (aristocracy, middle class, working class), 'The boundaries of the classes, particularly of the two lower ones, are rarely clearly or explicitly explained, and there is little general agreement among writers about the bases of classification. Nevertheless this model and these categories are regularly used in analysing the interplay of economic, social and cultural forces.'[150] He suggests discarding the three-class model altogether and substituting a basic model containing a minimum of five classes and employing the category of a middling class. His five classes are: upper class, middle class, middling class, working class A, working class B. This draws our attention to the possibility of divisions within classes themselves, and the idea of a labour aristocracy, concisely defined by R.J. Morris as, 'a section of the nineteenth century working class who were relatively better paid, more secure, better treated at work and more able to control the organisation of their work'.[151]

We have discussed the significance of E.P. Thompson's, now classic, study of class formation in previous chapters. However, despite his considerable achievements, he has been the subject of a number of critiques. Many critical appraisals of this work have centred on his neglect of the category of gender in his analysis. This brings us to the significance of gender in the formation of the British working class. A good starting point is: Joan Scott's *Gender and the Politics of History* (1988) in which she criticised E.P. Thompson's study from a feminist perspective. Scott says that in Thompson's famous study, *The Making of The English Working Class*, 'the male designation of general concepts is literalized in the persons of the political actors who are described in strikingly detailed (and easily visualized) images'. 'The book is', Scott asserted, 'crowded with scenes of men...talking, marching, breaking machines, going to prison, bravely standing up to police, magistrates and prime ministers', even though 'not all the actors are male'.[152] Scott acknowledges that women are present within the text of this work, but feels that Thompson always associates women with domesticity. So, although she cites Thompson's sympathetic treatment of women textile workers, who had to cope with the 'double burden' of home and work, she is also critical of the way Thompson deals with women's political activity. Thompson discusses women's involvement in politics, in trade unions and Female Reform Societies. However, he says that their trade unions were more concerned with immediate grievances, and were thus less political than the artisanal organisations, while their radicalism was based on nostalgia for a pre-industrial domestic economy. This glosses over the fact that all industrial unions in the 1820s and 1830s had similar concerns, and that the longing for the past was also an aspect of male artisans' political consciousness. He says that women's role in the emerging radical movement 'was confined to giving moral support to the men'.[153] Scott's analysis of Thompson's work basically comes down to the assertion that women are marginalised within the narrative of class formation he presents, while it is men who are the active participants in the 'making' of their own class.

Scott's critique of Thompson has raised the question: how do women fit into this narrative of class formation? Which, in turn, leads to a whole new set of questions as posed by Theodore Koditschek: 'Why were women excluded from certain types of economic roles and occupations? Why did class organization and class consciousness become increasingly cast in a masculinist frame? How did the entire process of proletarianization crystallize along gender's faultlines?'[154] Koditschek points to the importance of four recent works of British social history in forming answers to these questions, and says that, taken together, these four studies can tell us much about the gendering of the British working class. The central issue in this discussion is whether the period of industrialisation in Britain, although a time in which both men and women suffered immensely, was ultimately one in which men, of all classes, suppressed women. Let us, therefore, briefly look at each of these works in turn.

Deborah Valenze's *The First Industrial Woman* (1995) focuses on the eighteenth century and considers the impact of early industrialisation on women.[155] Valenze retains some of the Thompsonian tradition of working-class history and begins by pointing to the significance of waged labour in the process of industrialisation. She goes on to say that this was not just a question of class, but of gender, since it was women's labour that was most downgraded. The workings of both the industrial and the agricultural revolutions had the effect of forcing women out of employment. Enclosure drove women out of agricultural work, and the dairy industry, traditionally a mainstay of women's work, was transformed by the rationalization of agriculture, which displaced dairywomen. The mechanization of spinning, in particular, deprived women of a valuable source of income. Factories only offered women unsatisfactory dead-end employment, and the result was women did not benefit from industrialisation, but ended up at the very bottom of the class/gender hierarchy.

Valenze seeks to investigate the manner in which England changed from an essentially agricultural society in which female labour played an active and acknowledged part, to an industrialised nation based on a notion of male productivity. Or, as she puts it, 'Why were female workers praised for their industriousness in the eighteenth century, but a century later, damned or pitied?' This is not to say that pre-industrial production (typified by the spinning wheel) was a 'golden age' of women's work, as production was usually organised patriarchally by the male head of the household. However, female labour was recognised and acknowledged to be economically important, whereas, in the nineteenth century female workers were perceived negatively.

It is true to say that women's work did go from being an accepted part of economic life, to being perceived as a problem in the Victorian period. Women were excluded from employment during the nineteenth century due to the concerted effort to promote a domestic role for women that would take them away from activities outside the home. Deborah Valenze points out that women were seen as barriers to progress in the world of work. They were held to be unable to break free of outmoded traditions. She looks at the employment of women in cottage industries, and 'The Other Victorian Woman': the domestic servant. During the early modern period, service included young people of both sexes. During the nineteenth century, though, domestic service not only became an increasingly female occupation, but also formed the largest single category of women's employment. It reinforced an image of working-class women being engaged in non-productive activity. Marx said that servants did not create wealth themselves but lived off the surplus wealth created by the bourgeoisie, and that this placed them in a special parasitic category of labour. There was a plentiful supply of servants from the late eighteenth to the late nineteenth century, as poor rural women were left with little option other than to look for a 'place' in a nearby village or town. Domestic service propagated attitudes of deference and subordination amongst servants themselves, and it is highly questionable whether it served as a bridge between classes, as some have asserted. The overall result of the changes described by Valenze is a diminution in the status of labouring women, and a concomitant reduction in their opportunities.

Anna Clark focuses on the rise of class consciousness, class organisation and political radicalism.[156] It shows how class formation amongst the British working class was masculinist (it was based around male identity). The mid-Victorian equilibrium was the result of working-class leaders abandoning more radical alternatives to liberal individualist capitalism based on respectability and the acceptance of the Victorian ideal of separate gender spheres. Clark shows how there was a 'struggle for the breeches' behind the making of the British working class. Men began to form their own masculine version of class in the late eighteenth century. There was a counter-movement in the 1820s based on greater equality between the sexes, but this egalitarian trend was undermined in the 1830s by the rise of a new kind of masculinist working-class politics under the umbrella of Chartism (which was based on the Victorian ideal of separate spheres).[157] So Clark looks at the same period of working-class history as Thompson, but her reading of it is different, and she ends up by depicting the narrative as 'a tragedy rather than the melodrama of E.P. Thompson's story'.[158] Thus she considers working-class political activity, the formation of the industrial working class, and Thompson's radical artisan culture from a different perspective.

Clark contrasts the gender relations of artisans and textile workers in London, Lancashire and Glasgow, showing that textile workers and artisans found different ways of expressing their communal identity, and adopted different strategies to cope with the threat cheaper female labour posed to the status of male craftsmen. Artisan culture 'tended to be both exclusively masculine and exclusive in general'. By contrast, 'Textile workers were sometimes able to draw men, women, and children together in a kin, neighbourhood, and workplace community solidarity, but even then their actions pitted one group of workers against others who were more marginal and vulnerable.' However, as the development of new technology began to threaten the position of skilled, male factory workers, they often began to emulate traditional artisans by excluding women from their jobs. However, unlike artisans they accepted females as auxiliaries. Thus it is apparent that, in contrast to Thompson, Clark views artisan culture as a corrosive influence on the British working class. Artisans focused on the workshop and the pub. Drinking may have promoted a particular type of culture based on artisan solidarity but, from a woman's perspective, it sapped funds needed for family life, and engendered violence.[159]

Sonya O. Rose's *Limited Livelihoods: Gender and Class in Nineteenth Century England* (1992) considers the attempts to exclude women from paid employment. Rose demonstrates how exclusion was the result of both state legislation and the tacit alliance between employers and organised working men. Rose shows that Victorian men's aspiration to eliminate female competition was not just an attempt to protect their privileges and skills, but was an intrinsic part of their gender identity. From the 1840s onwards working men's sense of masculinity was increasingly based on the premise of the male breadwinner earning a 'family wage'.[160] Rose sees the ideology of separate spheres as a central organising motif in the worldviews of bourgeois men and women.

Rose points out that in many industries women and men were thrown into competition with each other, as employers used women to drive down men's wages. On occasion, women were substituted for men, performing the same task, but paid from one-third to one-half less than the men had been.[161] Employers also took it for granted that men should be hired to do skilled work, and it seems as if they would not even have thought of employing women for such jobs. She considers the various arguments workers and employers uses to justify lower wage rates for women. For example, some employers claimed that they also needed to employ costly male supervisors who could tune machines and do repairs, if they hired women.[162] Skilled workers in various industries sought to exclude women and to maintain strict divisions between women's and men's work. Added to this, was the fact that male unionists would not consider admitting women to their union. Rose says that union solidarity was based on masculine values, particularly that of the male provider, and it was secured by men appealing to other men. This marginalised women, were thus reluctant to become involved in trade unions.

Ellen Ross explores the different gender roles of working-class men and women within marriage. The division of labour was highly gendered, with wives having responsibility for childcare and domestic labour. Men's role was to bring home the income that it was their wives' job to spend, although many men regularly presented their wives with only that portion of their wages that remained after a visit to the pub. Husbands also tried to conceal the true extent of their earnings from their wives. Men and women had different priorities, while men wanted to spend money on personal luxuries like drink and tobacco, women's priority was to the maintenance of the family.[163] Marriage thus became the site of a continual struggle between the sexes over access to financial resources waged by a variety of means, involving both diplomacy and open conflict. So this is a study in working-class gender relations, which emphasises the difficulties of women's lives within marriage. In many ways, the working-class mothers in her study, their lives limited by lack of opportunity, poverty, and the demands of childcare and housework, while also being subject to the scrutiny of governmental bodies and private associations, seem to be highly restricted. Although these women played a key role in the survival of their families, which required considerable inventiveness, and they also benefited from the support of their immediate community, they are ultimately victims of both their class and their gender. Thus their situation is a result of their position at the bottom of the system of social relations.

These studies demonstrate that gender was of fundamental importance to the shaping of the British working class. Deborah Valenze has shown that attitudes to women's work altered during the eighteenth century. Women's labour was devalued, and the ideology of separate gender spheres became dominant. Going back to Thompson's point that the working class made itself as much as it was made, we have to consider that at various points the working class has defined itself in different ways. Class consciousness has been expressed as both a concept involving both sexes in a joint struggle to improve conditions for the class as a whole, and as a concept based on masculine identity, the male breadwinner role, and a defence of the rights of skilled men as against those of women workers. Unfortunately, it was the latter definition of class that was victorious in nineteenth-century Britain.

Many of the issues of identity and conflict are captured in the history of Irish migration to Britain during the nineteenth century, bringing us back to the question of divisions within the working class itself. Irish workers were resented by native workers who feared that they would take their jobs, and also encountered hostility as a result of working-class anti-Catholicism and anti-Irishness. The violence and antipathy that Irish migrants in Britain faced is well known. There is no doubt (indeed there can be no debate) that the Irish were most noticeable, in negative contexts, in terms of the application of negative stereotypes, at just this time. When commentators looked for poverty, crime and a demonised but renascent Catholic religion, they needed to look no further than the Irish. When contemporaries struggled to make sense of the Dystopian urban world that grew threateningly around them, they alighted on the Irish – scapegoats incapable of defending themselves. The way middle-class observers viewed the Irish, the language they used to describe them, was often stark. The Manchester doctor and educationist, J.P. Kay-Shuttleworth, like Thomas Carlyle, Friedrich Engels or the poet Ebenezer Elliott, shared a loathing and contempt for the Irish, which they expressed in a form of words that would today fall foul race relations legislation. But it is not this degree of loathing – the intensity of social comment – that is up for debate. No historian of the Irish in Britain disagrees with the general hypothesis that sees attitudes towards these settlers reaching a nadir in the famine period. In a whiggish formulation of national history, Irish immigration represents an interruption of otherwise normal relations. The Famine has an overbearing impact on both Irish and British society in this context and, when coupled with the 'Condition of England' crisis of industrialism and urbanisation, explains why the Irish were victimised. It is almost as though we are supposed to believe that the Irish were mistreated because they were in the wrong place at the wrong time.

In the 1850s, however, a radical change occurred. The hinge of the nineteenth century is often thought to have the year of revolutions, 1848, when Europe ruptured, Ireland rose and Chartism loomed. When the British ruling elite escaped the fate of Louis Philippe, when William Smith O'Brien's Confederate rising ended in abject defeat, and when Chartism was exposed by its divisions, the language of politics appeared to change. Instead of seeking to overthrow capitalism, working men are thought to have turned their attentions to acquiescence, to striking a bargain with the new system of production. This classic idea of history as a series of watersheds dominates labour history (an approach criticised in Richard Price's challenging new study).[164] The Irish fit into this line of thinking quite neatly, if we accept the still dominant view that, despite initial problems of settlement, the Irish sought, and were rewarded with, easy passage into host society. Chartism (so the theory goes) was killed off by economic prosperity, free trade and the railways. There is, of course, an element of truth in this perspective. For our purposes, such a schema sees the Irish become a reflection of troubled times in the 1830s and 1840s, but equally a measurement of more contented times in the 1850s. Less commented upon in these happier days, and affected by only sporadic incidents of violence, the Irish, like the 'Hungry Forties', are largely thought to have gone away. The ethnic tensions that marred communal life in the north of England in the 1850s and 1860s, and which saw episodic outbreaks of violence in a wide range of places, is somehow consigned to a place marked 'superficial'. Here, religious dispute and ethnicity are portrayed as cultural **superstructure**, secondary to more important and embedded material considerations (focusing on class relations and improving economic experiences). The Irish, then, are thought to have moved quickly from their position of inferiority. In the 1840s, they stand at a great distance from the indigenous working class: their history, culture, religion, poverty, and many other factors, made them different or 'other'. Yet, by the late 1880s – just slightly more than a single full generation after the final flurry of famine-related immigration in the 1850s – the Irish begin to emerge as activists and leaders in the unskilled unions. That the Labour Party of the 1920s could rely on so many sons and grandsons of Irish immigrants to swell its ranks or to be its representatives in parliament probably does attest to the degree of progress these immigrants made. It may not have matched Irish-American achievement through Tammany Hall or in the American Federation of Labor, but it was quite a notable success by the standards of an unyielding, conservative political establishment in Britain.

The prevalent notion, then, is that Irish workers could not achieve class consciousness until they had shaken off their ethnic identity. In this type of context, ethnicity becomes a poor relation of class. This idea is driven by a hard-nosed Marxist approach of the type that Marx himself might have disapproved. In recent times, Steve Fielding and John Belchem have done much in their writings to undermine this notion that Irish migrants' identities were singular, unyielding and impermeable entities.[165] Here we are reminded of Linda Colley's view: 'identities are not like hats. Human beings can and do put on several at a time'.[166] American scholarship on the twin or related questions of class and ethnicity offers a more perceptive fusion of ideas, a hybridity of identities in a way that enables them to be seen as mutually enforcing. This is certainly how the Marxist scholar, Eric Foner, has seen the role played in the 1880s by the American Irish in supporting the Land League, an organisation dedicated to winning radical economic and political reforms for their homeland, Ireland. For Foner, the successful mobilisation of the American Irish behind this essential Irish movement was the measure of another sort of coming of age: the welding together of class and ethnic imperatives. For the first time, the Irish were being introduced to the American reform tradition, railing against one form of monopoly, the British government, in such a way that would prepare them for an important role in the fight against another form of monopoly, American capitalism. The League is thus seen as an instrument in the American-Irish community's 'assimilation ... with a strong emergent oppositional working class culture'.[167] This view has certainly been supported by Kerby Miller, who writes: 'there is no doubt that bonds forged in steel mills, pitcrews, and working-class neighbourhoods among Irish-American labourers heightened ethnic as well as class consciousness'.[168] Moreover, Alan O'Day has utilised Miroslav Hroch's typology of ethnic groups (the need of leaders ethnic groups 'to maintain the way of life of and the value system of the established ruling class') to explain the 'apparent paradox' that ethnic groups simultaneously maintain incomers' identities and promoting assimilation.[169] While many Irish in Britain felt the same way as Foner's or Miller's American Irish, their organisation failed on both points: they could not break into the native political arena either by forming their own party or by dominating an existing party. The mature and conservative political culture of British life and the absence of a large Irish middle class in most towns (save for Liverpool and Glasgow) made the political achievements of their American cousins an enviable dream. Indeed, political recognition at the local or national level was something that would not be realised throughout industrial Britain until perhaps the 1920s when Irishmen were playing a significant role in the then mainstream British Labour Party.

▶ **Conclusion**

The specific manifestations of structure and **agency** we have considered in this chapter demonstrate the complexity of the historical process. At its most visible, social structure can be said to operate through domination, and human agency through resistance. This 'resistance' is not usually manifested in the form of open rebellion but can take a number of less dramatic forms. Social structures are also manifest in much less visible forms than that of open repression, and the existence of mental structures, and the role of ideologies is significant here. The insights offered by Antonio Gramsci are important to an understanding of the operation of social power. Social structures are also significant in the creation and the suppression of opportunities. Giddens' work on **structuration** is useful in drawing our attention to the positive as well as the negative features of social structures. However, we have to recognise that agency is quite often severely limited by structure. This is not to say that structure predetermines action, but that it sets limits upon action. Historical analysis must be concerned with the distinctive features of particular historical epochs, particularly in terms of their means of production of the necessaries of life, but must also be sensitive to the fact that societies are in a constant state of change.

It is possible to imagine a diagram that would depict the relative significance of various structural factors, the role of human agency and the impact of the unintended consequences of action. Having drawn up our model of the way that society operates, the only task remaining for the current authors would be to instruct readers to go away and apply it to the historical situation of their choice. The problem is, that despite some very determined attempts to offer a solution to the question of structure and agency in social theory, in the view of the current authors, no comprehensive solution has yet been suggested, which satisfactorily resolves all the issues discussed here. Most significantly, as far as the current authors are aware, the interaction of class, gender and ethnicity has not been successfully incorporated into a single theory of society. Instead, both historians and sociologists have offered us some very significant insights into the way that the historical process operates. Although there have been many attempts at presenting such a model in the past, and there are likely to be more in the future, given the nature of both history and sociology (and 'actually existing' historians and sociologists), it is very difficult to imagine a point in the future when a consensus will exist around such a model. The task of explaining society in both the past and the present is, thus, a 'work in progress' that will never be completed to the satisfaction of all the parties involved in its creation. However, such a conclusion should not make us pessimistic about the future of historical or sociological explanation. It is through this ongoing attempt to understand the historical process that we can come to a better understanding of both ourselves, and the society we live in.

5   Ideology, *Mentalité* and Social Ritual: From Social History to Cultural History

This chapter assesses an important historiographical development: the emergence of a 'New Social History' and, beyond that, of what is termed 'Cultural History'. The chapter's main aim is to explain, by drawing upon a wide range of examples, the linkages (and competition) between these more recent turns towards the cultural and the older forms of Marxist-inspired social history of the 1960s. In some respects, the two traditions have lived side by side: the keystones of Marxist social history, works by such influential writers as E.P. Thompson, were quickly assimilated into an Anglophone historiographic tradition. The Americans were particularly quick to seize the opportunities afforded by such analyses of workers' lives. Whilst many important *Annales'* social histories pre-dated the work of Thompson, the spread of their ideas in the non-Francophone world was initially restricted to those who could read French. Nevertheless, the two approaches were, as Lynn Hunt rightly argued, 'two dominant paradigms of explanation' in 'the move towards the social'.[1]

The turn to the 'cultural' in historical interpretation can, in many ways, be seen as a development of pioneering works of the *Annales* School and the British Marxists. Cultural history has developed a truly global momentum since its inception in the early 1970s and has, in some respects, eclipsed social history as the provider of cutting edge analyses that subvert traditionalist assumptions about the content and approach of 'new' history. And yet: radical departures in historiography, born as they are from critical perspectives upon existing methods and assumptions, risk a loss of freshness and vibrancy as they themselves become norms. Both the *Annales* and British Marxists suffered, perhaps, from what Peter Burke rather sharply called the move 'from the cellar to the attic' (i.e. the shift of emphasis from material conditions to **mentalities**).[2] By becoming accepted, popular, modish and even dominant, any historical approach is bound to meet with further radicalisms: this certainly happened to the Marxist-inspired social histories of the 1960s; and later generations of the *Annales* have abandoned some of their predecessors' aims and ambitions. At the very least, even where they remain dominant, proponents of a particular way of doing things can expect their ideas to be honed, re-conceptualised and utilised to answer different questions about new material. If writers such as Christopher Hill, George Rudé, E.P. Thompson and E.J. Hobsbawm helped to make Marxist social (and economic) history fashionable, and if Jacques Le Goff, Georges Duby and Emmanuel Le Roy Ladurie did the same for French social history, then their works provide an interesting plank to support a discussion of what happened to these most progressive forms of social history and why the study of cultural history moved into their space.

The British Marxist historians and their disciples clearly offered a radical reinterpretation of what was important in historical enquiry: a concern with the lives of ordinary people became their key impetus; analysis of class struggle, influenced by readings from Karl Marx and other Marxist writers, provided the prism through which the social life of ordinary people was viewed. A parallel force, the *Annales*-inspired cultural history, sometimes referred to as *les histoire des mentalités* (or *psychologie historique*) should be acknowledged.[3] Here, the central concern was also with ordinary lives; but in the case of the *Annales*, the key element of study was emphatically cultural. Both the *Annales* and the British Marxists sought their appreciation of past society in the darker recesses of lives of ordinary people. The *Annales*, and those inspired by that approach, focused most explicitly on the medieval and early modern period. Class was usually (though not completely) rejected as a mode of explanation and organisation, with the focus on pre-modern systems of thought and action underpinning this quite distinct approach to the rituals of belief and everyday life. The British Marxists were predominantly, though not exclusively, concerned with the later period, and the modern working class.

Inspired at first by the *histoires des mentalités* approaches of the *Annales* School, and later influenced by a diverse array of philosophers, theorists and historians – including Michel Foucault, Roland Barthes, Jacques Derrida, Hayden White Natalie Zemon Davis, Roger Chartier and Michelle Vovelle – cultural history has, in recent years, seen a distinct shift from a modernist (**empirical, materialist,** realist, **determinist**) approach to the past, as typified by classical social history, towards a postmodernist (**idealist, relativist, linguistic**) approach to the past, which stresses the importance of language as constitutive (rather than the product) of action.[4] With this shift, core elements of the historian's own mentality have shifted. Instead of being concerned with labour organisations, examples of class conflict and the **dialectic** of competing economic interest groups, once favoured by Marxist social historians, cultural historians have stressed the centrality of ritual, ceremony and shared cultural attributes in explaining the past. This can be seen in the shift, in labour history, from studies of worker organisations, trade unions and the importance of production in socio-economic lives, to an emphasis upon the culture of consumption, and the language, signs and social communication that can be 'read' in the development of such phenomena.

▶ Historic approaches to social and cultural aspects of the past

Whereas social history has long emphasised social relations and the lives of ordinary people, often heavily glossed with Marxist theory and invariably influenced by sociological approaches, cultural history has changed markedly in recent decades. During the nineteenth century – when, as we have seen, E.R. Green was emphasising the history of ordinary people – cultural history had very different connotations than today. It was formerly primarily concerned with either high culture, such as art and music: that is, the history of the sensibilities and ideas affecting given periods, much in the style of Matthew Arnold's most important critique.[5] We can see in Arnold, for example, a fear of swamping by mass culture that influenced many modernist writers who followed, such as D.H. Lawrence and George Bernard Shaw.[6] The essence here, however, is of culture as *zeitgeist* – the spirit of the age. In this way, the study of past cultures – cultural history – focuses on the importance, at any given time or in a particular place, of what Peter Burke called 'modes of thought'.[7] These 'modes of thought' were relative to their context; contingent upon time, place and tradition. In explaining the relativity of such thoughts, Burke quotes John Locke's humane viewpoint: 'Had you or I been born at the Bay of Saldanha, possibly our thoughts and notions had not exceeded those brutish ones of the Hottentots that inhabit there.'[8] Already in the early eighteenth century, there was an understanding that **mentalities** could be revealed in ritual and ceremony, something that was later stressed by historical anthropologists, such as Clifford Geertz, and historians of the *Annales*.[9]

The emphasis upon systems of thought and the primacy of human ideas in the shaping of cultures, a factor emphasised in **poststructuralist** analyses of the past, also had antecedents in the age of the **Enlightenment**. Hegel used the term culture quite clearly, and in so doing places distance between culture, with its emphasis upon ideas (e.g. Hegelian **idealism**) and the social, with its connotations of **historical materialism**, social change and the shadow of Marxism. One tension which emerges here, and one which has never really gone away, is the sense that culture (and therefore cultural history) seeks to encapsulate, possibly to freeze-frame, the essence of an age; where social history alights upon the tensions, often material in origins, which encourage social action in any given age and which ultimately explains the change from one mode of being to the other. The way in which cultural history and social history might spin on this difference of emphasis, and this relative imbalance between cultural encapsulation and social change, is a key difference between them, and a recurring theme in this chapter.

Jacob Burckhardt's study of the Italian Renaissance has been seen as a major development in cultural history. As a study of art and society this book was, in some respects, a major influence upon the entire discipline of art history.[10] Burckhardt's great work enjoys fame for its engagement with the widest contexts of the Renaissance: classical roots, humanist thought and the patronage of the arts (and its thus vital economic dimension). It was this attempt to understand the 'spirit of the age' of the Renaissance, Italy's *zeitgeist*, which marked what was a major contribution to human knowledge; but it is the combination of art history and cultural history that sets the work apart from that of the sixteenth-century writer, Giorgio Vasari, who sought trends and patterns in the art of the Renaissance, but not in wider implications for society. Indeed, 'his total lack of interest in the relationship between art and political and social development now appears as a grave omission'.[11] In both authors, though, we can detect sensitivity to the social implications and meanings of culture. And in Burckhardt we have an historian's spirit to match that of E.R. Green. A clear movement away from culture as 'lofty', 'high' or 'rarefied', was clearly signalled in the author's explication of his chosen themes for a course of lectures on the Middle Ages: 'Not politics but culture ... Not according to nations or chronology, but according to the pervasive spiritual currents ... Not princes and their dynasties but people and their development in a common spirit.'[12] Burckhardt was interested in collective beliefs or **mentalities**, with art 'not an isolated thing' but 'involved with the total life of a people'[13] At this point, however, there was no suggestion of class or popular politics; nor was there any indication of protest and the material world, at least not as the ultimate question for an historian.

Cultural approaches to the past, those typified by the 1920s Dutch medievalist, Jan Huizinga, and later the *Annales'* historians, focused upon the way of the past in terms of its mental frameworks, as well as the fundamental, anthropological, differences between the past and present – differences which become less pronounced the closer we move through history to our own ages. Jan Huizinga, in the preface to his classic study of medieval life, offers posterity this reminder of the nature of the medieval world, stressing this element of difference, of distance, from our own times: 'We, at the present day, can hardly understand the keenness with which a fur coat, a good fire on the hearth, a soft bed, a glass of wine, were formerly enjoyed.'[14] With their heavy focus on the medieval period, such historians grant the past a timeless quality, a less pronounced emphasis upon social change (or caesura) than would be found in later Marxist social history. It is certainly true that, the further back in time we go, the slower the pace of social change; but a failure to probe for the nature of change, rather than immediate culture of an age, presents us with one of the key differences between the modes of social and cultural history discussed here.

Burckhardt and Huizinga marked out major signposts in the development of cultural history and pre-warned, in some respects, of the tensions with social history that would later emerge. Both acknowledged the differences of epochs or ages; but explaining why the characteristics of those ages gave way to new formulations did not figure as highly on their agenda. For Burckhardt, there was no question that the

Middle Ages were different from, and by implication inferior to, the Renaissance: that present excelled the past. This is how he conceptualised that difference:

> In the Middle Ages both sides of human consciousness – that which was turned within and that which was turned without – lay as though dreaming or half awake beneath a common veil. The veil was woven of faith, illusion, and childish prepossession, through which the world and history were seen in strange hues. Man was conscious of himself only as a member of a race, people, party, family, or corporation – only through some general category. It is in Italy that this veil dissolved first; there arose an *objective* treatment and consideration of the State and of all things ... Man became a spiritual *individual* ...[15]

But how did 'Man' become this new vision of Burckhardt's? This preference for a reading that emphasised the triumph of the human mind over its earlier states of backwardness accords with a dominant theme in much cultural history: the emphasis upon collective psychology, and particular the influence of religion as a restraint upon modern modes of thought and action. Huizinga, too, recognised the need for human kind to outgrow the limits of the environmental and social circumstances. He wrote: 'To the world when it was half a thousand years younger, the outlines of all things seemed more clearly marked than to us. The contrast between suffering and joy, between adversity and happiness, appeared more striking.'[16]

In the period encompassed by these great works, the theorists most closely associated with social history (or, perhaps more properly social science history) also provide a link to the cultural approach at its juncture with the social. Karl Marx, Max Weber and Emile Durkheim underpin aspects of both social and cultural history in the sense that all three were interested in cultures and behaviour patterns; whilst the stress that each placed upon social change, and though the explanations for it may have differed, each would have claimed to be explaining cultures. In one respect, if we allow that culture is the deeply ingrained explanation of context and social action, then Marx's *Capital* was classically 'cultural', for it sought to explain dominant ideas about the rise of modern systems of production and exchange, looking at the way they affected people's beliefs as well as their material conditions. Weber's studies of society were focused, too, on explanations of dominant cultural as well as social or political expressions, such as the development of armies or bureaucracy. Durkheim was also centrally concerned with the norms and values of the societies he studied. In the previous chapter, we noted Durkheim's concern with the *conscience collective*, that he held to be the basis of solidarity in pre-industrial society. While he argues that the *conscience collective* becomes less significant in industrial society, he still maintained that it was a moral order based on commonly held beliefs and values.[17]

As this discussion begins to suggest, then, the axis for the meeting of social and cultural history is really the question of which explains the past most adeptly, and, possibly, which concerns the most important elements of the past. We can also see hints that it may be that cultural and social history are the same thing; but practitioners of each would deny that this is so. We must therefore spend the remainder of this chapter discussing the interstices between the disciplines to discover what features in the interplay between the two.

▶ Ideology and mentality

Our interest in the **mentalities** approach stems from a need to understand the men and women of the distant past: to get into their minds, to demonstrate the empathy that the philosopher of history, R.G. Collingwood, thought essential to his philosophy of history.[18] In forwarding such a desire, early cultural historians were moving away from the idea that material circumstances constituted the central narrative of the human condition. The early *Annalistes* began to move the historical viewfinder on to the way people thought rather than on the ways in which they live. This is a crucial juncture of social and cultural approaches; one which remains important today. Important works such as Georges Lefebvre's 1930s study of crowd in the French Revolution[19] which prefigured works, such as those of George Rudé, which in the 1950s and 1960s presented a Marxist concern with the social (and political) aspect of crowds.[20] The classic works of the founding phase of the *Annales* School – particularly Marc Bloch's study of popular beliefs in the healing powers of monarchs and Lucien Febvre's study of Lutheran beliefs[21] – moved the discussion of collective psychological aspects, the history of *mentalités*, on to a new level. Moreover, at the time Rudé was first becoming known as a writer on crowd action, the *Annales* was furthering its impact on the history of the Parisian crowd with the important work of Albert Soboul.[22]

Elsewhere in Europe, early medieval cultural historians, such as Huizinga, helped to chart new territory in the attempt to understand the collective cultural mores and psychological emotions that connected people. The interest in why people believed what they did, why they were superstitious, how they felt about pain and the prospect of death has, since the 1920s, offered a continuous thread in the *Annales* School and among the cultural historians they have influenced. Following the deaths of Bloch and Febvre, the mantle passed to historians such as Robert Mandrou, Georges Duby and Jacques Le Goff. Mandrou, for example, was especially concerned with the historical psychology approach, writing two important books that looked at the world of early modern France with an eye to health, emotions and mentalité.[23] These works, as Burke reminds us, sought to distinguish ' "the fears of the majority" (the sea, ghosts, plague, and hunger) from the fears of "the ruling culture" (Satan, Jews, women – and especially witches)'.[24]

In England, one of the great works of the post-war generation was Keith Thomas's study of religion and magic in the medieval and early modern world.[25] Engaging with a much broader range of issues of superstition and collective psychology, Thomas's book, *Religion and the Decline of Magic* instantly became a classic of cultural history because of the richness of its examination of the motivations, beliefs and fears of ordinary people. Its consciously cultural emphasis placed it neatly both in time and historical approach: like the *Annales* history, which inspired it, Thomas's work was located in the medieval and early modern periods; again, like the *Annalistes* approach it centred upon the shared mental structures of people whose views of the world were anthropologically 'pre-modern'. Thomas opens his account with an important claim about the importance of certain dead 'systems of belief which … no longer enjoy much recognition today'. 'Astrology, witchcraft, magical healing, divination, ancient prophecies, ghosts and fairies', Thomas explained, 'are now rightly disdained by intelligent persons … [b]ut they were taken seriously by equally intelligent persons in the past'. In noting this important point about the difference between past and present modes of thought, Thomas reminded his readers that 'it is the historian's business to explain why this is so'.[26] Indeed, Thomas's work clearly drew upon psychological and anthropological tendencies in historical enquiry.[27] Jacques Le Goff, a contemporary of Thomas's, captured the basis of pre-modern irrationality, whether the subject be a belief in magic or the 'royal touch': 'The **mentalities** and sensibilities of medieval men were dominated by a sense of insecurity which determined the basis of their attitudes.'[28] People thus held beliefs that differed greatly from those of modern man and woman; but such ideas did not exist in a vacuum.

Notable developments in the writing of history from the Marxist point of view brought cultural history approaches and social history closer together. E.P. Thompson, a pioneer of a cultural as well as Marxist **'history from below'** can be seen as a critic of harsh and unbridgeable divisions between the social and the cultural. Thompson's central interest, expressed in his classic work of the 1960s, was to imagine a working class that was constitutive of its own cultural life and social thought. While Thompson did not write in the argot of postmodernism, nor use the language of the linguistic theorists, he did stress language as constitutive of action, thus showing an appreciation of the importance of communication, language and symbols. Thompson, whose *Making of the English Working Class* long provided a focal point for Marxist social history, was in some ways critical of pure, or hard, Marxism that emphasised the rigid determinacy of **base-superstructure**. Thompson set out in the preface to his major work the problems associated with trying to imagine that blanket economic or environmental factors altered lives, ideologies and belief systems at a constant rate. To get round the problem of how and why some groups developed class-consciousness (as he saw it), Thompson stressed the importance of a 'cultural superstructure, through which recognition [class consciousness] dawns in inefficient ways'.[29] In other words, aspects of culture slow down, or accelerate, an individual or group's consideration and recognition of its class position. In passing from the objective location of being in a class (class in itself) to solidaristic action on the basis of that class position (class for itself), individuals and groups meet 'cultural lags and distortions'.[30] In fact, Thompson was critical of the **base** and **superstructure** model itself, and argued instead for the adoption of a much looser conception of the relationship between the ideology and the economy, also drawn from Marx.

▶ Marxist social history, 'history from below' and subordinate 'cultures'

The British Marxists were concerned mostly with the modern period and the age of revolutions, but notable contributors such as Rodney Hilton, who worked on medieval society, and Christopher Hill, whose central concern was with the political turmoil of the seventeenth century, offered perspectives from an earlier period. There was not, however, the same weighting of work on the earlier period; in this sense, the search for instances of class struggle and a vigorous application of Marxist methods, perhaps played a role in promoting work on the later period. Equally, the political context of the British Marxists themselves also shaped their agenda. They were all members of the Communist Party of Great Britain historians' group, which gave rise to the journal, *Past and Present* (1952); and some of the same people were among the more diverse group that founded the Society for the Study of Labour History (1960), which in turn spawned what is now the *Labour History Review*. The concern with political and industrial revolutions clearly helped to point then young Marxists, such as E.P. Thompson and Eric Hobsbawm, towards the crucible of the nineteenth century; but their own post-war/Cold War context also shaped their interests.

The study of the ordinary person occupied one of the first major names of the British Marxist school, George Rudé, who was concerned above all with the role of crowds, primarily because these offered a unique insight into what the protesting masses thought about their world.[31] What is more, crowds had tended to be ignored by historians, or else had been dismissed as brutish, unthinking, mobs. As one early sociologist argued: by joining a crowd, a man 'descends several rungs in the ladder of civilisation'.[32] Rudé's intention was to get away from such an uncritical reading of the crowd and to offer a more nuanced view of mass action.

Some of his earliest published work focused on the classic 'outsider' group in British history in the period of and following the French Revolution: convicts who were transported to the Australian colonies.[33] A large literature subsequently emerged in Rudé's wake, which began to unravel the hidden history of the convicts; the misery of their passage and incarceration; their toil and bolts for freedom; the role they played in shaping national identity in Australia; and, latterly, the opportunities that many of them seized to make new lives in the colonies once their time had been served.[34] These studies of ordinary men and women – deemed criminal by a savage penal code – were examples of those hidden from history, the victims of Thompson's 'enormous condescension of posterity'.[35] This was the stuff of radical social history.

By examining examples of popular, or people's history, Rudé was placing a marker that would be noticed by contemporary Marxist historians and others. The intention, in studying the crowd, was to get inside the minds of those past groups and peoples in order really to understand the crowd. He wanted to know of the crowd: 'how it behaved, how it was composed, how it was drawn into its activities, what it set out to achieve and how far its aims were realised'.[36] The focus of his work was shaped by the purpose of his enquiry. He concentrated upon ordinary urban and rural workers, 'participants through various forms of "popular action" in the great French and Industrial Revolutions which have shaped **modernity**'.[37] His interest was not with dominant elites. Whilst the crowds of interest to Rudé were mainly those that rioted, this was merely the first phase of what has since become a stream of studies, which have tackled the question of popular protest and crowd action. Rudé sat alongside Thompson and Hobsbawm, who shared this interest in the social and political importance of, what Hobsbawm called, 'collective bargaining riot'.[38] But none of them wrote about crowds, which protested peacefully, and more recent studies have stressed orderly mass expression and the importance of identifying the language of the non-riotous crowd. As one recent contributor to these debates has argued, the crowd is not only (nor perhaps primarily) riotous, but the crowd is a provider of symbolic nodes of reference: 'autonomous or quasi-autonomous vehicles for the expression of cohesion – for the expression of different versions of order'.[39]

Historians are conditioned by their own experiences, and this was no less true of these Marxist writers. Hobsbawm recalled how his military experiences during the Second World War helped him to develop an admiration for, and an interest in, the ordinary men – workers or soldiers – whom the war brought him into contact with. This certainly showed in Hobsbawm's early writings on workers, which he brought together in a seminal volume.[40] Ranging across themes as diverse as Tom Paine, machine-wreckers, wages, labour aristocrats, methodism and Marxism and fabanism, Hobsbawm's work was unified by his desire to explain the social and political consciousness of workers in the industrial period. Previously, little-studied (or else entirely neglected) themes, were brought to life by Hobsbawm and his colleagues; all these contained, concerned and had implications for ordinary people's lives. History had moved far on from the days when Charles Kingsley attacked the history of 'the little man' as 'no science at all'.[41]

It was as late as the 1960s, before this '**history from below**' made the transfer from formulation to fashion. The term 'history from below' is credited to the interwar

French historian, Georges Lefebvre,[42] but the parlance certainly did not achieve cult status in the Anglophone world till long after the Second World War. E.P. Thompson's espousal of the term, in a now famous essay in the mid-1960s, has been marked as a turning point, as 'the concept of **history from below** entered the common parlance of historians'.[43] The preface to Thompson's major work remained, for decades, a clarion call to like-minded scholars to pursue the under history of society: to bring light into the darkest recesses of the past; to uncover the meaning of life for the silent majority, rather than the noisy minority. His classic statement of the central philosophy of this new Marxist social history is well known but still compelling:

> I am seeking to rescue the poor stockinger, the Luddite cropper, the 'obsolete' handloom weaver, the 'utopian' artisan, and even the deluded follower of Joanna Southcott, from the enormous condescension of posterity. Their crafts and traditions may have been dying. Their hostility to the new industrialism may have been backward-looking. Their insurrectionary conspiracies may have been foolhardy. But they lived through these times of acute social disturbance, and we did not. Their aspirations were valid in terms of their own experience; and if they were casualties of history, they remain, condemned in their own lives, as casualties.[44]

The sentiment of this famous statement is human: but Thompson added further resonance when he explained how the experiences of the past might impact upon the present. He wrote: '... we are not at the end of social evolution ourselves. In some of the lost causes of the people of the Industrial Revolution we discover insights into social evils which we have yet to cure'. And he went on, '[c]auses which were lost in England [in the nineteenth century] might, in Asia or Africa, yet be won'.[45]

When Thompson visited India in the mid-1970s, his philosophy of history had a tremendous impact upon scholars working from a radical perspective; for them, 'history from below' opened up a whole world of struggle and resistance, which Thompson, Rudé, Hobsbawm and others can scarcely have envisaged. In a pertinent forecasting of styles of synthesis that would develop later in western historical research, Indian scholars also drew upon **poststructuralism** and **postmodernism** to elicit new ways of thinking about iconic figures such as Gandhi and those who resisted imperial domination by the British and subjugation by indigenous elites. But, set in its India context, 'history from below' also challenged notions that Indian nationalism was a 'top down' process, generated, controlled and delivered by elites. Instead, it drew on Thompson's work, and, importantly, key works by Eric Hobsbawm, to elicit more about ordinary peoples' lives.[46] Like Thompson's subjects, the Indian worker or peasant was voiceless in the historical vacuum. Thus, in making comparisons with Thompson's study and that of his Indian peers, we might argue that for Industrial Revolution we could read Empire; for Luddites we might read peasant rebels; but, in both cases, class and **hegemony** provided a codified theme for struggle and resistance. The result, in India, was the development of a school of historical enquiry which, in 1982, produced its own journal, *Subaltern Studies*, an act that clearly echoed the structural formulations of both the British Marxists and the French *Annales*.[47] It was the simultaneous chiming between past and present, from historian's craft to agitator's exhortation, that made Thompson, and his work, so important to subsequent generations of historians working on issues of class and anti-colonial struggle in current and former imperial possessions.

▶ From women's history to gender history

The task of rescuing the past experiences of the bulk of the population from 'the enormous condescension of posterity' was given an added dimension by the growth of the women's movement in the 1960s and 1970s. This revealed the necessity of recovering the experiences of women in past societies, which had previously been 'hidden from history'.[48] Feminist scholars argued that women had largely been omitted from previous accounts of the past, which resulted in a distorted vision of history, making it seem as if only the activities of men were worthy of preservation. This partial account of the past was subsequently added to by the activities of a number of historians of women during the 1970s and 1980s. Such work was initially conducted outside the academic establishment. In library and museum discussion groups, and evening classes organized by the Workers' Education Association and local authorities, women went about the business of creating their own feminist history groups.[49]

An understanding of the relationship between class and gender, and a desire to combine the insights of both Marxism and feminism was central to the development of women's history in this country. Catherine Hall explained that feminist history in Britain derived energy from a close relationship with socialism and the politics of class. Ruskin College was a focal point for early women's history, just as it had also long supported class-orientated social history and trade union studies. Raphael Samuel, who taught at Ruskin, was an important figure in the conflation of socialist and feminist histories. He was important in the History Workshop movement, whose publication, *History Workshop Journal* was, as the sub-title declared, dedicated to both feminist and socialist histories.[50]

The connection between Marxists, socialists and feminists was a vital development of the 1960s and 1970s. It is significant, for example, that Catherine Hall was herself taught by the eminent Marxist historian Rodney Hilton. Thus, the writing of the history of women, and of gender relations in general, has been informed by this earlier tradition, but, as we saw in the previous chapter, it has also become increasingly critical of it.[51]

During the 1980s, there was a tremendous growth in the whole area of women's history and women's studies in general. Academic institutions began to offer more courses dealing with the female experience, and women's studies created a major publishing industry around itself. A number of significant journals dedicated to feminist history subsequently appeared, most notably *Gender and History* (1989), *Journal of Women's History* (1989) and *Women's History Review* (1992). By 1983, Joan Scott could write that the challenges of early feminist had been met, partly at least through inspiration from women's political movements, so that 'historians have documented not only the lives of the average woman in various historical periods, but they have charted as well changes in the economic, educational and political positions of women of various classes in city and country and in nation states'.[52] This reflection on the current state of play led Scott to assert the need for a history of gender relations, a point which she developed more fully in her later work.

The approach Scott advocated was suggested to her in important articles, which Joan Kelly and Natalie Zemon Davis published in the mid-1970s. These pieces had begun to argue that women's history should be reconceived as the history of gender and that only by studying both sexes together could the dynamics of domination be understood. Natalie Zemon Davis had said that the aim was: 'to discover the range in sex roles and in sexual symbolism in different societies and periods, to find out what meaning they had and how they functioned to maintain the social order or to promote its change'.[53] Although Joan Kelly and Natalie Zemon Davis had previously voiced the need for a gendered approach to history, it was Joan Scott who really set the agenda for historians in this area for the next decade or so.[54] She argued that previous historians had used the word 'gender' descriptively, and that the use of the term simply meant that women were grafted on to existing explanations controlled by relatively traditional assumptions. Her search for a theory that would adequately explain the concept of gender led her towards some of the thinkers associated with **postmodernist** or **deconstructionist** approaches to history. Scott was concerned with language and discourse, and thus focused on discourses about women rather than on the lives of women themselves. She thus developed a definition of gender over several pages based on the ideas of Jacques Derrida and Michel Foucault. She argued: 'The core of the definition rests on an integral connection between two propositions: gender is a constitutive element of social relationships based on perceived differences between the sexes, and gender is a primary way of signifying relationships of power.' From this basis she concluded 'changes in the organization of social relationships always correspond to changes in the representations of power, but the direction of change is not necessarily one way'.[55] Scott critically discussed three uses of the word 'gender': feminist, Marxist and **poststructuralist**/psychoanalytical. Feminist theory is ultimately based on the physical difference between men and women, which makes it ahistorical, as it is based on an unchanging relationship. All the variants of Marxist theory ultimately rest on the causal role of economic factors. Despite efforts to break free from this assumption, gender roles are ultimately seen as determined by the economic relations of production. The Anglo-American school of psychoanalytic theory concentrated on the reproduction of gender relations within the family, and thus limited the concept of gender to the family. The Lacanian approach to psychoanalytic theory emphasises the centrality of language, and the unstable nature of gender identities, as the categories of 'man' and 'woman' are not fixed. Scott approved of this, but also saw it as unhistorical as it tends to universalise the categories and relationships of male and female. She says that what we needed instead was 'a refusal of the fixed and permanent quality of the binary opposition, a genuine historicization and deconstruction of the terms of sexual difference'.[56]

The intention of Scott's piece was to establish that there is little basis for an appeal to women's 'traditional' role. In other words, that there are no permanent, fixed gender identities. She intended to accomplish this 'genuine historicization and deconstruction of the terms of sexual difference' through an acceptance of Derrida and Foucault.[57] In assessing this approach we need to acknowledge that gender relations are subject to historical change, but are they also totally unfixed and do they contain no constant elements? The contradiction in Scott's approach was that, for Derrida, meaning is always continually deferred, so we can never know what the past really meant. Scott was not arguing that we should quit the archives or abandon the study of the past. However, she invoked Derrida as a means of investigating/'deconstructing' meaning systematically (though never definitively or totally). This led to a concern not with what happened, but with what was represented as happening through a focus on **discourses** about the subject, and the deconstruction of fixed categories of meaning. So there is no historical experience to attempt to recapture through conventional methods of historical research. If we cannot know about social relations, because there is nothing outside the text, as Derrida asserts, then why should we do historical research? How are we to explain anything at all? Although Scott has been criticised for her adoption of **poststructuralism**, her ideas have also been highly influential amongst feminist scholars.[58] Her work offers a sophisticated analysis of the role of gender relations in history, based on a rejection of traditional notions of the differences between men and women suggested by feminism. The question is, though: does Scott's approach actually resolve the tension between **postmodern** theory and historical practice? If not, have those who have adopted it taken onboard a fundamentally flawed approach to the study of gender?

▶ Cultural history as 'the history of mentalities'

In one of its most important manifestations cultural history focused upon 'the history of **mentalities**', what the French term *l'histoire des mentalités*. In this guise, the *Annales* and the British Marxists' '**history from below**' approaches are quite closely aligned. In one way, the 'history of **mentalities**' is the study of people's cultures – particularly ordinary people's cultures – in something of the same way as Thompson and his peers were concerned with the lives of the masses. In one sense, though, cultural history of this type and Marxist social history were distinct from each other. The centrality of material factors was not apparent in French cultural history. Whilst there are Marxist cultural historians of the French school, most were consciously avoiding a materialist reading of the past, and some were positively hostile to such Marxist re-enactments. Peter Burke partly explains this move away from Marxism by reference to the fact that the approach of certain cultural historians or social anthropologists meant they 'turned Marx on his head, in other words returned to Hegel, by suggesting that the really deep structures are not economic and social arrangements but mental categories'.[59] Other writers, however, have taken one of the dominant anthropological influences on historians – Claude Lévi-Strauss – arguing for the continued importance of Marx. An interest in totems and symbols in past cultural representation does not necessarily mean the obviation of Marxist notions of social evolution, with the stress upon material conditions, and so these remained important for such writers.[60]

Like its British Marxist equivalent, the cultural history of popular mentalities developed in the 1960s by such luminaries as Emmanuel Le Roy Ladurie, Robert Mandrou and Jacques Le Goff, was critical of previous approaches. French cultural history in this period sought to depart from the work of Lucien Febvre, which sought to contain religious psychology at a high and ultimately rigid level of analysis, largely excluding the values and beliefs of people at the bottom of society – the majority of people – from the picture. For the 1960s generation, earlier *Annales'* works tended to have a elitist feel; traditional notions of the history of ideas as collected primarily in the hands of educated, authority figures still seemed dominant. A history of cultures (as opposed to culture) required a new reading from the 'bottom up'. At the same time, a clear move was being made away from the sweeping Braudelian vista and the quest for '*histoire totale*'. These pioneers of a new type of cultural history, still clearly alive to the importance of the social and economic dimension, would begin to shape a micro-historical analysis of closely read texts of types that might illuminate the beliefs and fears of ordinary folk.

Their work, like that of the British Marxists, was to endorse clearly movement away from the idea that the lower orders or working class were simply hollow receptors for dominant ideologies. The world uncovered by these *Annales* historians in classic studies, such as Le Roy Ladurie's *Montaillou*, echoed the British Marxist social history primarily in the way they uncovered the needs, desires and views of the mass of people. Shorn of a Marxist interpretation such works as *Montaillou* emphasised the ritual, ceremony and culture of daily life. Both approaches – Marxist or otherwise, whether social or cultural in posture – tackled a similar, fundamental problem: how do we find sources to evoke the mindsets of ordinary people? For writers such as Christopher Hill or E.P. Thompson, literacy levels were such that an enormous print culture could be examined: chapbooks, broadside ballads, poems, journalism and so on. But for Le Roy Ladurie, uncovering the past value systems of medieval peasants was much more difficult. In using 'official' sources – in his case the diligently compiled records of inquisitorial trials of Cathar heretics – Le Roy Ladurie was able to breathe life into the ordinary folk whose religious world view was being measured against orthodox Catholicism, as determined by the Pope's secretariat. As people were accused of heresy, and their Catholicism was brought under the spotlight, a secondary and even tertiary evidence-base began to emerge, which painted a picture of life in a much fuller, more rounded way, than might ordinarily be expected from trial depositions and so on. In reading the records against the grain, Le Roy Ladurie was remembering early *Annalistes* and also echoing the likes of Thompson, who often had recourses to parliamentary investigations and other sources of information, because the 'top-down' view occasionally cast light on the 'bottom-up' value system. In a world often lit up by Rabelaisian indulgences, drink, sex, popular songs and ballads; 'rough music' and communal justice, ordinary people negotiated their own lives, and the world about them, on at least some of their own terms. Trickle-down concepts of culture were being undermined, or at least recast, by notions of a robust and seemingly independent existence on the ground.

At the heart of this *Annaliste* approach to popular culture is the desire to comprehend the **mentalités** of ordinary life. In seeking to make such discoveries, this sort of cultural history conformed to a threefold characterisation offered by Peter Burke in an important article.[61] First, he said, it stresses collective attitudes. Secondly, it concerns unconscious assumptions and everyday thought. Thirdly, it focused on the structure of belief. The influence of the *mentalités* approach to cultural history has increasingly given way to that of social anthropology in general, and the work of Clifford Geertz, in particular. Geertz's analysis of historical artefacts – texts and symbols – and collective rituals both added to social-anthropological-historical inquiry and posed an interesting reading of structures. Geertz argued that people's cultures are ensembles of texts, with anthropologists cast as sneaks trying to read over the owners' shoulders. Geertz's work employed what he called 'thick description' – a term now commonly used in the microanalysis of situations, cultures and materials.[62]

The essence of Geertz's method involved treating other cultures as 'texts' that the anthropologist can interpret through finding the meanings behind socially established patterns of behaviour. Geertz borrows the term 'thick description' from Gilbert Ryle, who also supplied a celebrated example of how a wink was to be interpreted: 'But the point is that between what Ryle calls the "thin description" of what the rehearser (parodist, winker, twitcher. …) was doing ("rapidly contracting his right eyelids") and the "thick description" of what he was doing ("practising a burlesque of a friend faking a wink to deceive an innocent into thinking a conspiracy is in motion") lies the object of ethnography.'[63] In other words, thick description means describing events in terms of their meaning to the 'native' actors, rather than just their external features, in order to gain an understanding of how a particular society works. The next stage is explanation: trying to see overall themes in thickly described events. It is a question of relating very small social occurrences ('ethnographic miniatures') to big themes ('grand realities' or 'wall-sized culturescapes of the nation').[64] It could be said that this is where this approach falls down, as it offers the observer/anthropologist/historian the opportunity to impose their own meanings on the social rituals they are describing, with no apparent means of validating their interpretation. Geertz acknowledges that anthropologists' interpretations can always be contested, so interpretation is always provisional.[65] Thus Geertz's approach, while it may have much to offer, is essentially relativistic.

Cultural history is, on one level, the history of popular ideas; in such a respect it represents a significant departure from the traditional history of ideas, with its emphasis upon seminal individuals and their canonical texts.[66] Cultural history can be called 'history of ideas from below', though, because it concentrates on the shared framework of ideas and notions shaping everyday actions, whether the more mundane playing out of marital ceremonies, the indulgence in carnival-like play, or the embarkation upon serious riots or risings. Peter Burke claims that the history of **mentalities** grew up to fill a conscious gap between narrow definitions of the history of ideas and social history.[67] Miri Rubin pointed out that the 'cultural turn' has been most prominent in the works of historians of the late medieval and early modern periods. As she argued: 'In these periods of seemingly such uneven cultural production, within powerful religious cultures that perpetuated the dichotomy of Latin/vernacular, priesthood laity, Christian/other, there was most reason to place the process of cultural production under the microscope.' For here, she contended, 'The encounter between the historian – product of an unenchanted world – and religious cultures humbles and encourages the search for equivalents or analogies elsewhere.'[68]

A consideration of popular culture and carnival-like festivities, brings us to another significant influence within the 'new cultural history', the ideas of the Russian literary theorist Mikhail Bakhtin (1895–1975). Bakhtin's writings are concerned with the nature of literature and language, and have been influential across a range of disciplines including philosophy, semiotics, cultural studies, anthropology, and, as we shall see, history. He uses very many terms in his work that may seem quite obscure and require elucidation such as: **heteroglossia**, **dialogism**, **polyphony**, carnival and the grotesque, and the **chronotope** to name but a few, all of which are primarily associated with language and different types of discourse.[69] The question of which discipline Bakhtin belongs to is not quite as complicated as with Foucault (e.g. he could not be described as a historian), but it is still somewhat ambiguous. He is usually seen as a literary theorist, but he repeatedly claimed that he was a philosopher.[70] Literary critics have been attracted by the centrality of the novel (as opposed to poetry) in Bakhtin's work.[71] His work has obvious relevance for English scholars, but his significance for historians may not be immediately apparent. Peter Burke reminds us that Bakhtin was only really discovered by western scholars – people such as Carlo Ginzburg, Bob Scribner and many others – in the 1970s. But, as Burke also stated that 'today, however, Bakhtin's concepts of "carnivalization", "uncrowning", "the language of the marketplace", "grotesque realism" and so on are so frequently employed that it is difficult to remember how we managed without them, while his view of the importance of the subversion and penetration of "high" culture by "low" is in danger of becoming a new orthodoxy'.[72]

For historians, it has been his concept of the **carnivalesque** that has thus far proven to be the most fruitful for historical research. '**Carnival**' is one of Bakhtin's central concepts.[73] This is to do with the festivals of popular culture (including the pre-Lent carnivals and the celebrations associated with marriages, midsummer and Christmas). Bakhtin uses the term 'carnivalesque' to refer to the varied popular festive life of the Middle Ages and the Renaissance, but it can also be used to refer to carnivalized writing. Raman Selden says: 'Carnival is *collective* in feeling and popular, reflecting values which ruling-class ideology tends to ignore or patronise. An essential feature is the reversal of all hierarchies and conventional attitudes. Hierarchies are turned on their heads – fools become wise; kings become beggars; separate spheres are flung together.' In other words, 'everything which asserts authority, everything fixed, rigid or serious, is mocked and treated with insulting and violent abuse'.[74] Bakhtin was concerned with the way these values were expressed in what he classed as 'carnivalised' literature. The materiality of the body is central to Bakhtin's conception of carnival. Grotesque realism, and gay relativity are the key terms in carnival. Bakhtin emphasised the importance of the special type of social relationships created by the suspension of the rules of normal life during the period of the carnival:

> The suspension of all hierarchical precedence during carnival time was of particular significance. Rank was especially evident during official feasts; everyone was expected to appear in the full regalia of his calling, rank, and merits and to take the place corresponding to his position. It was a consecration of inequality. On the contrary, all were considered equal during carnival. Here, in the town square, a special form of free and familiar contact reigned among people who were usually divided by the barriers of caste, property, profession and age.[75]

In this sense carnival is an Utopia in itself. Carnival takes the form of various performances. Laughter as a means of mocking of authority has an important subversive effect in carnival. Carnival is essentially 'popular humour'. In some ways the content of this has never changed, and it is worth remembering when considering the significance of 'carnivalesque inversion', 'gay relativity' and 'grotesque realism' that we are talking about humour at the level of a British 'Carry-on' film.

These ideas have been utilised by a number of historians, as Peter Burke points out earlier. R.W. Scribner describes how images from the world of play (or the 'carnivalesque') were used in the visual propaganda for the spread of the Reformation in Germany. In these illustrations, the Catholic Church was usually depicted in a derogatory manner. Scribner draws on Bakhtin's notion of the **carnivalesque** reducing the high and serious to the level of the comic and the mundane: 'This was a form of popular criticism of the mighty, robbing them of their aura of sanctity.'[76] Scribner posited an illustration of a cardinal, a leading dignitary of the Roman Catholic Church, which could be inverted to show a fool. The tournament was also treated in a similarly irreverent fashion. Although it was normally the preserve of the social elite, it was parodied at a popular level in mock tournaments, such as those found in the Nuremberg **carnival**. This can be seen in the battle between Carnival and Lent depicted by Brueghel.[77]

Natalie Zemon Davis, an early modern historian whose work is characterised by a concern with carnival and ritual, discusses the popular festivals found in all the cities of France at that time. In 'The Reasons of Misrule', she quotes the French lawyer Claude de Rubys writing at the end of the sixteenth century: 'It is sometimes expedient to allow the people to play the fool and make merry, lest by holding them in with too great a rigor, we put them in despair ... These gay sports abolished, the people go instead to taverns, drink up and begin to cackle, their feet dancing under the table, ... and draft scandalous defamatory leaflets.'[78] She points out that Keith Thomas also sees carnival as a pre-political safety valve characteristic of 'a preindustrial sense of time', but there are other views of this, such as those of the anthropologist Victor Turner and Mikhail Bakhtin, who 'see topsy-turvy play or rite as present in *all* societies'. In Bakhtin's study of Rabelais, Davis contended, 'the carnival is always a primary source of liberation, destruction and renewal, but the scope it is allowed changes in different periods'.[79] Thus, the Bakhtinian notion of carnival, like Victor Turner's concept of *communitas*, allows people to experience life without hierarchy.[80] We must remember, of course, that Bakhtin's writings on carnival only form a fraction of his total work, and Peter Burke argues that his other concepts could be just as fruitfully employed, not least his work on the novel, collected and translated in *The Dialogic Imagination* (1981).[81] These, Burke argued, provide vital insights into the 'social history of language'. Challenging Saussure's writing on language for paying 'insufficient attention to social context', Bakhtin's works 'emphasise the importance of different voices within the literary text, its "heteroglossia" ... or its "dialogic" '. For Burke, the conclusion is clear and exciting: 'If social historians decide to follow them in this direction ... they may well find the notions of '**heteroglossia**' and '**dialogic**' as useful as '**carnivalisation**' has already proved itself to be.'[82]

This is an interesting proposition, but one that also carries with it an inherent problem. How can theoretical terms specifically designed to be applied to the language of imaginative literature, be used to understand the past? Do such ideas have wider applicability outside of the understanding of cultural artefacts? (There is, of course, no reason why they should just be confined to the understanding of novels. Films e.g. may well benefit from a Bakhtinian analysis.)

For Bakhtin, **heteroglossia**, or the many discourses that exist within a single national language, enables people to hold other views of the world, than those that are dominant at any given moment. Thus, it allows for the possibility of freedom of thought, or a challenge to **hegemony**. This is what leads Marc W. Steinberg to assert that Bakhtin's ideas can be wedded to a Thompsonian Marxist approach to history.[83] If this were the case, it would mean that Bakhtin was the key to uniting language and experience in cultural history. There are problems with the notion of heteroglossia for historians though. First, it privileges language over actual experience. We have to situate the role of language within that of a particular culture in order to determine the importance of linguistic diversity in combating a dominant ideology. Even in the most repressive regimes, individuals can find ways of expressing themselves outside of the dominant ideology, but can this be said to constitute resistance in itself? Finally, whether or not the ideas of the Bakhtin circle can be incorporated into a Marxist framework is an open question, as is the issue of whether Bakhtin's texts are themselves 'Marxist'.

In many ways, the work of Natalie Zemon Davis epitomises the approach adopted by the 'new cultural historians'. Davis chose to focus on the common people (peasants and artisans) and popular culture of the period. Suzanne Desan points out that Davis turned towards anthropology early in her career. It provided a way to understand ritual in her work on early trade unions, and, later, to explore religious practice. Desan also explained how Davis's employment of this discipline was accompanied by critical reflection: 'Davis expresses certain reservations about the shortcomings of anthropology and particularly criticizes its tendency to ignore change. In her own work, she consistently seeks to combine anthropological insights with a greater sensitivity to the historical dynamic.'[84] The influence upon Davis of Clifford Geertz can be seen in the way she reads social rituals like texts. As she herself put it: 'It was also a matter of recognizing that forms of associational life and collective behaviour are cultural artefacts...A journeyman's initiation rite, a village festive organization, an informal gathering of women for a lying-in or of men and women for story-telling, or a street disturbance could be 'read' as fruitfully as a diary, a political tract, a sermon, or a body of laws.'[85]

The changing dynamics of gender relations is also central to her work, but this is also combined with an awareness of other forms of social division. In *Society and Culture in Early Modern France*, she discusses the common people of that time, but does not take for granted that the people she is discussing are defined by a single feature, whether it be gender, their wealth or social status. So, for example, she looks at the sort of social experience that might help form Protestant consciousness among male artisans, and whether or not their fight against the Catholic clergy connects with economic conflict. In the essay 'Women on Top' she discusses sex-role reversal in rite and festivity. This reflects her concern with **carnival** and ritual and the influence of Mikhail Bakhtin in her work.

In her subsequent work, Davis began to blur the boundaries between history and fiction. As Daniel Snowman noted, 'There is an element of storytelling – of "fiction", indeed – in much of her writing.'[86] Although this certainly did not entail an abandonment of archival research, it did bring in an element of invention to compensate for gaps in the source material, most famously in *The Return of Martin Guerre*. Thus, she worked extremely hard to track down sources, relating both to individuals and their contexts. Ultimately, though, she declared: 'What I offer you here is in part my invention, but held tightly in check by the voices of the past.'[87] Martin Guerre was a sixteenth-century French peasant who left his family to become a soldier of fortune. A few years later an impostor (Arnaud du Tilh) appeared, who successfully lived as the husband of the real Martin Guerre's wife (Bertrande de Rol) for three years, after which time the real husband reappeared and the impostor was tried and executed. Davis was consultant to the film depicting these events, and her written account of the story has enjoyed considerable success. However, Davis's admission that her account was partly invention has attracted considerable comment.

Some of this 'invention' involved providing a historical context for the story itself. As Snowman puts it, 'On the basis of her intimate knowledge of not only all the historical sources but also the location and its modern-day denizens, she was able to portray, like a novelist, the day-to-day texture of life in Martin's part of France...'[88] To take a minor example, it does seem that Martin Guerre was impotent, so Martin and Bertrande's marriage remained unconsummated for eight years. As Davis says, 'A married couple who had not had a pregnancy after a certain period of time was a perfect target for a charivari, a *caribari* or *calivari*, as it was called in the area around Pamiers.'[89] For Davis to say that the couple 'must have' been subject to this humiliating ritual is not stretching historical credibility too far, as this was obviously a fairly common practice in that time and place.[90] A more controversial issue is: did Bertrande know that the man she took to be her husband was not the real Martin? In other words, did Martin's wife collude with the impostor in this deception? Davis says that she did, and since there is no mistaking 'the touch of the man on the woman', she would have known that the man she took to be her husband was not Martin.[91] One of Davis's sternest critics, Robert Finlay, disagreed with such an interpretation, pointing out that: 'the historical record indicates that Bertrande was universally regarded as the impostor's victim, not his accomplice'.[92] Finlay's contention that Davis was indulging in speculation, particularly in regard to Bertrande's character and motives, is quite pertinent. Davis's interpretation does, indeed, make a good story, but it does seem that she lost sight of the boundary line between history and fiction in the writing of this work. As Finlay puts it: 'What Davis terms "invention", the employment of "perhapses" and "may-have-beens", is, of course, the stock in trade of historians, who are often driven to speculation by inadequate and perplexing evidence. Depth, humanity, and color in historical reconstruction are the products of imagination and do not flow from a vulgar reasoning upon data.' Equally, he went on, 'speculation, whether founded on intuition or on concepts drawn from anthropology and literary criticism, is supposed to give way before the sovereignty of the sources, the tribunal of the documents. The historian should not make the people of the past say or do things that run counter to the most scrupulous respect for the sources.'[93]

As the earlier account should make clear, Davis has not wholeheartedly embraced the **poststructuralist** approach to history, in which the quest for historical 'truth' is abandoned, but she does come perilously close to it. Works such as Davis's *The Return of Martin Guerre* or Robert Darnton's *The Great Cat Massacre* (described later), can be classed as 'micronarratives' or 'microhistories,' ably defined by Willie Thompson as 'the study of very limited and localised areas of investigation (with no necessary adherence to Rankean norms – plausible invention being permitted), since this is the only basis upon which even a provisional and aesthetically satisfying truth might be established'.[94] As Richard Evans points out, both works 'have been sharply criticised by historians for their allegedly cavalier handling of the evidence, and it is possible here that the influence of **postmodernist** theory has played a questionable role'.[95] Although not necessarily written as specifically 'postmodern' histories, such works do, nevertheless, conform to the idea that historians should abandon attempts at large-scale explanation and focus on small-scale stories, Lyotard's micro-narratives, or what, a notable advocate of the postmodern approach to history, F.R. Ankersmit, calls 'historical scraps'.[96]

As well as being a good example of 'microhistory', Darnton's study is also an important contribution to our expanded comprehension of different layers of meaning in cultural history. Darnton's desire was to show 'how' people thought, not just 'what' they thought. It is concerned with people's construction of their world, 'how they invested it with meaning' and 'infused it with emotion'.[97] In addition to Geertz, Darnton acknowledged the influence of Lévi-Strauss, whose work on Amazonian totems and taboos in the 1960s was the kind of **ethnohistory**, which might usefully be used to understand the dead world of European culture. Building on such insights, Darnton argues that cultural history is not simply the history of 'high culture', of the type envisaged by Burckhardt, but instead concerns the 'cosmology' of past peoples, 'to show how they organised reality in their minds and expressed it in their behavior'.[98] Cultural history thus raised the age-old issue of theorists versus **empiricists**.

Historical relativism – the lack of fixity of meaning in past phenomena – is a key philosophical issue for the cultural historians who took on the challenge of addressing the problems of anachronism and the role of the author as a filter for historical meaning, much more seriously, perhaps, than previous generations of social historians. An acknowledgement of the relativity of cultures and their historians was, for Peter Burke, an acceptance that reality is socially constituted, and that: 'What had previously been considered as unchanging is now viewed as a "cultural construction," subject to variation over time as well as in space.'[99] This approach to history owes much to the two key **postmodern** thinkers discussed in the previous chapter: Michel Foucault and Jacques Derrida. We shall presently consider the influence of Foucault on historians, Derrida's influence on the writing of history is perhaps even more diffuse and elusive than Foucault's. Derrida, the **poststructuralist** linguistic philosopher and his disciples rejected representational theories of meaning.[100] They shared a 'concern for unravelling their [texts'] contradictions, directing attention to their ambiguities, and reading them against themselves and their authors'.[101] This in turn questions the very essence of what is central and what is peripheral to history. Darnton argues that all historians who have read documents should realise that 'other people are other', that historical actors do not think the way we do. To capture the essence of the past, Darnton claims, is to capture 'otherness'. At the same time, this is not simply a 'familiar injunction against **anachronism**'.[102] All historians recognise the impact their own, contemporary culture might have on their reading of the past; but poststructuralist, postmodern critiques of the historian go far beyond simply demanding that historians issue a health warning with their writings.

Cultural historians, however, are also historians of 'below' in that they are anxious to bring back to life those seemingly unimportant events, such as the ribald customs of the past and the ritual massacring of cats. In Darnton's evocative study of just this phenomenon – an incident of cat massacring in Paris in the mid-eighteenth century – the very value of the work is not in its singular cultural reading. Darnton opens up a world we cannot easily comprehend, where starving apprentices took out their disillusionment with the master and mistress on all the cats they could find. In a ribald pageant of slaughter, the lads, soon accompanied by the journeymen, rounded up the cats and killed them in a variety of horrific ways. Some were put through mock trials, others were burned, still others were cut to pieces. Among the dead felines was the mistress's favourite grey. Instead of concentrating purely upon the ritual, Darnton's great strength is his reading of the text on several levels and he offers a pyramid of explanations as to why a printer's apprentices killed dozens of cats. The explanation touches upon material conditions: hunger, the denuding of craft independence and the hopelessness of the apprentices, condemned to a life of wage-labour, with no prospects of themselves becoming independent printers. The explanation also takes in questions of surrogacy, and the expression of a desire to kill the printer and his wife through the slaughter of cats. Cultural readings of the text evoked, in Darnton's eyes, questions of superstition, witchcraft, black magic, and the role of cats in folklore. In this respect, then, the great feature of Darnton's work is that it seems perfectly to mix Marxist social history with a newer cultural history, although it is not without its critics.[103]

Another great influence on recent currents of historical thinking is that of Michel Foucault. His full impact is difficult to deduce for a number of reasons. To begin with, he does not offer an easily identifiable method, or a coherent body of knowledge that can readily be applied to a range of historical contexts. Alan Sheridan goes as far as to argue: 'there is no "Foucault system"', in that, 'one cannot be a "Foucauldian" in the way one can be a Marxist or a Freudian' because, unlike Foucault, 'Marx and Freud left coherent bodies of doctrine (or "knowledge") and organizations which, whether one likes it or not (for some that is the attraction), enjoy uninterrupted apostolic succession from their founders'.[104] By comparison, Foucault's legacy is as 'a slayer of dragons, a breaker of systems'.[105] This has not prevented historians applying his insights to a range of historical situations, but this is usually accomplished through the selection of a single aspect of his work, rather than a concerted attempt to write 'Foucauldian' history. Patricia O' Brien says that Foucault's influence is now most often identified with a range of topics rather than a method: 'He sought to undermine the assumptions of a discipline that still ghettoises histories of women, homosexuals, and minorities, a discipline that still understands power, for the most part, as an attribute of a nation or class.'[106] Even where he was weak, Foucault has certain strengths, as O'Brien again articulated: 'Although Foucault was blind to gender as an analytic category, his method of studying power through discourse holds great promise for work in this area.'[107]

Foucault's reception amongst historians has varied greatly. Clare O' Farrell points out: 'Foucault's work was the subject of sympathetic and enthusiastic discussion and indeed application in avant-garde historical circles in France during the 1970s.'[108] He was particularly well received by members of the *Annales* School, attracting praise from no less a personage than Fernand Braudel.[109] Alan Megill has described the response of historians to Foucault as passing through stages, from what he calls 'non-reception' though 'confrontation' to partial 'assimilation'.[110] He has certainly attracted a certain amount of criticism from the historical profession, whilst he himself has not been above making scathing comments about historians.[111] As R.A. Houston has pointed out, much of the hostility displayed by historians towards Foucault stemmed from the fact that 'Foucault was really a philosopher whose grip on, and interest in, historical fact and method was slight.'[112]

For historians studying certain topics, or the development of particular social institutions though, it is now almost impossible to ignore Foucault. To take two notable examples, his ideas have permeated the study of criminal justice, and the development of prisons in particular, as well as that of madness and the growth of asylums. This awareness has often taken the form of critical engagement with Foucault, as illustrated by J.A. Sharpe's comment: 'Perhaps for our immediate purposes, the most important issue is not whether Foucault's views on the prison are correct, but to grasp the underlying importance of his formulation of the changes in the way in which power, and in particular the power to punish criminals is expressed.'[113] Sharpe sees a great deal of value in Foucault's arguments about the rise of the prison, but also points to the places in which it has been undermined by **empirical** research.[114] R.A. Houston offers a similar evaluation of Foucault's writings relating to madness and society: 'Rather than pronouncing Foucault right or wrong, it may be more fruitful to pick up the questions he has raised and to ask what positive contribution *Histoire de la folie* has made to debate.' On this score, Houston compares Foucault to Marx. Just as Marx's writings 'shaped the way all historians approach social and economic processes', Foucault 'set an agenda for scholars who wish to understand social and intellectual change, and to identify the underlying structures behind thought and action'.[115] Again, Houston acknowledges the value of Foucault's contribution in this area, but also asserts his determination not to let his ideas dominate the research, or obscure the importance of other scholars in other disciplines who have also displayed a critical approach to conventional notions of mental illness.[116] Foucault has famously drawn historians' attentions to bodies, 'in hospitals, in clinics, in asylums, and in prisons'.[117] Foucault's ideas on power are continually being applied to new contexts. Sheila Fitzpatrick points out that he has been a major influence on recent studies of Stalinist Russia, 'particularly for his view of power, sexuality, and the construction of self'.[118]

Perhaps the last word on the importance of Foucault to historical studies belongs to Marnie Hughes-Warrington. She acknowledges that Foucault opened up new areas of study, showed us that 'many of our "enlightened practices" restrict the freedom of individuals,' and offers us the opportunity 'to lay bare the chains that bind us'. She nevertheless concludes that his work is 'plagued by problems'. Ultimately, she argued, 'Foucault's use of evidence is selective, and it often seems as if he has forced his interpretation on his materials. He also tends to favour the idea that an argument can be made convincing if it is delivered forcefully.'[119]

▶ 'New cultural history' and the eclipse of 'old social history'?

Driven by perspectives from linguistics and the philosophy of history, the new cultural history has challenged the fundamental premises of history in a way that the *Annales* and the British Marxists clearly did not. Whilst Thompson and Le Roy

Ladurie clearly challenged, they did not question the idea of historical texts and artefacts, but instead looked for new ones. The Marxists were **positivists** in the sense that they shared with nineteenth-century icons such as Marx and Auguste Comte a belief that the structures of history could be uncovered: that we could plot the course of historical change because it was governed by scientific principles. **Poststructuralists** and **postmodernists**, however, challenge these fundamentals: the role of the author; the reality of historical production; the objective of the historian's method; the scientificity of historical knowledge. In addition, they reject systemic theories, **metanarratives**, such as (but not exclusively) Marxism, with their implication of hierarchies of explanation (**base** over **superstructure**, society over culture). Instead, postmodernists stress the relativity of knowledge, the subjectivity of the author, the literary invention (as opposed to historical reality) of the historian's outpourings and the constitutive power of language over some 'anterior social reality'[120] in explaining the nature of human society, past or present.

Yet, it was not merely Marxist verities that would be challenged by the new cultural history. A conscious effort was being made to shift emphasis from social structure to other determinants of historical process. Lynn Hunt captured the mood well in placing clear ground between herself and E.H. Carr: 'where he saw the epic advance of social and economic history, the heroic historian marching hand in hand with the forces of progress, I tell the perpetual romance, the quest without end, the ironic doubling back of territory presumably covered'.[121] The 'doubling back' might be read as a simple revisionism; the revisiting of old themes with a new method, theory or tub to thump. But this was about more than mere correction of detail; it was about the correction of the subject's philosophical disposition. For Hunt, history was to be treated 'as a branch of aesthetics rather than as the handmaiden of social theory'.[122] The departure from the old social history could not be clearer.

Yet, elements of social history were themselves infused with the new vogue of **poststructuralism** and the '**linguistic turn**'. Labour history provides a good example. The list of contributors to the development of a new cultural history of labour, with an emphasis upon the constitutive powers of language, rapidly gained new disciples, is significant. One of the first attempts to structure such a new approach to territories dominated by Marxist social and labour historians came with Gareth Stedman Jones' important contribution. The essential feature of Jones' work – a book which took Chartism as its centrepiece for explanation – was a critique of Marxist notions of the immutable and immediate linkage between social existence and consciousness. Jones appeared to be pushing apart the age-old concepts of base and structure (the latter shaped directly by the former) in order to find a place for discourses of power and the dynamic of language. Jones' privileging of the power of language strays a long way from orthodox Marxism, prompting Lynn Hunt to ask whether 'such a radical displacement of the Marxist agenda can still be considered Marxist?'[123] The preference to place language, not materiality, at the core of social explanation, has been stressed more recently by other scholars in the broad fields of labour and working-class history, notably Patrick Joyce and James Vernon. A series of important debates in the various social history journals concerning the primacy of language over the material life suggested that the interstices of social cultural history were where the battle-lines were most clearly drawn. Joyce, like Stedman Jones made his name as an historian of the British working class.[124] Part of the anxiety over the challenges of both Stedman Jones and Joyce to Marxist accounts of class formation derived from the unwritten assumption that somehow both are poachers turned gamekeepers. Joyce's work, with its suggestion of the manifold (rather than singular) formulations of identity, stresses gender, ethnicity and other social concepts at the expense of a totalising notion of class.[125] Indeed, Joyce has been provocative in suggesting that, with class at its heart and Marx on its sleeve, social history is all but dead.[126]

Running alongside the '**linguistic turn**' in social history, the same period witnessed the production of important books, which continued to stress community formation and the emergence of collective consciousness which still saw Marxism as the favoured tool and class determinants as being of central explanatory importance.[127] Whilst new approaches to social history have adopted a broader idea of social and cultural identities – drawing upon gender, race and ethnicity as well as class – there has also been a reorientation in terms of focus for studies of the working class. In practical terms, the development of cultural history approaches, and this interest in language and modes of expression other than class, have had a fundamental impact upon the types of studies now produced in the area of working-class history. Many scholars previously associated with classical approaches to ordinary people's histories, where class consciousness and new political formations were held to be essential, have moved towards new conceptions of the determinants of the historical process, often radically so. In the context of this final section, only a flavour of such changes can be given.

One important feature of the turn to culture has been a *volte-face* in terms of the significance accorded to aspects of life. Labour history for more than a century concentrated on production-side interpretations: by this we mean that work, work conditions, and the lives of people when shaped by the manufacture of things, generally assumed a high level of historical significance. The centrality of the Industrial Revolution meant that people were seen primarily as workers; their lives were viewed in terms of social phenomena – for example, living and working conditions – and their responses to such phenomena were usually considered in political terms. Thus, the misery of life in the early years of industrialism was taken as read, and the emphasis upon trade unions and the formation of working-class political parties was not only seen as central but was also regarded as inevitable, perhaps even to the point of being teleological.

Recently, emphases have shifted from production to consumption; from an assumption of economic and social life as determining all things, to one where responses to daily life, and aspects of culture, were seen to be encoded with a much more complex series of messages. An example of this is the shift into areas such as leisure, consumer spending, shopping and the rise of a retail culture: for much of the work in these areas has been conducted by scholars who themselves were trained in more traditional labour history. The study of consumption switched the emphasis from those who made things to those who bought them, although the creation of new industries related to shopping and fashion are by no means ignored in such a formulation. The result, moreover, was a kind of history that by no means abandoned concepts of production and work in favour of consumption and leisure. As a notable representative of this trend, Bill Lancaster, wrote: 'British social history in recent years has moved away from its post-1960s focus upon work and working-class life. Interest in sport, leisure and gender has accelerated and many social historians are paying increasing attention to the world of goods.'[128] Writers such as Lancaster clearly demonstrated an appreciation of tensions between drudgery and pleasure, and realised that a culture of high street consumption could not be fed if work, distribution and marketing (as examples) were not in line with desired outcomes. Workers thus fought for time, as well as money, when they battled for shorter working weeks as well as higher hourly rates; and new types of work sprang up in shops and stores, seaside resorts, holidays, and in the provision of transport, in order that people might enjoy the leisure they demanded. In this respect, we might well argue that the old social history – a Marxian labour history – had been dovetailed with (not eradicated by) a new cultural history, which was bent on seeing the synergies and tensions between the worlds of work and play, whilst bringing the latter to the fore in our modes of explanation.[129]

We can see a similar switch from production to consumption in the history of reading, an area of study perhaps first made fashionable by cultural historians of France, notably Robert Darnton.[130] Utilising the tools of anthropology, Darnton and others began to offer perspectives on the past, which looked beyond the production of books as the focal point of historical meaning to the consumption of those books as the important indicator of past **mentalities**. This is not to say that such scholars were uninterested in the industrial production of books, or the impact of new printing technologies and transport could have upon the price and availability of the written word. But their work contrasted most clearly with that of pioneering Marxist historians, notably Christopher Hill's exhaustive study of the political voice within the enormous pamphlet tradition of Civil War England. The politics of reading is also to be found in the reading, as well as in the writing, of literature such as this. An important new study of working-class reading habits in Britain has, as its intellectual centre-point, the very idea of what the reading matter ordinary people consumed tell us about their lives and aspirations. Again, the intention is not to push the creators of literature out of the viewfinder; instead, the aim is to suggest that working people were made to think about their world by writings other than those with an express political purpose. Here, then, we have a meeting place for Hill's radical pamphleteers and the wider literary ambitions of the ordinary men and women who clubbed together, joined reading societies, subscribed to *Household Words*, and made their social superiors restive by reading Pope's edition of the *Iliad*.

In his *Intellectual Life of the British Working Classes* – a huge, scholarly book, enormously researched from the entirety of known British working-class autobiographies – Jonathan Rose follows Robert Darnton's path into the reading culture of the ordinary man and woman. Darnton, a pioneer of work in the history of reading, began to develop confidence that it would be possible to develop, through a creative *Annales*-style counter-reading (i.e. reading against the grain) of the sources 'a history as well as a theory of reader response'.[131] In other words, Darnton began to understand how reading affected people's mentalities. As Rose said of this book, the reminiscences of these working-class autobiographers and memoirists 'makes possible a broader kind of reading history, which could be called a history of audiences'. He goes on: '[p]ut simply, a history of audiences reverses the traditional perspectives of intellectual history, focusing on readers and students rather than authors and teachers'.[132] This switch in emphasis enables intellectual history to move from a focus upon elite culture towards a cultural history of the daily worlds of ordinary people. Rose's multi-layered study revealed that women, as well as men, immersed themselves in the written word. There was surprise in the early eighteenth century that women accounted for 8 and 13 per cent, respectively of subscribers to Pope's *Illiad* and *Odyssey*. Thomas Burnet and George Duckett mocked reading, arguing sardonically that, because of Pope's appeal, 'every Country Milkmaid may understand the *Illiad* as well as you or I'.[133] They did not believe it was that grave, of course, but a grain of unease caused the comment in the first place. Such snobberies also affected well-regarded men above the rank of common farm servant. Francis Place, the noted nineteenth-century political activist and tailor, for example, had to countenance middle-class clients cancelling orders because they could not stomach the idea of a needle-smith like him being in possession of more than 1000 books.[134]

Yet, where social historians of the earlier generations may have focused upon the class imperatives of literary culture, examining the text as a measure of class consciousness, the cultural approach of Rose is more in keeping with the recent mood. Whilst keen to make clear the importance of reading in the creation of political classes, and in the formation of critical visions of the world, Rose notes that the obvious political pathways were not always followed. Reading and learning could (and did) create tory and conservative workers as well as socialists.

▶ Conclusion

The rise of cultural history was due in part to a frustration with what were seen as the limitations of social history, particularly its stress upon materiality in the explanation of historical change. Proponents, such as Peter Burke, admire the mixing of approaches seen in the works of E.P. Thompson and Natalie Zemon Davis, thus maintaining a certain faith in the centrality of structural factors in explaining the historical process, despite a deep commitment to cultural history. Burke considered that Thompson, Chartier and others in their respective moulds were 'largely successful in revealing the inadequacies of traditional materialist and determinist explanations of individual and collective behaviour over the short term and in showing that in everyday life and in moments of crisis alike, it is culture that counts'. Yet, he also suggested that social historians of this type had 'done little to challenge the importance of material factors, of the physical environment and its resources, over the long term'. Not that Burke would cast out the material features of life when seeking for the meaning of cultures. He wrote: 'It still seems useful to regard these material factors as setting the agenda, the problems to which individuals, groups and, metaphorically speaking, cultures try to adapt or respond.'[135]

Critics such as Lynn Hunt, on the other hand, hold the twin paradigms of Marxist and *Annales* social history, of the type defended by Burke, to be flawed. In place of these social history approaches, such cultural historians have stressed culture as the vital spark of past society, laying emphasis upon ritual, ceremony, language and communication, belief systems and superstition, in the explanation of past societies. In this sense, cultural history has developed from anthropological approaches. This chapter sought to denote some of the important considerations for social historians that are captured by this changing vista. At the same time, it should also have become clear that we do not necessarily regard social and cultural interpretations as entirely distinct. We presented ideology and mentality as two hinges upon which critical perspectives have turned, and suggested that a division between **idealism** (a focus upon ideas) and materialism in pursuit of the past has been influential. In stressing language over material realities, in arguing for the fictive quality of history, post-modernists have helped to drive the culturalist agenda. However, we suggest that culture is not the sole property of those who have embraced the linguistic turn and is present in many reworkings of the major Marxist themes, especially studies of non-elite culture. In essence, we have sought to give credence to both social and cultural approaches by suggesting that far from them being entirely separate, each paradigmatic stronghold is encrusted with deposits of the other. This is ultimately due to the difficulty of resolving the explanatory question at the heart of this chapter: is it ideas or material factors that determine the course of historical development? Culture and ideology, in the broadest sense of those words, obviously plays a key role in historical development, but where do ideas come from? In answering the latter question, we have to return to the importance of structural factors in history, thus suggesting a reciprocal process of interaction between the two that, ultimately, may be impossible to completely disentangle.

Conclusion

Most historians, if asked, would declare social history to be a relatively modern invention, one associated strongly with the growing influence of the *Annales* School, or Marxist approaches in the post-1945 period. In general, social history is considered to be the attempt of historians to appreciate 'the social' (however that might be defined), though it is often quite narrowly conceived. In some respects, social history has been relegated to a listing of things with a particularly 'social' bent: class struggle; the history of the family and affective relations; the impact of great caesura, such as the Industrial Revolution and so on. For others, social history is primarily at the interplay between historical methodologies and sociological theories. Certainly, sociologists of history or historical sociologists have produced some of the most important works of social history. There can be no doubting the influence of theory in shaping the precise nature or approach of social historians, particularly since the Second World War. But, as we have seen, aspects of social history have deeper roots – some lie in the Enlightenment and the ways in which philosophers envisioned human culture; other elements, perhaps more prosaic, can be traced back to early historians, such as J.R. Green, who, in the mid-Victorian years, was seeking to emphasise ordinary people and social occurrence at the expense of Great Men and the lofty events of state.

As we have seen, history and sociology have always enjoyed a 'special relationship', and the crossover between the two disciplines steadily increased during the second half of the twentieth century. The application of social theory to historical evidence has been a decisive aspect of the attempt to strengthen the interpretative power of the historian's craft. Sociologists, on the other hand, have renewed their interest in historical questions. This has led to a great deal of discussion of the 'convergence' of the two disciplines, although there is still considerable disagreement amongst both historians and sociologists as to what the relationship between the two disciplines should actually be. The cross-pollination between the two disciplines has led to the creation of the hybrid discipline: historical sociology. We have reconsidered the question of which scholarly works belong in this category. There is an 'agreed core' of historical sociologists, largely operating within the tradition of 'grand historical sociology'. However, we have also argued that scholars from both sides of the disciplinary divide, often working on a much smaller canvas, deserve inclusion as 'honorary' historical sociologists.

The important point is that both history and sociology are concerned with understanding the way that people's actions (human **agency**) are influenced by social structures and the way that social structure is changed by people's actions. Sociology cannot solely concern itself with the search for general laws, while history cannot concern itself simply with the study of unique persons or situations. Sociology must be concerned with events and specific circumstances, and history must be concerned with theory in order to understand the **structuration** of social action. Power, defined as the capacity to control and define our environment and command social resources, is one factor limiting human agency. 'Action depends upon the capability of the individual to "make a difference" to a pre-existing state of affairs or course of events', to borrow a phrase from Giddens.[1] There is obviously a connection between action and power, and we have suggested that class is central to an understanding of this relationship, although other social divisions also have a decisive impact upon an individual's freedom of action. Society sets limits upon our actions in such a way as it may seem that we 'have no choice' about our decisions. But this is not necessarily the same as saying that action has been replaced by reaction in such situations. Both history and sociology are about the purposive actions of human beings, but those actions take place within certain constraints and, as Weber makes us aware, often have consequences that were never foreseen.

There are many issues facing both historians and sociologists today, not least the question of responding to the **postmodern** critique of conventional academic practice alluded to throughout this text. This, in itself, offers a number of challenges to those concerned with the history of society, not least at the fundamental level of the possibility of ever knowing the 'truth' about the past. It also questions the possibility of theorising about society, or creating any sort of explanatory framework for the understanding of both past and present. There are those who feel that some sort of accommodation can be reached with this 'new approach', and suggest that it can be incorporated into our existing practices. This is not the position of the current authors, although we do acknowledge that this development has raised many interesting questions, and indicated areas of study that have previously been neglected. Postmodernism's rejection of traditional **metanarratives**, particularly those of class, and its concern with difference and otherness has led it to embrace diversity and, 'ride the crest of the explosively increased interest in feminism, multiculturalism, and whatever had been marginalized by mainstream culture'.[2] Although historians by no means needed the prompting of postmodernists to begin the investigation of these issues, their emphasis on fragmentation and diversity requires a measured response. We urgently need a new approach to the social structuring of different forms of identity in past societies. Those involved in the study of the past must take seriously the issue of the relative importance of various social divisions, and particularly how class, gender and ethnicity interact with each other.

Both of the dominant traditions of social history, the *Annales* School, and the Marxist approach, have come under attack from various quarters in recent years. Some of these criticisms have been justified. The *Annales* approach has been more suited to studying long-term continuities than conflict and revolution, and is unable to offer an explanation of social change. *Annales* scholars are also divided between those who favour a Braudelian three-tiered level of analysis (economic, social, socio-psychological) and those primarily concerned with the history of **mentalities**. The divisions within this School are such that it no longer seems to offer a unified approach.[3] The Marxist approach, on the other hand, can be justifiably accused of placing too much emphasis on instances of class conflict, and neglecting periods of stability in social relations. Also, aside from any criticism from postmodernists, Marxists have to come to terms with both the importance of relatively autonomous state apparatuses to the shaping of capitalist society, and the notion that economic coercion is just one of the several significant sources of power within society.[4] This does not detract from the fact that both approaches have produced works of history of lasting value, whether as a result of the ambitious quest for a 'total history', or the desire to reinsert the common people back into the story of the past, and recapture the dignity of their daily lives.

Thus the efforts of past scholars can provide us, not just with worthy examples, but with models of historical scholarship that we can use as our inspiration and, hopefully, build upon. The situation of the individual scholar today is hampered by the increasing specialisation of history as a discipline, which makes it more difficult to see 'the big picture'. However, it is also much improved in terms of the increased range and scope of the discipline, which has brought a much wider range of topics into the historian's viewfinder. What is required now is more theoretically informed work at different levels of historical enquiry. As we stated earlier, this does not mean that historians need to be continually engaging with 'grand theory', or providing readers with elaborate diagrammatic representations of social structure within their works. It is a question of historians being able to engage with a theoretical framework that is appropriate to the particular problem being discussed. In other words, offering 'adequacy at the level of theory'.

A consideration of the other aspect of this task, engaging with the past at different levels of historical enquiry, merely highlights the necessity for works to offer a variety of perspectives, from a local to a global level. Thus, to begin with, we need studies at a micro-level that seek to reconstruct the detail of a particular historical experience, but without losing sight of broader forces of social change. We have already suggested that comparative approaches to history can offer a number of advantages to scholars, as well as carrying with them a new set of problems. This is one way to overcome the increasing specialisation of the discipline, and make wider links between either different societies or different parts of the same society. Comparison can be carried out at a number of levels, and for a number of different purposes, as Charles Tilly and others have pointed out.[5] Less fashionable now, are the attempts to offer explanations on a grand scale, those systemic, 'total' and comparative attempts at an all-encompassing explanation we have discussed within this book. So, while long-term explanations of social change may no longer appear to be on the agenda of most scholars, the need for studies at this level is ever more pressing, and we should not shy away from the challenge they present. Social history is now an established part of the discipline of history, and social theory has played an essential part in its development. Historians are continuing to investigate new areas of past societies, and expand the range of the discipline. Social theory offers us a means of orientation in this infinitely expanding historical universe, and allows us to see history as more than a series of 'unique' unconnected events.

Glossary

Agency Ascribes to the individual or group some degree of independence of thought in relation to actions. Agency is central to Marxist considerations of class in which working people are considered to have been conscious of their ability to act through the assertion of ideas, rights and intentions, thus demonstrating consciousness of their class and participation in the formation of that class.

Anachronism The tendency in historical analysis to consider past societies in the light of contemporary values and ideas (see also **presentism**).

Base-superstructure The model of society associated with Marxism in which the economic system (the base) is argued to determine other aspects of life, which are shaped by, and built upon, it (superstructure): that is, institutions, governance, social relations and cultural life. Changes to the base accordingly effect changes in society. This process of development, with economic systems at the explanatory heart of the matter, is central to **historical materialism (the material conception of history)**.

Carnival, Carnivalesque, Carnivalised A Bakhtinian term denoting the varied, popular festive life of the Middle Ages and the Renaissance, including the pre-Lent carnivals and the celebrations associated with marriages, midsummer and Christmas, which can also be used to refer to carnivalised writing. The essential features of carnival and carnivalesque literature are: an irreverent spirit that inverts hierarchies and mocks authority, a mentality of collective celebration and free association, which reflects popular culture, and an assertion of values, which ruling-class ideology tends to ignore or patronise.

Chicago School Founded in 1892 at the University of Chicago, and associated with Albion Small, W.I. Thomas, R.A. Park, Ernest Park and others. It was the first department of sociology in America and gained a reputation for path-breaking works of urban sociology.

Chronotope A Bakhtinian term that literally means 'time-space' and denotes the specific time and place in which any narrative text is located. Its uniqueness lies in the fact that it privileges neither category, as both time and space are seen as totally interdependent.

Constructionism, constructionist This term embraces a wide range of approaches to the past involving the assumption that meaningful historical interpretation could not be based on observable evidence alone, therefore a general theory of historical explanation should be used to explain the past, such as that offered by the Marxist or *Annaliste* schools. This term is used by Alun Munslow to denote one of his three basic categories of history.

Counterfactual analysis 'What if?' history. An approach to history associated most closely with the economic historian F.W. Fogel in which alternative historical pathways are posited to shed light of things that actually did eventuate. Fogel, for example, sought to assess the impact of the American railways by creating an economic forecast based on the development of alternative transport systems, had railways not been invented.

Deconstructionism, deconstructist This approach to historical analysis questions traditionalist (**constructionist** and **reconstructionist**) notions of history. It seeks to expose as flawed, notions of the truthfulness, objectivity and factuality or historical knowledge. Instead, it stresses language as the central element in historical (and other) forms of knowledge and analyses the use of language as constitutive of explanation. This term is used by Alun Munslow to denote one of his three basic categories of history.

Determinism, determinist A term applied to theories of history and society that are held to allow no room for human **agency**. Marxists have often been accused of economic determinism in which all social phenomena are explained in terms of the economy. *Annaliste* historians, such as Fernand Braudel, on the other hand, have been accused of a geographical determinism, in which the role of the physical environment is accorded primacy.

Diachronic The tendency to consider historical issues chronologically across time, as opposed to synchronically, which refers to society as a static entity. Also applied to those analytical perspectives that privilege historical development (see also **synchronic**).

Dialectic In historical analysis, the suggestion that human society progresses through phases of development driven by the tension between opposing forces. In Marxism, this is usually explained in the competition of economic and political control between classes. Thus, thesis is set against antithesis and the resulting tension creates a new order (synthesis). Class struggle – between bourgeoisie and proletariat – was therefore supposed to create the synthesis of socialism and communism as society moved, in Marxist terms, towards a perfectible end point.

Dialogism   A Bakhtinian term that literally means 'double-voicedness', and is often seen as Bakhtin's central concept. In essence, it means that every speech act is related to previous utterances, and is structured in expectation of a future response. The term refers to the way in which a single statement can embrace more than one meaning, words become an arena of struggle in which there is a continuous interaction between meanings. Bakhtin's use of the term is ambiguous, however, as it is used to refer to particular examples of linguistic utterance and also to a quality of language itself. This ambiguity in Bakhtin himself has led to critical debate about dialogism in which various different meanings have been attributed to the term. However, it would seem that the notion of dialogism is expressive of various properties of everyday and literary language.

Discourse   Analysis of the meaning of texts, actions and contexts according to the meaning associated with them by both author and reader. Discourse applies to languages but also locates itself within other contexts.

Empiricism, empiricists, empirical   An approach that holds that true knowledge of the world ultimately stems from experience or observation, as opposed to speculation or theory. This belief has informed the practice of most historians for about the last 200 years (see also: **Historical relativism**).

Enlightenment, The   A Europe-wide intellectual current spreading during the seventeenth and eighteenth century from England to Scotland and France, and beyond. The Enlightenment is associated with a flight from irrationality and superstition of the medieval period and the emergence of reason. It affected all features of life at this time.

Ethnohistory   A branch of cultural history in which social anthropology is used to decode the sign, symbols of past societies with the intention of getting 'inside' the mental structures of the people studied.

Ethnomethodology   A term that literally means 'people's methods', and is associated with a sociological approach primarily developed by Harold Garfinkel in the late 1960s. It is concerned with the rules and types of knowledge that govern people's everyday interactions, which enable them to make their activities comprehensible to others, and also make sense of what others say. Thus, it focuses on the way in which individuals construct their social realities mainly through the medium of conversation and face-to-face interactions.

Figurations   A term employed by the sociologist Norbert Elias to denote the interdependence of individuals in a society, and the manner in which the interweaving of individual motivations can produce an outcome that was not intended by any of the social actors involved. The term could be applied at any social level, from a class in a school, to a village, a city, or a nation.

Functionalism, functionalist   A sociological approach primarily associated with Talcott Parsons, Robert K. Merton and their followers, usually referred to as structural functionalists. In the social sciences, functionalism sees social practices as enduring because they fulfil useful functions, and thereby contribute towards the continuity of society. Functionalism is essentially concerned with the interdependence of the various elements within a society, thus it accounts for a social activity by referring to its impact upon another social activity or institution.

Hegemony   Popularised by the Italian Marxist, Antonio Gramsci, hegemony comprises the dominant value systems and ideologies, which according to this approach, are imposed onto subordinate classes, and which are thus inculcated into them. However, it also presupposes that the wishes of the non-hegemonic groups are taken into account through a form of negotiation.

Heteroglossia   A Bakhtinian term that expresses his view that **discourse** always expresses a particular ideological position. The term heteroglossia first appears in the key essay 'Discourse in the Novel' (1935). This essay is concerned with the nature of language and consciousness and the interaction of contradictory and differing voices in social discourse. The basic struggle is between a centripetal force that seeks to centralise and unify meaning, which is utilised by any dominant social group to impose their own monologic perception of the world, and a centrifugal force – the force of heteroglossia – that stratifies and fragments ideological thought into multiple views of the world. Not to be confused with **polyphony**.

Histoire év\u00e9nementielle   A term popularised in English-speaking historiography because of its associations with the *Annales* School. When Marc Bloch and Lucien Febvre led the *Annales* revolution against (then) historiographical orthodoxy they were positing a problem-oriented history *against* a 'history of events' (***histoire événementielle***) and narrative history.'

Histoire sérielle   A term coined by the *Annaliste* historian, Pierre Channu in 1960, and subsequently adopted by other exponents of this approach. It refers to trends over the ***longue dureé*** that are explored through the use of homogenous units of data such as wheat prices, dates of wine harvests, annual births and so on. *Annaliste* historians have used this approach to tackle a wide range of historical issues, not least changes in attitudes towards death.

Historical materialism (also known as: **the material conception of history**, and **dialectical materialism**)   A thesis strongly identified with Karl Marx and Friedrich Engels, which argues that material conditions of the world at any given time determine the shape and structure of institutions, social relations and cultural life.

Historical psychology   (See: **Mentalities,** *mentalité*).

Historical relativism   The term associated with **post-structuralist/post-modernist** critiques of traditional, that is, **empirical** approaches. Whilst **empiricists** have argued that there exists an objective, knowable past, the former assert that history is relative (i.e. changeable, unfixed) and that historical writing is a creation of the historian's mind, not of some universal truth.

'History from below'   A term used to describe the study of the lives of lower- or working-class people in the past. Associated with the British Marxists, particularly E.P. Thompson, 'history from below' grew to incorporate a whole generation of social historians, both Marxists and non-Marxists, and has certain resonance with the *Annales* school's work on peasant societies, and with the scholarship of, for example, Carlo Ginzburg.

Idealist, idealism   Associated first with Enlightenment thought, not least F.W.G. Hegel, idealism suggests that human ideas hold primacy in the explanation of historical phenomena. Usually set up in counterpoint to **positivism**.

Ideal types   A term associated with the sociologist Max Weber. An ideal type is a hypothetical description of the essential characteristics of a particular phenomenon. They are not merely descriptions of things that exist in the real world, but theoretical devices that help us to think about those objects. An ideal type is formed by exaggerating particular features of a historical phenomenon to an extreme and leaving out other accompanying features. No actually existing social phenomenon will conform exactly to the features of an ideal type.

Idiographic   An approach which attempts to particularise explanation (see also **nomothetic**).

Interdisciplinary   An approach that combines elements from more than one academic discipline.

Linguistic, 'linguistic turn'   In historical analysis, the preference for associating explanatory primacy with language rather than material circumstances. **The linguistic turn** implies a new direction in historical analysis towards a fluidity of interpretation in which meaning is not fixed and verbal exchanges, signs, codes and people's articulation assumes importance in the stead of fixed, material, objective points of analysis (see also: **postmodernism**).

Longue Dureé A phrase coined by the *Annaliste* historian, Fernand Braudel in 1958 in an important article. It denotes a long period of historical time covering several centuries in which certain continuities can be observed. Braudel saw the classic *longue dureé* as extending from the fifteenth to the end of the eighteenth century. He sought to jettison **unilinear** time in favour of the 'plurality of social time', which conceived of movement on three planes, the short term, the medium term and the *longue dureé*.

Marxist-humanist A term used to describe American Marxists who were influenced by E.P. Thompson. As with the British Marxists, these historians (e.g. Eugene Genovese) were considered with the human face of history, with the lives of ordinary people and subordinate groups, not least slaves.

Mentalities, *mentalité* The study of mental and intellectual conditions within past persons and societies, associated with the work of Emile Durkheim and Lévy-Bruhl, and developed most widely by the *Annales* School. Lucien Febvre called for a 'historical psychology' as a way of avoiding psychological **anachronism**. Marc Bloch's *Royal Touch* (1924) is seen as one of the pioneering works in the history of mentalities.

Mercantilism An economic theory, approved by the Scottish Enlightenment of Adam Smith, etc., which favoured trade policies that would increase the possession of gold as the only form of wealth.

Metanarrative(s), *grandes histoires* A term meaning literally a narrative about narratives, popularised by Jean-François Lyotard. Master narratives, or over-arching stories of the direction of human history; these grand stories involved a notion of progress. The Enlightenment notion of progress through the application of reason to society, and the emancipation of the proletariat in Marxism are both examples of metanarratives. Postmodern theory rejects all metanarratives in favour of *petites histoires* or micronarratives (see also: **postmodernism**).

Mode of production A Marxist term used to describe a particular stage of history in which a specific form of production predominates. It denotes a particular relationship between the relations of production and the forces of production (e.g. primitive communism, Asiatic mode of production, ancient mode of production, feudalism, capitalism, socialism, communism).

Modernism In the historical sense, modernism is associated with grand narrative, **empirical**-objective history and the idea that human history was developing, evolving and improving, leaving behind lesser, or lower, forms of civilisation. **Postmodernists** reject the 'idea of progress' inherent in modernism and seek to undermine the intellectual assumptions underpinning this condition. (see also: **modernity**).

Modernity A term used to refer to a period of historical development, which is difficult to date, but is generally held to have begun around the time of the **Enlightenment**, and can be seen as continuing to the present day. It is associated with the twin upheavals of the French and the Industrial Revolution, and the patterns of social life that emerged from those events. (see also: **modernism**).

Monocasual A type of explanation that sees historical events, or social phenomena, as the result of a single cause. Historians and social scientists, on the other hand, need to deal with a multiplicity of causes in order to provide a convincing explanation.

Nomothetic Seeking to generalise explanation (see also: **idiographic**).

Overdetermination First used by Sigmund Freud to indicate how a symbol or act could have more than one meaning and popularised by the French Marxist philosopher, Louis Althusser. Althusser used it to describe the existence of multiple sources of causation in history, which he saw as too complicated to be simply reduced to a simple determination of the **superstructure** by the **base**.

Panopticon An important concept in Michel Foucault's social theory in which disciplinary power is based on the notion of continuous surveillance. The design for the panopticon came from Jeremy Bentham and was very influential on nineteenth-century views of the prison system. The term literally means 'all-seeing' and is based upon the idea of a tower situated in a courtyard from which prison guards could observe prisoners' cells 24 hours a day without being seen themselves. The prisoners would thus modify their behaviour in the belief that they were being watched, regardless of whether they were actually under surveillance at the time.

Physiocrats Eighteenth-century French philosophers associated with Enlightenment thought; critics of **mercantilism**.

Political economy The forerunner to modern economics, political economy stressed that economic theory, activity and behaviour could only be understood in relation to other spheres of life, not least social effects and politics. In this sense, it was quite different from the emerging, modern economics, which stressed the scientific dimension of the new discipline.

Polyphony A term employed by Bakhtin mainly to describe Dostoevsky's 'multi-voiced' novels. Not to be confused with **heteroglossia**, which is primarily used to highlight the clash of antagonistic social forces.

Positivism, Positivists   Associated with the founding father Auguste Comte, positivism is today something of a term of abuse aimed at those who stress the **structuralist**. Positivists asserted that the history of human society was governed by laws of social change and that if these laws could be discerned, then a predictive approach could come into play. It is clear, then, why Marx is often labelled 'positivist'.

Postmodernism   An umbrella term, covering most subjects, which brings together those who reject **modernist** notions of historical explanation, particularly grand-scheme narratives of historical development, objectivity, **empiricism** and the fixity of meaning. It involves a critique of conventional academic practice, which essentially asserts that, since language is unable to represent the real world accurately, and knowledge about the world is intrinsically linked with power, we can never attain objective knowledge about the past (see also: **metanarrative**).

Postmodernity   A term used to refer to a new phase of historical development, which is alleged to have occurred in the latter part of the twentieth century, and involves a movement beyond both the institutions of **modernity**, and the cultural assumptions of **modernism**. (see also: **postmodernism**).

Poststructuralism   Associated with the **linguistic turn**, a part of the wider **postmodernist** movement, post-structuralism is, as its name suggests, a reaction against **structuralism**. Its proponents consider language to be central to power relations and exchanges of power and knowledge. Developed from the work of Friedrich Nietzsche, and especially Michel Foucault, poststructuralism is an important part of debates about the nature of any form of historical enquiry.

Presentism   The tendency to view the past in the context of present issues and viewpoints (see also: **anachronism**).

Reconstructionism reconstructionist   Also known as the realist, common-sense, or **empiricist** approach to history, this approach to history asserts that the historian offers an unmediated, objective account of the past, as the skills of the 'professional' historian allow them to deal with the evidence impartially, thus it is possible for the historian to discover the truth about the past. The most notable exponent of this approach was G.R. Elton, and this term is used by Alun Munslow to denote one of his three basic categories of history.

Relativism, relativist   Premised upon the notion that phenomena, whether past or present, and the explanation of those phenomena and their relations, are relative. Thus, meanings are not fixed and permanent but changed according to who is observing them, and the period in which they are being studied.

Structuralism, structuralist. A term embracing a multiplicity of meanings, the precise significance of which depends upon the context within which it is employed. In essence, it holds that social life is heavily influenced by certain patterns or rules. Structuralism in history is primarily associated with the *Annales* and Marxist approaches to history, and those scholars who are usually classed as 'historical sociologists.' In the social sciences, the term is applied to a number of approaches that emphasise the significance of structural factors in social life, most notably Marxism, Emile Durkheim and functionalists, such as Talcott Parsons. In anthropology, the term is primarily associated with the method of cultural analysis developed by the structural anthropologist, Claude Levi-Strauss in the 1950s and 1960s in his study of myths and legends. Structuralism in linguistics is mainly associated with the ideas of the Swiss linguist, Ferdinand de Saussure, who argued that language is based on a knowable (if highly complex) set of rules. The central idea of linguistic structuralism, that language works according to its own internal regulations and is not directly connected to external reality, was challenged by the Bakhtin Circle of authors. **Poststructuralism** developed as a critique of the varieties of structuralism described above.

Structuration, theory of Developed by the notable British sociologist, Anthony Giddens, this theory states that there is a duality of structure between the impersonal forces that shape human action and the human action itself. Giddens seeks to develop a theory for understanding society through this duality, and in so doing seeks to develop recognition of the concept, 'that structure is simultaneously the unintended "outcome" of human activity and the "medium" of that activity'.

Synchronic An approach which considers a society at a single instant, as opposed to across a period of time (see also **diachronic**).

Total History, *histoire totale* The aim of historians of the *Annales* School of history, known collectively as *Annaliste* historians, has been to write a history that would encompass every aspect of human life. The founders of this approach, Lucien Febvre and Marc Bloch, wanted to replace a history that concentrated on a narrative of events with one that would be primarily concerned with 'structures'. The key to this new history was an **interdisciplinary** approach. The ideal of 'total history' is often said to have been most fully realised in Fernand Braudel's *The Mediterranean and the Mediterranean World in the Age of Philip II* (1947). Critics have pointed to the impossibility of ever writing a 'total history' that would offer a coherent account of the past.

Unilinear A term applied to evolutionary theories of historical development that posit a single path of progress. This accusation is often levelled at Marxism, which has been depicted as offering a developmental route that all societies must inevitably follow.

Notes

▶ Introduction

1 E.H. Carr, *What is History?* (1988), p. 56. Carr makes this comment in relation to the issue of whether history is a science. A useful discussion is contained in R.J. Evans, *In Defence of History* (1997), pp. 45–74.

2 A. Giddens, *Sociology* (Cambridge, 1997), p. 586.

3 J. Tosh, *The Pursuit of History* (Harlow, 2000 edn), p. 135.

4 Carr, *What is History*, p. 89.

5 For a discussion of differing definitions of social history see: P. Cartledge 'What is Social History Now?', in D. Cannadine (ed.), *What is History Now?* (Basingstoke, 2002), pp. 19–35.

6 The most celebrated example of a counterfactual model of economic development is, Fogel's *Railroads and Economic Growth* (1964). His disciplinary borrowing was from economics, and econometric methods, in particular. See Tosh, *Pursuit of History*, pp. 171–72. The term 'thick description' was popularised by the American cultural anthropologist Clifford Geertz. For general introductions to Geertz's work see 'Clifford Geertz' in A. Edgar and P. Sedgwick, *Cultural Theory: The Key Thinkers* (2002), pp. 82–84, and 'Thick description' in N. Rapport, Nigel and J. Overing, *Social and Cultural Anthropology: The Key Concepts* (2000), pp. 349–52; also, F. Inglis, *Clifford Geertz: Culture, Custom and Ethics* (Cambridge, 2000).

7 P. Burke, *New Perspectives on Historical Writing* (Cambridge, 1997), p. 1.

8 Ibid.

9 See, for example, the various studies in the Macmillan series, 'Social History in Perspective' (General Editor: Jeremy Black) or, the Oxford University Press series, 'Oxford Studies in Social History' (General Editor: Keith Thomas).

▶ 1 Cinderella Gets Her Prince? The Development of Social History

1 H. Perkin, 'What is social history?', *Bulletin of the John Rylands Library*, 36 (1953), reprinted in his *The Structured Crowd* (Brighton, 1981). The final version of this essay dates to 1962.

2 E.P. Thompson, *Making of the English Working Class* (1963).

3 Ibid., pp. 9–14.

4   C. Lloyd, *The Structures of History* (Oxford, 1993), pp. 11–12.

5   See later Chapter 6 for a discussion of the interface between social and cultural history in the modern period.

6   E. Roll, *A History of Economic Thought*, 5th edn (1992), p. 4.

7   Lloyd, *Structures of History*, p. 12.

8   Ibid., p. 12.

9   Roll, *History of Economic Thought*, pp. 119–20; Lloyd, *Structures of History*, pp. 12–13.

10   P. Burke, *History and Social Theory* (Oxford, 1992), p. 4.

11   R. Griffin, *The Nature of Fascism* (1993), pp. 8–13.

12   S. Pollard, *The Idea of Progress* (1968), p. 104.

13   Ibid.

14   Ibid., p. 280.

15   R. Williams, *Keywords* (1988), p. 295.

16   S. Gordon, *The History and Philosophy of Social Science* (1991), pp. 276–77.

17   A. Giddens, *Sociology: A Brief but Critical Introduction* (1984), p. 12. For a discussion of the different usages of the term 'positivism' by sociologists. See, P. Halfpenny *Positivism and Sociology: Explaining Social Life* (1982).

18   Gordon, *History and Philosophy*, p. 282.

19   F. Engels, 'Socialism: utopian and scientific', in *Karl Marx and Friedrich Engels: Selected Works in One Volume* (1991 edn), p. 380.

20   Ibid., p. 378.

21   Ibid., 'Manifesto of the Communist Party', p. 35.

22   J.R. Green, *A Social History of England* (1874), p. v.

23   Drawing its influences, too, from the 'Historical School' in Germany. See Roll, *Economic Thought*, pp. 276–83.

24   J.E. Thorold Rogers, *Six Centuries of Work and Wages: The History of English Labour* (1884; 1919), p. 8.

25   A. Toynbee, cited in B. Inglis, *Poverty and the Industrial Revolution* (1971), p. 13.

26   On Booth and Rowntree, and their traditions, see R.A. Kent, *A History of British Empirical Sociology* (Oxford, 1981), and D. Englander and R. O'Day (eds), *Retrieved Riches: Social Investigation in Britain 1840–1914* (Aldershot, 1996).

27   *The History of Trade Unionism* (1894) and *English Poor Law History* (1927); and J.L. and B. Hammond's *The Village Labourer* (1912) and *The Town Labourer* (1917).

28   Hammond, *Town Labourer*, I, p. 29.

29   Ibid., II, p. 146.

30   As one scholar says, 'The vogue for disguise in order temporarily to become a slum dweller probably began with J. Greenwood's *A Night in a Workhouse* (1866).' R.A. Kent, *A History of British Empirical Sociology* (Aldershot, 1981), p. 52.

31   'Economic history: Unwin and Clapham', in F. Stern (ed.), *The Varieties of History: From Voltaire to the Present* (London, 1970), p. 305.

32   Ibid.

33 Ibid., p. 306.

34 H.L. Beales, *The Industrial Revolution, 1750–1850: An Introductory Essay* (1928; New York, 1967), p. 20.

35 Ibid.

36 See his *Economic History of Britain*, 3 vols (1926–38).

37 'Clapham: economic history as a discipline' in F. Stern (ed.), *The Varieties of History: From Voltaire to the Present* (1970), p. 308.

38 Ibid., p. 309.

39 Inglis, *Poverty and the Industrial Revolution*, p. 16.

40 J.C.D. Clark, 'What is social history…?', Juliet Gardiner (ed.), *What is History Today?* (Basingstoke, 1988), p. 52.

41 R.H Tawney, *The Agrarian Problem in the Sixteenth Century* (1912).

42 R.H. Tawney, *The Acquisitive Society* (1921; 1961 edn), p. 36.

43 Tawney, *Acquisitive Society*, p. 36.

44 Ibid., pp. 36–37.

45 R.H. Tawney, *Religion and the Rise of Capitalism* (1926).

46 Notably Weber's *The Protestant Ethic and the Spirit of Capitalism* (1904–05).

47 Cole's major work of this type was written with his brother-in-law. See, G.D.H. Cole and R. Postgate, *The Common People 1746–1945* (1938).

48 For the Coles, see M. Margaret. The Life of G.D.H. Cole. (1971); L.P. Carpenter, *G.D.H. Cole: An Intellectual Portrait* (Cambridge, 1973); A. Wright, *G.D.H. Cole and Socialist Democracy* (Oxford, 1979); and B. Vernon, *Margaret Cole 1893–1980: A Political Biography* (1986).

49 Cole and R. Postgate, *The Common People*, p. 688.

50 Ibid.

51 G.M. Trevelyan, *English Social History* (1941), p. vii.

52 Ibid., p. x.

53 Ibid., p. xi.

54 Ibid.

55 Hunt, *New Cultural History*, p. 4.

56 On which concentration of interest in the early modern period, see K. Wrightson, *Earthly Necessities: Economic Lives in Early Modern Britain* (2000). A clear exposition of Wrightson's vision of social history (sometimes dubbed the 'new social history') can be found in the prefatory statements in his enormously successful and important book, *English Society, 1580–1680* (1982).

57 R. Price, *English Society, 1680–1880: Dynamism, Continuity and Change* (Cambridge, 1999) contains one of the best attempts to understand the balance between these factors.

58 The society produced a publication, the *Bulletin of the Society for the Study of Labour History*, which in recent times has become known as the *Labour History Review*.

59 E.P. Thompson, 'History from below', *Times Literary Supplement*, 7, April 1966.

60 For outstanding histories of crowds, see G. Rudé, *The Crowd in History* (1964; 1995 edn); E.J. Hobsbawm, *Primitive Rebels* (Manchester, 1959); Rudé and Hobsbawm, *Captain Swing* (1969); and Thompson, 'The moral economy of the English crowd in the eighteenth century', *Past and Present*, 50 (May, 1971).

61 This can be seen, for example, in almost any edition of the journal, *International Labor and Working Class History*.

62 For example, E. Genovese, *Roll Jordan Roll: The World the Slaves Made* (New York, 1974); Herbert H.G. Gutman, *Work, Culture and Politics in Industrializing America* (1966).

63 Ibid., p. 11.

64 I. Pinchbeck, *Women Workers and the Industrial Revolution, 1750–1850* (1930).

65 A point made with some clarity in J. Tosh, *The Pursuit of History*, 3rd edn (2000), p. 84. For the demographic approach to household and women, see P. Laslett and R. Wall (eds), *Household and the Family in Past Time* (Cambridge, 1972).

66 A. Macfarlane, *Witchcraft in Tudor and Stuart England* (1970). More recently, see M. Hester, *Lewd Women and Wicked Witches* (1992).

67 Clio, the muse of history: ergo, econometrics *is* history – a somewhat fanciful claim.

68 J.A. Henretta, 'Social history as lived and written', *American Historical Review*, 84, 5 (1979), p. 1315.

69 N.F.R. Crafts, 'What is economic history … ?', in Gardiner (ed.), *What is History Today*, p. 39.

70 R.W. Fogel, *The Railroads and American Economic Growth* (1964).

71 S.L. Engerman and R.W. Fogel, *Time on the Cross: The Economics of American Negro Slavery* (1974).

72 P.A. David, H.G. Gutman, R. Sutch, P. Temin and G. Wright, *Reckoning With Slavery: A Critical Studies in the Quantitative History of American Negro Slavery* (1976).

73 T.R. Malthus, *Essay on the Principle of Population …* (1798).

74 F. Engels, The Origins of the Family, Private Property and the State (1884), preface, in *Selected Works of Marx and Engels*, p. 430.

75 Indeed A. Marwick considers historical demography to be 'the most important single development [in the study of the past] in the immediate post-war years': *The New Nature of History* (Basingstoke, 2001), p. 129.

76 E.A. Wrigley, D.E.C. Eversley, R.S. Schofield and P. Laslett. An important book outlining the early research of this group is E.A. Wrigley (ed.), *An Introduction to English Historical Demography* (Cambridge, 1966).

77 E.A. Wrigley and R.S. Schofield, *The Population History of England, 1541–1871: A Reconstruction* (1981). An important recent study using reconstitution techniques is E.A. Wrigley (ed.), *English Population History from Family Reconstitution, 1580–1837* (Cambridge, 1997).

78 P. Laslett, *The World we have Lost* (New York, 1965).

79 *Centuries of Childhood* (1961).

80 L. Stone, *The Family, Sex and Marriage, 1500–1700* (1977).

81 A. Briggs, in H.J. Dyos (ed.), *The Study of Urban History* (London, 1968), p. v?

82 Marwick, *New Nature of History*, p. 130.

83 For example, his 'The Metropolis and Mental Life' (1903), in R. Sennett (ed.), *Classic Essays on the Culture of Cities* (New York, 1969).

84 W.I. Thomas and F. Znaniecki, *The Polish Peasant in Europe and America*, 2 vols (New York, 1927); O. Handlin, *Boston Immigrants* (1941) and *The Uprooted* (Boston, 1951).

85 S. Thernstrom, *Poverty and Progress: Social Mobility in a Nineteenth Century City* (Cambridge, Mass, 1964).

86 See, for example, A. Briggs, *Victorian Cities* (1963; Berkeley, CA, 1993 edn); H.J. Dyos (ed.), *Exploring the Urban Past* (Cambridge, 1982).

87 M. Anderson, *Family Structure in Nineteenth-Century Lancashire* (Cambridge, 1971). An example of recent innovation, this time in comparative urban history, is A. Mayne, *The Imagined Slum: Newspaper Representations in Three Cities, 1870–1914* (Leicester, 1993).

88 L.H. Lees, *Exiles of Erin: Irish Migrants in Victorian London* (Manchester, 1979). At the same time, R.A. Burchell produced a similar study of for the Irish in an American city: *The San Francisco Irish, 1848–80* (Manchester, 1979), which also leant heavily on the demographers techniques of large-scale census analysis.

89 K. Thomas, *Religion and the Decline of Magic* (1973).

90 Wrightson, *English Society*, p. 12.

91 Ibid., p. 223.

92 J. Langton, 'The Industrial Revolution and the regional geography of England', *Transactions of the Institute of British Geographers*, 9 (1984), p. 157.

93 On reading culture, see J. Rose, *The Intellectual Life of the British Working Classes* (New Haven, Conn., 2001). For examples from Hill's seventeenth century, see L. Stone, 'Literacy and education in England, 1600–1900', *Past and Present*, 42 (1969); K. Thomas, 'The meaning of literacy in early modern England', in G. Baumann (ed.), *The Written Word: Literacy in Transition* (London, 1986); Jonathan Scott, *England's Troubles: Seventeenth Century English Political Instability in European Context* (Cambridge, 2001), pp. 231–33.

94 F.M.L. Thompson, *The Cambridge Social History of Britain, 1750–1950*, 3 vols (Cambridge, 1990).

95 Review in *Labour History Review*, 57, 3 (1992), p. 112.

▶ 2 Fruit of a 'special relationship'? Historical Sociology

1 J. Tosh (ed.), *Historians on History* (Harlow, 2000), p. 219.

2 G. Stedman Jones, 'From historical sociology to theoretical history', *British Journal of Sociology*, 27, 3 (1976), p. 295.

3   G. Stedman Jones, 'From historical sociology to theoretical history', *British Journal of Sociology*, 27, 3 (1976), p. 295.

4   Giddens quoted by P. Abrams, 'History, Sociology, Historical Sociology', *Past and Present*, 87 (1980), p. 14.

5   P. Abrams, *Historical Sociology* (Bath, 1982), pp. 43–50.

6   P. Burke, *History and Social Theory* (Cambridge, 1992), p. 10.

7   P. Burke, *Sociology and History*, pp. 11–12.

8   Ibid., p. 12.

9   L. Lyon, *The Community in Urban Society* (Lexington, MA, 1987), p. 34.

10 R.A. Kent, *A History of British Empirical Sociology* (Aldershot, 1981), pp. 89–99.

11 Ibid., pp. 1–9.

12 S. Mennell, *Norbert Elias: Civilization and the Human Self-Image* (Oxford, 1989), pp. 3–23; Elias, Norbert, *The Civilizing Process* (Oxford, 1994).

13 S. Mennell, Ibid., pp. 16–17; N. Elias, *The Court Society* (Oxford, 1983).

14 Elias, *Court Society*, p. 27.

15 See, for example, J. Hughes, 'Norbert Elias' in R. Stones (ed.), *Key Sociological Thinkers* (Basingstoke, 1998).

16 D. Smith, *The Rise of Historical Sociology* (Philadelphia, PA, 1991), p. 2.

17 T. Skocpol (ed.), *Vision and Method in Historical Sociology* (Cambridge, 1984), p. 2.

18 C. Wright Mills, *The Sociological Imagination* (Oxford, 2000), pp. 22–24.

19 Ibid., p. 31.

20 Ibid., p. 31.

21 Ibid., p. 33. These points have been made by a number of commentators. For example, Christopher Lloyd says that, 'Talcott Parsons was never a historian, remaining as an abstract grand theorist of social change, insofar as he considered the question of change at all.' See, C. Lloyd, *The Structures of History* (Oxford, 1993), p. 77.

22 Ibid., p. 55.

23 Ibid., p. 146.

24 For a history of the development of historical sociology, see, D. Smith, *The Rise of Historical Sociology*; for an historian's point of view, see, 'Historical Sociology' in A. Green and K. Troup (eds), *The Houses of History* (Manchester, 1999), pp. 110–18.

25 P. Burke, Peter, *Sociology and History* (1980), p. 2.

26 Ibid.

27 G.R. Elton, *The Practice of History* (1967), pp. 20–42.

28 Stedman Jones, 'Historical Sociology ', pp. 295–305.

29 Burke, *Sociology and History*, p. 19.

30 Abrams, *Historical Sociology*, p. x.

31 Abrams, 'History, Sociology, Historical Sociology', p. 7.

32 Ibid., p. 6.

33 J.H. Goldthorpe, 'The uses of history in sociology: reflections on some recent tendencies', *British Journal Of Sociology*, 42, 2 (1991), pp. 211–30.

34 Goldthorpe's article triggered a debate in a subsequent issue of the *British Journal Of Sociology*. A particularly telling response came from Bryant Joseph M. 'Evidence and explanation in history and sociology', critical reflections on Goldthorpe's critique of historical sociology', *British Journal Of Sociology*, 45, 1 (1994), pp. 1–19.

35 T. Skocpol (ed.), *Vision and Method*, p. 1.

36 Green and Troup (eds), *Houses of History*, pp. 110–18.

37 Skocpol, Theda (ed.), *Vision and Method*, intro, pp. 5–6.

38 Wright Mills, *Sociological Imagination*, pp. 22–24; R. Collins, *Four Sociological Traditions* (Oxford, 1994), pp. 242–43; A. Giddens, *Sociology* (Cambridge, 1997), p. 567.

39 Ibid., p. 5.

40 F.K. Trimberger, 'E.P. Thompson: Understanding the Process of History', in Skocpol Theda (ed.), *Vision and Method*.

41 I. Kershaw, *The Hitler Myth: Image and Reality in the Third Reich* (Oxford, 1990), pp. 1–2.

42 Kershaw, *Hitler* (Harlow, 1991), p. 10.

43 Kershaw, Ian, *Hitler*, 2 vols (Harmondsworth, 1998 and 2000), quotation from vol. I, p. xxi.

44 Kershaw, *Hitler*, vol. I, xii.

45 Abrams, *Historical Sociology*, pp. 16–17.

46 Ibid., pp. 3–4.

47 Ibid., p. 5.

48 Ibid., pp. 6–7.

49 F. Braudel, *The Mediterranean and the Mediterranean World in the Age of Philip II* (1949); Abrams, *Historical Sociology*, pp. 333–35.

50 Lloyd, *Structures of History*, p. 81.

51 Ibid., p. 6.

52 Ibid., pp. 47–48.

53 Ibid., pp. 48–49.

54 Clifford Geertz's work, including 'Deep Play: Notes on the Balinese Cockfight', Emmanuel le Roy Ladurie's *Montaillou* is a classic of this type; Robert Darnton's work, especially, *The Great Cat Massacre* is also important. For a discussion of these works see, ch. 5, pp. 132–3, 138–40.

55 Lloyd, *Structures of History*, p. 101. The works of Eric Hobsbawm include: *The Age of Revolution, 1789–1848* (1995 edn), *The Age of Capital, 1848–1875* (1995 edn) and *The Age of Empire, 1875–1914* (1995 edn). To these should be added the even more magisterial *Age of Extremes: The Short History of the Twentieth Century, 1914–1991* (1994).

56 Ibid., pp. 74–75.

57 An example of this type of wide-ranging treatment of migration can be found in T. Sowell, *Migrations and Cultures: a World View* (1996), a book of systemic sweep and with a powerful desire to explode the negative mythologies of the impact of migrations in modern times.

58 C. Tilly, *As Sociology Meets History* (New York, 1981), p. 43.

59 Ibid., p. 44.

60 Abrams, *Historical Sociology*, pp. xii–xiii.

61 J.H. Goldthorpe *et al.*, *The Affluent Worker in the Class Structure* (Cambridge, 1969), pp. 1–2.

62 Ibid.

63 R. Sennet and J. Cobb, *The Hidden Injuries of Class* (New York, 1973), p. 74.

64 Ibid., pp. 71–73.

65 Ibid., pp. 10–18, 166.

66 C. Wright Mills, *Sociological Imagination*, p. 143.

67 G. Pearson, *Hooligan: a History of Respectable Fears* (Basingstoke, 1982), pp. 1–11.

68 Ibid., p. 21.

69 Ibid., pp. 74–75.

70 A. Taylor, *Working Class Credit and Community Since 1918* (Basingstoke, 2002).

71 Collins, *Four Sociological Traditions*, p. 108.

72 Goldthorpe 'The uses of history in sociology', pp. 211–30.

73 T. Skocpol, *States and Social Revolutions: A Comparative Analysis of France, Russia, and China* (Cambridge, 1990).

74 T. Skocpol, 'France, Russia, China: a structural analysis of social revolutions', in Green and Troup (ed.), *Houses of History*, p. 124.

75 Skocpol, *States and Social Revolutions*, p. 17.

76 Ibid., p. 23.

77 Ibid., p. 29.

78 Ibid.

79 Ibid., p. 30.

80 Green and Troup, *Houses of History*, p. 112.

81 I. Wallerstein, *The Capitalist World-Economy* (Cambridge, 1979), p. vii.

82 Collins, *Four Sociological Traditions*, p. 109.

83 Tilly, *Sociology Meets History*, p. 41.

84 I. Wallerstein, *The Modern World System*, 3 vols (Orlan. do, FLA, 1974, 1980, 1989).

85 Ibid., vol. I, p. 15.

86 The discussion that follows draws heavily on the summary offered by: Ragin, Charles and Chirot, Daniel 'The World System of Immanuel Wallerstein: Sociology and Politics as History' in Skocpol (ed.), *Vision and Method*, pp. 276–312.

87 Wallerstein, *The Modern World System*, vol. I, pp. 57–61.

88 Ragin and Chirot, 'World System of Immanuel Wallerstein', p. 294.
89 Wallerstein, *Modern World System*, vol. II, pp. 3–9, 130–31.
90 Ragin and Chirot, 'World System of Immanuel Wallerstein', p. 299.
91 Ibid., p. 306.
      The continuing influence of Wallerstein's approach can be seen in:
      R.A. Denemark, *et al.* (eds), *World System History: The social science of long-term change* (2000).
92 Originally outlined in E. Durkheim, *Suicide: A Study in Sociology* (New York, 1966), first published as *Le Suicide: Etude de sociologie* (Paris, 1897).
93 M. Halbwachs, *The Causes of Suicide* (New York, 1978), first published as *Les Causes du Suicide* (Paris, 1930), Halbawchs, though not uncritical of Durkheim, and less rigidly structuralist in his argument, was also Durkheim's strongest subsequent supporter.
94 V. Bailey, *This Rash Act: Suicide Across the Life Cycle in the Victorian City* (Stanford, CA., 1998), p. 16.
95 Ibid., p. 33.
96 Ibid., p. 19.
97 Bailey, *Rash Act*, p. 28; A. Giddens, *The Constitution of Society: Outline of the Theory of Structuration* (Cambridge, 1984), p. 2.
98 Bailey, *Rash Act*, pp. 60–65.
99 Ibid., p. 258.
100 Ibid., p. 266.
101 See, Giddens, Anthony, *Profiles and Critiques in Social Theory* (Berkeley, CA, 1982).
102 Bailey, *Rash Act*, p. 29.
103 Lloyd, *The Structures of History*, esp. ch. 5 (quotation from p. 183).
104 Smith, *Rise Of Historical Sociology*, p. 1.
105 Ibid., p. 184.

► **3 'A mass of factors and influences?' Systemic, 'Total' and 'Comparative' Histories**

1 T. Zeldin, 'Social history and total history', in *Journal of Social History*, 10 (1976), pp. 243–44.
2 Though Zeldin was not, himself, a friend of the social sciences and was sceptical of the impact they might have on history. See the useful discussion and extract in J. Tosh (ed.), *Historians on History* (Harlow, 2000), pp. 245, 265–70.
3 See, for example, G. Stedman Jones, 'From historical sociology to theoretical history' *British Journal of Sociology*, 27 (1976).

4 Karl Marx, *Contribution to the Critique of Political Economy* (1859), preface.

5 For a sympathetic reading of Marx's approach to history see: Matt Perry, *Marxism and History* (Basingstoke, 2002). For a critical perspective, see S.R. Rigby, *Marxism and History* (1987; 1998 edn).

6 'Engels to Joseph Bloch', 21–22 September 1890, *Karl Marx and Friedrich Engels: Selected* Works (1968; 1991 edn), pp. 651–52.

7 Written in December 1851–March 1852. See ibid., pp. 93–171.

8 Hugh Trevor-Roper, 'Fernand Braudel, the *Annales* and the Mediterranean', *Journal of Modern History*, 44 (1972).

9 J.H. Hexter, 'Fernand Braudel and the *Monde Braudelllien*', *Journal of Modern History*, 44 (1972), p. 523.

10 For more on this structural interpretation, see C. Lloyd, *The Structures of History* (Oxford, 1993), pp. 80–82.

11 W.G. Hoskins, *The Making of the English Landscape* (1955); N.J.K. Pounds, *An Historical Geography of Europe*, 3 vols (Cambridge, 1973–85).

12 D. Smith, 'History, geography and sociology: lesson from the Annales School', *Theory, Culture and Society*, 5 (1988), p. 144.

13 J.A. Henretta, 'Social history as lived and written', *American Historical Review* (1979), p. 1297.

14 See the Preface to F. Braudel *The Mediterranean and the Mediterranean World in the Age of Philip II.*

15 J.H. Hexter *On Historians* (1979), pp. 132–40.

16 Smith, 'History, geography and sociology', p. 144.

17 Henretta, 'Social history as lived and written', p. 1299; Hexter, 'Fernand Braudel and the *Monde Braudellien*', p. 534.

18 Henretta, 'Social history as lived and written', p. 1299.

19 E. Fox-Genovese and E.D. Genovese, 'The political crisis of social history: a Marxian perspective', *Journal of Social History*, 10, 2 (1976), p. 209.

20 Ibid., p. 209.

21 Lloyd, *Structures of History*, p. 81.

22 E. Le Roy Ladurie, *Peasants of the Languedoc* (1974). First published in French in 1966.

23 Ibid., p. 289.

24 R.W. Fogel, *The Railroads and American Economic Growth* (1964).

25 W.W. Rostow, *The Stages of Economic Growth* (Oxford, 1960).

26 D. Cannadine, 'The present and the past in the English revolution', *Past and Present*, 103 (May 1984), p. 13.

27 E.J. Hobsbawm, 'From social history to the history of society', *Daedelus*, C, 1971, p. 26.

28 T. Pakenham, *The Year of Liberty* (1969), title page. See also J.C. Belchem, 'Nationalism, Republicanism and exile: Irish emigrants and the revolutions of 1848', *Past and Present*, 146 (1995), p. 106.

29 C.Tilley, *Big Structures, Large Processes, Huge Comparisons* (New York, 1984), p. 147.

30 G. Arrighi, *The Long Twentieth Century* (1994), p. ix.

31 Ibid., p. xi.

32 Tilley, *Big Structures*, pp. 70–71

33 Arrighi, *Long Twentieth Century*, p. xi.

34 Ibid., p. xi.

35 Ibid., p. ix.

36 Ibid., pp. ix–x.

37 For which see ibid., pp. 85–158.

38 L. Colley, *Captives: Britain, Empire and the World, 1600–1850* (2002), Part 1.

39 Ibid., pp. 33–34.

40 Ibid., p. 33.

41 We can, of course, note that Braudel's study was both diachronically and synchronically wide-ranging: from the Ottoman Empire in the East to the that of Spain in the East, as well as across time almost to a point of environmental timelessness.

42 A.A. Van Den Braembussche, 'Historical explanation and the comparative method: towards a theory of the history of society', *History and Theory*, 28, 1 (1989), pp. 9–10.

43 D. Englander (ed.), *Britain and America: Studies in Comparative History, 1760–1960* (New Haven, CT, 1997), p. ix.

44 M Bloch, 'A contribution towards a comparative history of European society', his *Land and Work in Medieval Europe: Selected Papers by Marc Bloch* (1967), trans. J.E. Andersen.

45 Van Den Braembussche, 'Historical explanation and comparative method', p. 10.

46 Bloch, 'Comparative history', p. 46.

47 Ibid.

48 First published in 1924.

49 M. Bloch, *Feudal Society* (1940).

50 Fernand Braudel, *Civilisation and Capitalism* (1979; 1984 edn).

51 W.H. Sewell, 'Marc Bloch and the logic of comparative history', *History and Theory*, 6 (1967), pp. 208–18.

52 Van Den Braembussche, 'Historical explanation and comparative method', p. 11.

53 Barrington Moore, *Social Origins of Dictatorship and Democracy* (1966); T. Skocpol, *States and Social Revolutions: A Comparative Analysis of France, Russia and China* (Cambridge, 1990); and in E.J. Hobsbawm's classic four-volume account of European History: *Age of Revolution, The Age of Capitalism, The Age of Empire, The Age of Extremes*.

54 Hobsbawm, 'Social history to the history of society', p. 29.

55 Ibid., pp. 29–30.

56 Skocpol, *States and Social Revolutions*, p. xiv.

57 Moore, *Social Origins*, pp. x–xi.

58 T. Skocpol and M. Somers, 'The Uses of Comparative History', *Comparative Studies in Society and History*, 22, 2 (1980), p. 175.

59 Ibid., pp. 176–78.

60 Ibid., p. 181.

61 Ibid., p. 182.

62 In contrast to Skocpol and Somers, Charles Tilly distinguishes four types of comparison, and Van Den Brambussche identifies five: 'Historical explanation and comparative method', pp. 13–15.

63 See, for example, Max Weber, 'Social psychology of the world religions', in H.H. Gerth and C. Wright Mills, *From Max Weber: Essays in Sociology* (1991 edn), pp. 267–301.

64 Social Psychology of the World Religions' (1915), in Gerth and Wright Mills, *From Max Weber*, pp. 267–301.

65 M. Mann, *The Sources Of Social Power*, 2 vols (Cambridge, 1988, 1993), I: p. 2.

66 Ibid.

67 Ibid., pp. 1–2.

68 Ibid., p. 3.

69 K. Marx, 'The Eighteenth Brumaire of Louis Boneparte' in *Karl Marx and Friedrich Engels: Selected Works* (1968; 1991 edn), p. 93.

70 The discussion of the changing relationships between the different sources of social power he identifies is evident throughout his work, but a good summary is offered in Mann, *The Sources of Social Power*, I: pp. 518–41.

71 In some ways his essay discussing changing forms of state power throughout history is more convincing than *The Sources of Social Power* itself, precisely because of its narrower focus. Mann considers two dimensions of state power, despotic and infrastructural, in relation to different periods of history. See M. Mann 'The autonomous power of the state: Its origins, mechanisms and results' in J.A. Hall (ed.), *States in History* (Oxford, 1986), pp. 109–36.

72 D. Armitage and M. Braddick (eds), *The British Atlantic World, 1500–1800* (Basingstoke, 2002).

73 P. Linebaugh and M. Rediker, *The Many-Headed Hydra: Sailors, Slaves, Commoners, and the Hidden History of the Revolutionary Atlantic* (Boston, 2000).

74 Ibid., p. 2.

75 S. Berger, 'Working-class culture and the labour movements in the south Wales and the Ruhr coalfields, 1850–2000: a comparison', *Llafur*, 8, 2 (2001).

76 N. Vall, 'The regional apparel: urban aggrandisement and regionalist aspirations in Malmö and Newcastle', *Scandinavian Journal of History*, 26 (2001).

77 N.L. Green, 'The comparative method and post-structural structuralism: new perspectives for migration studies' in J. Lucassen and L. Lucassen (eds), *Migration, Migration History, History: Old Paradigms and New Perspectives* (Bern, Berlin, Frankfurt, New York, Paris, Vienna, 1997), pp. 57–72.

78 See, for example, D.M. MacRaild, 'Wherever Orange is worn: The Orange Order and Irish Migration in the nineteenth and early twentieth centuries', *Canadian Journal of Irish Studies*, 2003.

79 An example of which would be Nancy L. Green (ed.), *Jewish Workers in the Modern Diaspora* (1998).

80 Braudel, *Mediterranean*, preface.

81 G. Roth, 'History and sociology in the work of Max Weber', *British Journal of Sociology*, 27, 1976.

82 See T. Woods, *Beginning Postmodernism* (Manchester, 1999), pp. 1–17.

83 A. Giddens, *The Consequences of Modernity* (Cambridge, 1990), p. 45.

84 Ibid. p. 149. For a critical discussion of the idea that we are now living in a 'post-modern era' see A. Callinicos, *Against Postmodernism: A Marxist Critique* (New York, 1999), pp. 121–71.

85 K. Jenkins, *On 'What is History'? From Carr and Elton to Rorty and White* (1995), p. 6.

86 T. Noble, *Social Theory and Social Change* (Basingstoke, 2000), p. 237.

87 On which view, see, for example, B. Southgate, *History: What and Why? Ancient, Modern and Postmodern Perspectives* (1996), p. ix.

88 P. Abbott and C. Wallace *An Introduction to Sociology: Feminist Perspectives* (1997), pp. 45–47.

89 H. Bertens, *The Idea of the Postmodern: A History* (1995), pp. 20–36.

90 For example, see Woods, *Postmodernism*, pp. 18–48 and Bertens *Idea of the Postmodern*, pp. 3–19. For a critical discussion of the central tenets of postmodern theory see Callinicos, *Against Postmodernism*, pp. 62–91.

91 Ibid., p. 3.

92 J-F. Lyotard quoted in K. Jenkins (ed.), *The Postmodern History Reader* (1997), p. 36.

93 Tim Woods, *Beginning Postmodernism* (Manchester, 1999), p. 20.

94 Ibid.

95 K. Jenkins, *Why History? Ethics and Postmodernity* (1999), p. 75.

96 N. Mouzelis, *Sociological Theory: What Went Wrong? Diagnosis and Remedies* (1995), pp. 48–49.

97 Ibid., p.152. The social realist position in relation to postmodernism is discussed in: J. Parker, *Structuration* (Buckingham, 2000).

98 Colley, *Captives*, p. 66; F. Braudel, *Perspective on the World* (1984), p. 467.

99 Charles Tilly, *Big Structures Large Processes Huge Comparisons* (New York, 1984), p. 77.

▶ **4   Social Structure and Human Agency in Historical Explanation**

1   For Secondary Education provision before 1944 see, for example: D. Wardle, *English Popular Education 1780–1975* (Cambridge, 1976), pp. 116–39.

2   Glasser's autobiography is in three volumes: *Growing up in the Gorbals* (1986), *Gorbals Boy At Oxford* (Thirsk, 2001), *Gorbals Voices, Siren Songs* (Thirsk, 2001).

3   Glasser, *Gorbals Boy*, pp. 1–2.

4   J. Tosh, *The Pursuit of History* (Harlow, 1999), p. 146.

5   P. Abrams 'History, Sociology, Historical Sociology', *Past and Present*, 87 (1980), p. 5.

6   D.F. Walsh, 'Structure/Agency' in C. Jenks, (ed.), *Core Sociological Dichotomies* (1998), pp. 8–9.

7   Ibid., p. 9.

8   See, Abrams, 'History', p. 8 who also suggests that 'the two sociologies are matched in historical work by "two histories"'. Also see Walsh, 'Structure/Agency', pp. 15, 21; M. Waters, *Modern Sociological Theory* (1994), pp. 15–55, 92–129.

9   See, for example: Abrams, 'History', pp. 13–14; Cohen, Ira J. 'Anthony Giddens' in R. Stones (ed.), *Key Sociological Thinkers* (Basingstoke, 1998), pp. 138–50; W. Outhwaite, 'Agency and Structure', in J. Clark *et al.* (eds), *Anthony Giddens: Consensus and Controversy* (Basingstoke, 1990), pp. 63–72.

10   N. Gash, 'A Modest Defence of Historical Biography' in idem, *Pillars of Government* (1986), p. 179.

11   See, R.J. Evans, 'Prologue: What is History Now?' in D. Cannadine, (ed.), *What is History Now?* (Basingstoke, 2002), p. 9.

12   J. Black and D.M. MacRaild, *Studying History* (Basingstoke, 2000), p. 98.

13   C. Lloyd, *The Structures of History* (Oxford, 1993), p. 78.

14   A. Munslow, *The Routledge Companion to Historical Studies* (2000), pp. 53–55, 194–98.

15   Ibid., pp. 69–74.

16   The issue of whether postmodern ideas can be somehow integrated within, and reconciled with, the way in which historians have traditionally studied the past is a thorny one. Richard J. Evans suggests that, 'Postmodernism in its more constructive modes' has been of benefit to historians. Evans, *Defence of History*, pp. 248–49. His 'assimilationist' perspective is explicitly rejected by Keith Jenkins, who makes it clear that he does not see the ideas of postmodern historians and 'traditional' historians as being compatible: *Why History?: Ethics and Postmodernity* (1999), pp. 95–114.

17   H. Bertens, *The Idea of the Postmodern: A History* (1995), p. 207; T. Noble, *Social Theory and Social Change* (Basingstoke, 2000), p. 235.

18 N. Elias, *The Court Society* (Oxford, 1983), p. 11.

19 Ibid., p. 13.

20 Walsh, 'Structure/Agency', p. 11.

21 D. McLellan, *The Thought of Karl Marx* (1995), p. 127.

22 Walsh, 'Structure/Agency', p. 17.

23 McLellan, *Marx*, p. 123.

24 Tosh, *Pursuit*, p. 143.

25 S.B. Smith, *Reading Althusser: An Essay on Structural Marxism* (1984), p. 157–59; also see Perry, *Marxism and History* (Basingstoke, 2002), pp. 39–42.

26 McLellan, *Marx*, p. 233.

27 Ibid., p. 225.

28 Ibid., p. 128.

29 D. McLellan, *Marx's Grundrisse* (1971), pp. 17–18.

30 D. Sayer, (ed.), *Readings From Karl Marx* (1989), p. 19.

31 Ibid., p. 17.

32 McLellan, *Grundrisse*, p. 125.

33 Perry, *Marxism and History*, pp. 42–43.

34 D. Frisby and D. Sayer, *Society* (1986), p. 35.

35 Ibid, p. 35–36.

36 E. Durkheim, *The Rules of Sociological Method* (1964), p. 3.

37 Ibid., p. 1–2.

38 A. Giddens, *Capitalism and Modern Social Theory* (Cambridge, 1992), p. 88.

39 Irving M. Zeitlin argued: 'The active, creative side of human conduct disappears in Durkheim's scheme', in his *Ideology and the Development of Social Theory* (Englewood Cliffs, NJ, 1968), p. 268; Lewis A. Coser has argued that Durkheim's innate 'conservativism' led him to see social constraint as both necessary and desirable. A. Giddens (ed.), *Emile Durkheim Selected Writings* (Cambridge, 1972), p. 44. For a further discussion of this aspect of Durkheim's thought see A. Giddens, *The Constitution of Society: Outline of the Theory of Structuration* (Cambridge, 1984), pp. 169–74.

40 M. Waters, *Modern Sociological Theory* (1994), p. 136.

41 Walsh, 'Structure/Agency', p. 19.

42 Abrams, *Historical Sociology*, p. 27.

43 Walsh, 'Structure/Agency', p. 20.

44 Noble, *Social Theory*, pp. 118–19.

45 Frisby and Sayer, *Society*, p. 68.

46 Ibid., p. 69. For a further discussion of the way Weber viewed the relationship between the individual and society see Weber, Max *Economy and Society: Volume One* (Berkeley, Los Angeles, London, 1978), pp. 3–62.

47 H.H. Gerth and C. Wright Mills (eds), *From Max Weber* (1991), p. 181. Despite their differences, the pronouncements of Marx and Weber on class do look

remarkably similar at times, as Derek Sayer points out: 'The question of exploitation aside, what is most significant here is surely the extent of agreement between Marx and Weber on what class is, how it differs from pre-modern social relations, and its centrality to modern, capitalist society.' *Capitalism & Modernity: An excursus on Marx and Weber* (1991), p. 108. For a further discussion of this issue, see ibid., pp. 92–133.

48 This suggestion is made by Rosemary Crompton in, *Class and Stratification: An Introduction to Current Debates* (Cambridge, 1993), p. 30.
49 Gerth and Wright Mills, *Weber*, pp. 184–85.
50 G. Roth, 'History and sociology in the work of Max Weber' *British Journal of Sociology*, 27, 3 (1976), p. 306.
51 Gerth and Mills, *Weber*, pp. 57–58.
52 Ibid., p. 55.
53 Ibid., p. 14.
54 R. Bocock, *Hegemony* (1986), pp. 33–35.
55 Ibid, p. 35.
56 Ibid, p. 27.
57 D. Forgacs (ed.), *A Gramsci Reader: Selected Writings 1916–1935* (1988), p. 173.
58 R. Williams, *Marxism and Literature* (Oxford, 1977), p. 108.
59 Forgacs (ed.) *Gramsci*, p. 423.
60 Ibid, pp. 432–44.
61 Ibid, pp. 211–12.
62 Smith, *Reading Althusser*, p. 157.
63 S.H. Rigby, *Marxism and History: A critical introduction* (Manchester, 1998), p. 196.
64 C. Rojek, *Capitalism and Leisure Theory* (1985), p. 129.
65 Ibid.
66 A. Callinicos, *Althusser's Marxism* (1978), p. 43.
67 Smith, *Reading Althusser*, p. 159. This suggestion is made by the classical scholar E.R. Dodds in relation to the historian of the Grecian period, Herodotus (*c*.484–*c*.424 BC).
68 P. Ricoeur, 'Althusser's Theory of Ideology' in G. Elliot (ed.), *Althusser: A Critical Reader* (Oxford, 1994), p. 45.
69 Smith, *Reading Althusser*, p. 160.
70 Ricoeur, 'Althusser', p. 47.
71 L. Althusser, *Lenin and Philosophy and other essays* (New York, 1971), p. 143. These ideas are expounded in the essay 'Ideology and Ideological State Apparatuses (Notes towards an Investigation)', p. 127–86 in the aforementioned collection of essays.
72 Rojek, *Capitalism and Leisure Theory*, p. 131. The most celebrated, and controversial, critique of Althusser is offered by E.P. Thompson in: 'The Poverty of Theory: or an Orrery of Errors' in E.P. Thompson, *The Poverty of Theory and Other*

Essays (1980) pp. 193–397. Thompson takes Althusser to task for both his methodology, which constructs theory without reference to actual historical examples, and his denial of the role of human agency in the historical process. It is worth noting that even Ted Benton, in his recent, and more sympathetic, reading of Althusser, is forced to conclude that 'In rejecting the "voluntarism" of the humanists, Althusser seems to have gone over to the opposite extreme of a "structuralist" denial of human agency.' See his, 'Louis Althusser' in Stones, (ed.), *Key Sociological Thinker*, p. 200.

73 On the question of how to classify Foucault, see C. O'Farrell, *Foucault: Historian or Philosopher?* (1989), A. Sheridan, *Michel Foucault: The Will to Truth* (1980), pp. 2, 225. Patricia O'Brien argues that, 'The body of Foucault's writing has seldom been recognized for what it is: an alternative model for writing the history of culture, a model that embodies a fundamental critique of Marxist and Annaliste analysis, of social history itself.' See her 'Michel Foucault's History of Culture' in Hunt, Lynn (ed.), *The New Cultural History* (Berkeley and Los Angeles, 1989), p. 25.

74 Lloyd, *Structures of History*, pp. 82–83. Foucault's work needs to be approached quite carefully, not least because he uses terms like 'archaeology' and 'geneal-ogy' in quite an idiosyncratic manner, which many readers may find confusing. In addition, he strongly resisted any attempt that was made to label him, even with his own appellations. For example, he asserted: 'This business about dis-continuity has always rather bewildered me. In the new edition of the *Petit Larousse* it says: "Foucault: a philosopher who founds his theory of history on discontinuity." That leaves me flabbergasted. No doubt I didn't make myself suf-ficiently clear in The Order of Things, though I said a good deal there about this question.' P. Rabinow (ed.), *The Foucault Reader: An introduction to Foucault's thought* (1991), pp. 53–54. For general introductions to Foucault's work see 'Michel Foucault', in M. Hughes Warrington, *Fifty Key Thinkers on History* (2000), pp. 93–101; L. Barth, 'Michel Foucault' in Stones, *Key Sociological Thinkers*, pp. 252–65; 'Michel Foucault' in Munslow, *Routledge Companion*, pp. 107–11.

75 O'Brien, 'Foucault', p. 36.

76 Sheridan, *Foucault*, p. 184.

77 Rabinow (ed.), *Foucault Reader*, p. 7. Clare O'Farrell points out that this state-ment came as a considerable surprise to Foucault's followers, as it represented, not only a change in focus from his previous preoccupation with power rela-tions, but also yet another of the 'famous mutations' his work periodically underwent. O'Farrell, *Foucault*, p. 113.

78 Walsh, 'Structure/agency', p. 31.

79 O'Farrell, Clare op. cit. p. 104.

80 L. Barth, Lawrence in Stones (ed.), *Key Sociological Thinkers*, p. 255.

81 M. Foucault, 'Panopticism' in Rabinow (ed.), *Foucault Reader*, pp. 206–13.

82 Ibid., p. 22.

83 A. Giddens, *The Constitution of Society* (Cambridge, 1984), pp.153–54. Giddens compares Foucault with the American sociologist Erving Goffman (1922–82), and makes the valid point: 'reading Goffman on "total institutions" can be more instructive than reading Foucault,' p. 154. For a discussion of this aspect of Goffman's thought see: 'The Mortified Self' in C. Lemert and A. Branaman (eds), *The Goffman Reader* (Oxford, 1997), p. 55–71.

84 For a succinct discussion of Foucault's conception of power see A. Edgar, P. Sedgwick, *Cultural Theory: The Key Thinkers* (2002), pp. 73–76.

   The suggestion that Foucault's work ultimately leaves little room for human agency has been made by a number of authors. see: O'Farrell, *Foucault*, pp. 107–108.

85 Edgar and Sedgwick, *Cultural Theory*, pp. 67–68. For a summary of this work see 'An outline of The Civilizing Process', in J. Goudsblom, S. Mennell (eds), *The Norbert Elias Reader* (Oxford, 1998), pp. 39–45.

86 N. Elias, *What is Sociology?* (1978), p. 12.

87 Ibid., p. 131.

88 Goudsblom and Mennell, *Norbert Elias*, p. 131. For a more detailed exposition of the concept of figuration see Elias, Norbert *What is Sociology?* (1978), pp. 128–33.

89 Christopher Lloyd points out that the writings of Weber's contemporary, Georg Simmel (1858–1918), also prefigures much of what Giddens was later to say about structure and agency. Lloyd, *Stuctures of History*, pp. 90–91. Arthur Stinchcombe has made much the same point in relation to the work of Gerth and Mills, and Derek Sayer has pointed out that Marx's writings also anticipate the central arguments of structuration theory. Clark *et al.* (eds), *Anthony Giddens*, pp. 48, 235.

90 Edgar and Sedgwick, *Cultural Theory*, p. 84.

91 For general introductions to Gidden's work see ibid., pp. 84–85; I.J. Cohen, 'Anthony Giddens', in Stones (ed.), *Key Sociological Thinker*, pp. 279–90; P. Cassell, *The Giddens Reader* (Basingstoke, 1993), p. 1–37.

92 A. Giddens, *The Constitution of Society* (Cambridge, 1984), p. 25.

93 Ibid., pp. xxii-xxiii.

94 Cassell, *The Giddens Reader*, pp.10–11.

95 Ibid., p. 119.

96 Giddens, *Constitution of Society*, p. xxxi.

97 Ibid.

98 Ibid., p. 169.

99 V. Bailey *'This Rash Act': Suicide Across the Life Cycle of the Victorian City* (Stanford, CA, 1998), p. 29.

100 Cassell, Philip, op. cit. p. 119.

101 D. Sayer, 'Reinventing the wheel: Anthony Giddens, Karl Marx and Social Change' in Clark *et al.* (eds), *Anthony Giddens*, p. 246.

102 A. Giddens, *Constitution of Society*, p. 169. For a summary of the criticisms that have been made of structuration theory see Waters, *Modern Sociological Theory*, pp. 52–54. Waters points to a number of significant criticisms of structuration theory, not least that the definition of structure that it offers is unclear, and that it ultimately reduces structure to action/agency.

103 Ibid., pp. 177, 256–58.

104 Miliband, Ralph, *Divided Societies: Class Struggle in Contemporary Capitalism* (Oxford and New York, 1991), p. 104.

105 J. Alberti, *Gender and the Historian* (Harlow, 2002), p. 45.

106 R. Miliband, op. cit. p. 106.

107 I. Whelehan, *Modern Feminist Thought: From the Second Wave to 'Post-Feminism'* (Edinburgh, 1995), p. 109.

108 L. Segal, *Why Feminism?* (Cambridge 1999), p. 47.

109 For a useful account of divisions within the workforce in the shipbuilding see I. Roberts, *Craft, Class and Control: The Sociology of a Shipbuilding Community* (Edinburgh, 1993). Chapter Four 'Craft Workers and the Negotiation of Control' is particularly revealing on this issue.

110 A good example of divisions within a particular ethnic group are the tensions and divisions that existed within the Jewish community in Nineteenth Century London between the wealthy elite, and the poor members of the community. For a perceptive account of this issue, see M. Rozin, *The Rich and the Poor: Jewish Philanthropy and Social Control in Nineteenth-Century London* (Brighton and Portland, Oregon, 1999).

111 Joyce, Patrick, 'The end of social history', in Tosh, John (ed.), *Historians on History* (Harlow, 2000), p. 274.

112 Ibid., p. 278.

113 E.J. Hobsbawm, 'Marx and History', in Tosh, John (ed.), op. cit. p. 95.

114 Scott quoted in J. Tosh (ed.), *Historians on History* (Harlow, 2000), p. 285.

115 C. Calhoun (ed.), *Social Theory and the Politics of Identity* (Oxford, UK and Cambridge, USA, 1994), p. 14.

116 For example T.E.J. Wiedemann says: 'A great deal of productive work was at all times done by people who were not slaves. Smallholders and day-labourers existed even in first-century Italy, when large-scale slavery was once supposed to have monopolized agricultural production. In building, handicrafts, and even mining, free craftsmen are found working alongside slaves.' T. Wiedemann, *Slavery* (Oxford, 1987), p. 5. Such arguments are essentially a challenge to the classical Marxist interpretation of antiquity.

117 T. Weideman, *Greek and Roman Slavery* (1981), p. 15.

118 Ibid., p. 1–35. K.R. Bradley, *Slaves and Masters in the Roman Empire: A Study in Social Control* (Brussels, 1984), p. 50.

119 Y. Garlan, *Slavery in Ancient Greece*, Janet Lloyd (trs.) (1988), pp. 23, 41.

120 M.I. Finley (ed.), *Slavery in Classical Antiquity* (Cambridge, 1964), p. 68.

121 T.E.J. Wiedemann, *Slavery* (Oxford, 1987), p. 28.

122 J. Peradotto and Sullivan (eds), *Women in the Ancient World: The Arethusa Papers* (Albany, New York, 1984), pp. 2–3.

123 J.P. Hallett, 'The Role of Women in Roman Elegy: Counter-Cultural Feminism' in ibid., p. 243.

124 Murnaghan and Joshel, *Women and Slaves*, p. 3.

125 Ibid., It is worth noting that the authors borrow this phrase from Anne Mclintock's description of race, class and gender in the British Empire. See her *Imperial Leather: Race, Gender and Sexuality in the Colonial Context* (1995).

126 P. Clark, 'Women, slaves and the hierarchies of domestic violence: the family of St Augustine', in Murnaghan and Joshel (eds), *Women and Slaves*, pp. 109–29.

127 R.P. Saller, 'Symbols of Gender and Status Hierarchies in the Roman Household' in ibid., pp. 85–91.

128 W.G. Thalmann, 'Female Slaves in the Odyssey' in ibid., p. 23.

129 Ibid.

130 M. Bloch, *Feudal Society*, I: *The Growth of Ties of Dependence* (1989), p. xiii. There has been some questioning of his use of the term 'feudalism', most notably by the Belgian historian Francois Ganshof in 1944, but it is difficult to argue with the broad outline of Bloch's definition. For the debate: see Brown, T.S. 'Foreword', pp. xi–xxi in ibid.

131 S.H. Rigby, *English Society in the Later Middle Ages: Class, Status and Gender* (Basingstoke, 1995), pp. 182–83.

132 M. Keen, *English Society in the Later Middle Ages 1348–1500* (1990), pp. 1–24.

133 R.H. Hilton, 'The Peasantry as a Class', in *The English Peasantry in the Later Middle Ages* (Oxford, 1975), pp. 3–19.

134 Ibid., p. 9.

135 Ibid., p. 12.

136 S.H. Rigby, *English Society in the Later Middle Ages: Class, Status and Gender* (Basingstoke, 1995), pp. ix–x.

137 Ibid., p. 9.

138 For a good summary of Frank Parkin's ideas see Frank Parkin 'Strategies of social closure in class formation', in Frank Parkin (ed.), *The Social Analysis of Class Structure* (1974).

139 Rigby, *English Society*, p. 12.
    For an account of W.G. Runciman's ideas see *A Treatise on Social Theory, vol. II* (Cambridge, 1989).

140 Rigby, *English Society*, p. 326.

141 Ibid., pp. 246–47.

142 M.E. Mate, *Women in Medieval English Society* (Cambridge, 1999), p. 2.

143 Rigby, *English Society*, p. 261.

144   Ibid., p. 325.

145   H. Perkin, *The Origins of Modern English Society 1780–1880* (1969), p. 176. See also the the summary of this work in, R.S. Neale, *Class In English History 1680–1850* (Oxford, 1981), pp. 106–109.

146   Ibid., pp. 218–70 (quotation: p. 256).

147   Ibid., p. 255.

148   Ibid., p. 219.

149   Neale, *Class*, p. 107.

150   R.S. Neale, 'Class and class consciousness in early nineteenth century England: three classes or five?', in R.S. Neale, *History and Class: Essential Readings in Theory and Interpretation* (Oxford, 1984), p. 143.

151   R.J. Morris, 'The labour aristocracy in the British class structure', in A. Digby, Anne and C. Feinstein, *New Directions in Economic and Social History* (Basingstoke, 1989), p.170.

152   J.W. Scott, *Gender and the Politics of History* (New York, 1988), p. 72.

153   Ibid., p. 73.

154   T. Koditschek, 'The gendering of the British working class', *Gender & History*, 9, 2 (1997), p. 342.

155   D. Valenze, *The First Industrial Woman* (New York and Oxford, 1995).

156   A. Clark, *The Struggle for the Breeches: Gender and the Making of the British Working Class* (Berkeley and Los Angeles, California, 19XX).

157   Koditschek, 'Gendering', pp. 342–45.

158   Clark, *Struggle for the Breeches*, p. 271.

159   Quotations from ibid., pp. 6, 25, 41, 140.

160   Koditschek, 'Gendering', pp. 345–46.

161   Ibid., p. 6.

162   Ibid., p. 28.

163   E. Ross, *Love and Toil: Motherhood in Outcast London, 1870–1918* (New York and Oxford, 1993), pp. 42–44.

164   R. Price, *British Society, 1680–1880: Dynamism, Containment and Change* (Cambridge, 1999).

165   S. Fielding, *Class and Ethnicity: Irish Catholics in England, 1880–1939* (Buckingham, 1993). Also see J.C. Belchem, John, Nationalism, 'Republicanism and exile: Irish emigrants and the revolutions of 1848', in *Past and Present*, 146, Feb. (1995).

166   L. Colley, *Britons: Forging the Nation, 1707–1837* (New Haven and London, 1992), p. 6.

167   E. Foner, 'Class, ethnicity and radicalism in the Gilded Age: the land league and Irish America', *Marxist Perspectives*, 1 Summer 1978, pp. 6, 43.

168   K.A. Miller, *Emigrants and Exiles: Ireland and the Irish Exodus to North America* (Oxford and New York, 1985), p. 550.

169 A. O'Day, 'Irish Diaspora politics in perspective: The United Irish Leagues of Great
Britain and America, 1900–1914', in D.M. MacRaild (ed.), *Great Famine and
Beyond: The Irish in Nineteenth and Twentieth Century Britain* (Dublin, 2000), p. 217.

▶ **5 Ideology, *Mentalité* and Social Ritual:
From Social History to Cultural History**

1 L. Hunt (ed.), *The New Cultural History* (Berkeley and Los Angeles, 1990), p. 1.
2 P. Burke, *The French Historical Revolution: The Annales School, 1929–89* (Oxford,
1990): this is the title used for ch. 4, pt i.
3 R. Chartier, *Cultural History* (Oxford, 1988), p. 3.
4 This development is captured in Victoria E. Bonnell and Lynn Hunt (eds),
Beyond the Cultural Turn (Berkeley, CA, 1999), esp. intro.
5 M. Arnold, *Culture and Anarchy* (1882).
6 A discussion of the Arnoldian fear of mass culture can be found in J. Carey,
*The Intellectuals and the Masses: Pride and Prejudice Among the Literary
Intelligentsia, 1880–1939* (1992).
7 'Modes of thought' constitutes but one possible definition of the origins of
cultural history, as it has developed over time, deployed by Peter Burke in his
Varieties of Cultural History (Oxford, 1997). The others are: 'the history of
artists, art and music', 'the history of doctrine', 'the history of disciplines' and
'the history of culture' (pp. 1–22).
8 Ibid., p. 14, quoting John Locke.
9 Again Burke is instructive here: see ibid., p. 14.
10 J. Burckhardt, *The Civilisation of the Renaissance in Italy* (New York, 1961 edn).
First published in 1860. The judgement about Burckhardt's importance in the
creation of art history as a distinct discipline is that of the editor of this edition, Irene Gordon.
11 George Bull, Introduction, G. Vasari, *Lives of the Artists* (London, 1965 edn),
p. 17.
12 Gordon, editor's introduction, *Renaissance*, pp. xvii–xviii.
13 Irene Gordon, Introduction, *Renaissance*, p. vii.
14 J. Huizinga, *The Waning of the Middle Ages* (1924; 1990 edn), p. 9.
15 Burckhardt, *Renaissance*, p. 121.
16 Huizinga, *Waning of the Middle Ages*, p. 9
17 A. Giddens, *Capitalism and Modern Social Theory: An Analysis of the Writings of
Marx, Durkheim and Max Weber* (Cambridge, 1992), pp. 77–81.
18 For him 'it is necessary to ask, first, "What did Plato think?" and secondly,
"Was he right?" ' T.M. Knox, editor's introduction, R.G. Collingwood, *The Idea
of History* (Oxford, 1946; 1992 edn), p. xi.

19   G. Lefebvre, *La Grande Peur de* 1789 (1932).

20   See below, pp. 125–6.

21   M. Bloch, *Royal Touch* (1924; London, 1973); L. Febvre, *The Problem of Unbelief in the Sixteenth Century* (1942; Cambridge, Mass, 1983).

22   A. Soboul, *Les Sans-Culottes Parisien en l'an II* (Paris, 1962).

23   R. Mandrou, *Introduction to Modern France, 1500–1640* (1961) and his *Magistrates and Sorcerers in Seventeenth-Century France* (1968).

24   Burke, *French Historical Revolution*, p. 70.

25   K. Thomas, *Religion and the Decline of Magic* (1971; 1991 edn).

26   Ibid. p. ix.

27   The case for Thomas's anthropological sense is well made, and clearly contextualised, in A. Green and K. Troup, *The Houses of History: A Critical Reader In Twentieth Century History and Theory* (Manchester, 1999), ch. 7.

28   J. Le Goff, *Medieval Civilisation* (1964), p. 325.

29   E.P. Thompson, *The Making of the English Working Class* (1963; 1980 edn), p. 9.

30   Ibid.

31   See, for example, Rudé, *The Crowd in the French Revolution* (1959) and his *The Crowd in History* (1964).

32   G. LeBon, *The Crowd: A Study of the Popular Mind* (1896), p. 13.

33   He began publishing on this theme in the 1950s. A more general study is G. Rudé, *Protest and Punishment The Story of the Social and Political Protesters Transported to Australia, 1788 1868* (Oxford, 1978).

34   For example, R. Hughes, *The Fatal Shore* (1988).

35   Thompson, *Making*, p. 12.

36   Rudé, *The Crowd in the French Revolution*, p. 1

37   F. Krantz, *History From Below: Studies in Popular Protest and Popular Ideology* (1985).

38   Hobsbawm, 'The machine breakers' in *Labouring Men: Studies in the History of Labour* (1964; 1968 edn), pp. 5–17 (quotation on p. 7). See, too, E.P. Thompson, 'The moral economy of the crowd', Past and Present, 50 (Feb. 1971).

39   M. Harrison, *Crowds and History: Mass Phenomena in English Towns, 1790 1835* (Cambridge, 1988), p. 7.

40   Hobsbawm, *Labouring Men*.

41   Quoted in J. Black and D.M. MacRaild, *Studying History* (Basingstoke, 2000), p. 46.

42   E.P. Thompson, 'History from below', *Times Literary Supplement* (1966).

43   J.A. Sharpe, 'History from below', in Peter Burke (ed.), *New Perspectives on Historical Writing* (Cambridge, 1991), p. 25.

44   Thompson, *Making*, p. 12.

45   Ibid.

46   E.J. Hobsbawm, *Primitive Rebels* (1959).

47 The term 'subaltern' was used, euphemistically (in order to defy detection by the authorities), in Gramsci's prison notebooks. See, for example, A. Gramsci, *Selections from the Prison Notebooks* (ed.) Quintin Hoare and Geoffrey Nowell Smith (New York, 1973), pp. 52–55, 323–43.

48 The title of a seminal work: S. Rowbotham, *Hidden From History* (1973).

49 For a general discussion of the development of women's history see: Gerry Holloway, 'Writing women in: the development of feminist approaches to women's history' in W. Lamont (ed.) *Historical Controversies and Historians* (1998), pp. 177–87.

   For a comprehensive survey of the development of women's history and its evolution into gender history see: J. Alberti *Gender and the Historian* (Harlow, 2002).

50 On the importance of this, see C. Hall, *White, Male and Middle-Class: Explorations in Feminism and History* (Cambridge, 1992) p. 10.

51 Catherine Hall and L. Davidoff collaborated on one of the most significant works of British gender history produced so far: *Family Fortunes: Men and Women of the English Middle Class 1780–1850* (1987). They point out that 'even E.P. Thompson's classic study of England in this period, with its important stress on cultural aspects of class, pays scant attention to the different positioning of men and women within the working class. Our focus is on the gendered nature of class formation and the way sexual difference influences class belonging', p. 30.

52 J.W. Scott, 'Women in history: the modern period', *Past and Present*, 101 (1983), p. 141.

53 N. Zemon Davis, 'Women's history in transition: the European case' *Feminist Studies*, 3–4 (1976), p. 90.

54 Particularly in her 'Gender: a useful category of historical analysis', *American Historical Review*, 91, 5 (1986), pp. 141–57.

55 J.W. Scott, *Gender and the Politics of History* (New York, 1999 edn), pp. 42–43.

56 Ibid., pp. 40–41.

57 Ibid., pp. 36, 41.

   Scott's embrace of the post-structuralist position is spelt out particularly clearly in the 'Introduction' to this volume. pp. 1–11.

58 Scott's views have been discussed by a number of authors, but a particularly significant exchange of views appeared in *Comparative Studies in Society and History*, 35 (1993): Laura Lee Downs, 'If "woman" is just an empty category, then why am I afraid to walk alone at night? Identity politics meets the post-modern subject' (pp. 414–37); J.W. Scott 'The tip of the volcano' (pp. 438–43); Downs 'Reply to Joan Scott' (pp. 444–51).

59 Burke, *History and Social Theory*, p. 14.

60 See C.R. Badcock, *Lévi-Strauss: Structuralism and Sociological Theory* (1975), pp. 72–76.

61 Peter Burke, 'Strengths and weaknesses of the history of mentalities', *History of European Ideas* (1986).

62 Clifford Geertz, 'Deep play: notes on the Balinese cockfight', in *The Interpretation of Cultures: Selected Essays* (1993 edn), pp. 412–53. 'The Balinese cockfight' is Geertz's most influential piece of writing, and a good example of how the technique of 'thick description' works in practice. See also his 'Thick description: toward an interpretive theory of culture', pp. 3–30.

63 C. Geertz, *The Interpretation of Cultures: Selected Essays* (1993), p. 6.

64 Ibid., p. 21.

65 A. Edgar and P. Sedgwick, *Cultural Theory: The Key Thinkers* (2002), pp. 82–84. Fred Inglis *Clifford Geertz: Culture, Custom and Ethics* (Cambridge, 2000), p.128.

66 For further context, see W. Scott, 'Cultural history at the crossroads: a local experience and a personal view', *Tidskrift Kultur Studier, I: Cultural Change in Theory and Practice*, May 1995.

67 As is demonstrated in his 'history of mentalities'.

68 Miri Rubin, 'What is Cultural History Now?' in David Cannadine (ed.), *What is History Now?* (Basingstoke, 2002), pp. 80–81.

69 For general introductions to Bakhtin's work, see 'Mikhail Bakhtin' in Edgar and Sedgwick, *Cultural Theory: The Key Thinkers*, pp. 14–16 and P. Morris 'Introduction' *The Bakhtin Reader: Selected Writings of Bakhtin, Medvedev, and Voloshinov* (2002), pp. 1–24. Sue Vice, *Introducing Bakhtin* (Manchester, 1997).

70 Ken Hirschkop *Mikhail Bakhtin: An Aesthetic for Democracy* (Oxford, 1999), p. 15.

71 Vice, *Introducing Bakhtin*, p. 13.

72 P. Burke, 'Bakhtin for Historians', *Social History*, 13, 1 (1988), p. 85.

73 The concept of carnival is discussed in both: M. Bakhtin, *Rabelais and His World* (Cambridge, Massachusetts, 1968) and M. Bakhtin, *Problems of Dostoevsky's Poetics* (Minneapolis, 1984). The 'Introduction' to *Rabelais and His World* offers a comprehensive discussion of his notion of the 'carnivalesque'.

74 R. Selden, *Practising Theory and Reading Literature: An Introduction* (Hemel Hempstead, 1989), p. 167.

75 Bakhtin quoted in Morris (ed.), *The Bakhtin Reader*, p. 199.

76 R.W. Scribner, *For the Sake of Simple Folk: Popular Propaganda for the German Reformation* (Cambridge, 1981), p. 62.

77 Ibid.

78 N. Zemon Davis, *Society and Culture in Early Modern France* (Cambridge, 1995), p. 97.

79 Ibid., p. 103. It has to be pointed out that Davis mistakenly calls Bakhtin a 'structuralist', in this connection, as his ideas were developed in opposition to the structural linguistics of Ferdinand de Saussure.

80 On Victor Turner's notion of *communitas*, see the entry on 'Liminality', in N. Rapport and J. Overing, *Social and Cultural Anthropology: The Key Concepts* (2000), pp. 229–36.

81 M. Bakhtin, *The Dialogic Imagination: Four Essays* (Austin, TX, 1981).

82 P. Burke, 'Bakhtin for Historians', *Social History*, 13, 1 (1988), p. 90.

83 M.W. Steinberg, 'Culturally speaking: finding a commons between post-structuralism and the Thompsonian perspective', *Social History*, 21, 2 (1996), pp. 193–228.

84 Hunt, *New Cultural History*, p. 52.

85 Zemon Davis, *Society and Culture*, pp. xvi–xvii.

86 D. Snowman, 'Natalie Zemon Davis', *History Today*, 52, 10 (2002), p. 19.

87 N. Zemon Davis, *The Return of Martin Guerre* (1983; Cambridge, MA, 2001 edn), p. 5.

88 Snowman, 'Natalie Zemon Davis', p. 19.

89 Zemon Davis, *The Return of Martin Guerre*, p. 20.

90 Ibid., p. 21.

91 Ibid., p. 44.

92 R. Finlay, 'The Refashioning of Martin Guerre', *American Historical Review*, 93, 3 (1988), p. 557.

93 Ibid., p. 571. See also Zemon Davis, 'On the Lame', in the same issue of this journal (pp. 572–603).

94 W. Thompson, *What Happened To History?* (2000), p. 68.
     For a fuller discussion of 'microhistory' see: G. Levi 'On Microhistory', in P. Burke (ed.), *New Perspectives on Historical Writing* (Cambridge, 1991), pp. 93–113.

95 R.J. Evans, *In Defence of History* (1997), p. 246.

96 For a summary of Lyotard's argument that the postmodern era is characterised by scepticism towards 'metanarratives' and the acceptance of 'micronarratives' in their place, see: Tim Woods, *Beginning Postmodernism* (Manchester, 199), pp. 20–23. Ankersmit cites several examples of 'microhistory' that conform to his vision of a postmodernist history, including, N. Zemon Davis's *The Return of Martin Guerre*. F.R. Ankersmit 'Historiography and Postmodernism', *History and Theory*, 28 (1989), p. 149. Evans also cites *The Return of Martin Guerre*, along with Darnton's *The Great Cat Massacre*, among his examples of, 'What a postmodernist history might look like': *Defence of History*, p. 300.

97 R. Darnton, *The Great Cat Massacre and other Episodes in French Cultural History* (1984), p. 11.

98 Ibid.

99 Burke (ed.), Introduction, *New Perspectives*, p. 3.

100 See W. Thompson, *Postmodernism* (Basingstoke, 2004), ch. 5, for a wide-ranging discussion of the Foucauldian influence.

101 Burke, *History and Social Theory*, p. 120.

102 Darnton, *Great Cat Massacre*, p. 12.

103 Willie Thompson makes the point that Darnton's account of the massacre is based on an insufficient amount of primary source material, as it is derived from a single questionable source, so 'It is an open question whether the great cat

massacre ever actually occurred.' W. Thompson *What Happened To History?* (2000), p. 58. Raphael Samuel has pointed out that the episode could be interpreted in a number of ways, which raises issues about the difficulties of 'reading' social rituals. See John Tosh *The Pursuit of History* (Harlow, 2000), pp. 186–87.

104 A. Sheridan, *Michel Foucault: The Will to Truth* (1980), p. 225.

105 Ibid.

106 Hunt, *New Cultural History*, p. 45.

107 Ibid.

108 C. O' Farrell, *Foucault: Historian or Philosopher?* (Basingstoke, 1989), p. 27.

109 Ibid.

110 Hunt, *New Cultural History*, p. 28.

111 Ibid., p. 30.

112 R.A. Houston, *Madness and Society in Eighteenth-Century Scotland* (Oxford, 2000), p. 12.

113 J.A. Sharpe, *Judicial Punishment in England* (1990), p. 86.

114 Ibid., pp. 82, 87.

115 Houston, *Madness and Society*, pp. 12–13.

116 Ibid., p. 13.

117 Hunt, *New Cultural History*, p. 34. M. Rubin 'What is Cultural History Now?' in D. Cannadine (ed.), *What is History Now?* (Basingstoke, 2002), p. 83.

118 S. Fitzpatrick, *Stalinism: New Directions* (2000), p. 8. For example, she cites the young German historian, Jochen Helbeck (b. 1966) who draws on Michel Foucault, as well as literary scholars such as Stephen Greenblatt. Ibid., p. 72. R.W. Thurston makes a fleeting, but illuminating, comparison between torture in Stalinist Russia and Foucault's description of torture in pre-revolutionary France. See his, *Life and Terror in Stalin's Russia 1934–1941* (1996), p. 66.

119 M. Hughes-Warrington, *Fifty Key Thinkers on History* (2000), pp. 98–99.

120 G.S. Jones, *The Languages of Class: Studies in English Working-Class History, 1832–1982* (Cambridge, 1983), p. 8.

121 Hunt, *New Cultural History*, p. 21.

122 Ibid.

123 Ibid., p. 6.

124 For Stedman Jones, the important early work was *Outcast London* (Oxford, 1971; 1986). For Joyce, *Work, Society and Politics: the Culture of the Factory in Later 19th-Century England* (Hassocks, 1980).

125 For an engaging debate with over the level of explanation accorded to Marxist approaches, see articles and rejoinders by Joyce and Richard Price in the journal *Social History* (see bibliography).

126 P. Joyce, 'The end of social history?', *Social History*, 20 (1995), pp. 73–91.

127 In this respect, we can point to T. Koditschek, *Class Formation and Urban Industrial Society: Bradford, 1750–1850* (Cambridge, 1990).

128 B. Lancaster, *The Department Store: A Social History* (Leicester, 1995), p. 1.

129 For example, despite his focus on the study of consumption, Lancaster maintains an awareness of class and conditions for those who worked in department stores, offering a 'labour history of the department store.' Ibid., Chapter 8 'Behind the counter: workers and the department store', pp. 125–58, 195–205.

130 See, for example, his *Forbidden Best-Sellers of Pre-Revolutionary France* (London, 1996).

131 Robert Darnton, *The Kiss of Lamourette* (New York, 1990), p. 212.

132 J. Rose, *The Intellectual Life of the British Working Classes* (2001), p. 3.

133 Ibid., p. 18.

134 Ibid., pp. 22–23.

135 Burke, *New Perspectives*, p. 18.

▶ Conclusion

1 A. Giddens, *The Constitution of Society* (Cambridge, 1984), p. 14.

2 H. Bertens, *The Idea of the Postmodern: A History* (1995), p. 13.

3 On the fragmentation of the *Annales* School, see L. Hunt, 'French history in the last twenty years: the rise and fall of the *Annales* Paradigm', *Journal of Contemporary History*, 21 (1986), pp. 209–24.

4 Dennis Smith points out that these challenges to the Marxist approach came from within the broader tradition of historical sociology. See D. Smith, *The Rise of Historical Sociology* (Philadelphia, 1991), p. 175.

5 A useful discussion of different types of historical comparison is offered in C. Tilly, *Big Structures, Large Processes, Huge Comparisons* (New York, 1984).

Further Reading

[Place of publication London, unless otherwise stated]

▶ Introduction

General works

The starting point for any reader wishing to learn more about social history and its linkages to the social sciences has to be Peter Burke's, *History and Social Theory* (Oxford, 1992). Our own study consciously seeks to complement that work. The way in which the discipline has moved on can be noted in the fact that this study is a significantly revised follow-up to his first work of this type, *History and Sociology* (1980). Key theorists such as Marx are required reading. Ideally, these should be read in their original form, though many useful commentaries are available. Matt Perry, *Marxism and History* (Basingstoke, 2002) is an excellent introduction to Marxist historical writings, though different in interpretation from S.R. Rigby, *Marxism and History* (Manchester, 2nd edn, 1998). For Max Weber, see H.H. Gerth and C. Wright Mills, *From Max Weber: Essays in Sociology* (1991 edn); and for interpretations of his canon, see G. Roth, 'History and sociology in the work of Max Weber', *British Journal of Sociology*, 27 (1976). Of the many sociologists who have focused upon the historical genesis of modes of social thought, A. Giddens is vital. A good starting point is A. Giddens, *Sociology* (Cambridge, 3rd edn, 1997). A companion volume of readings is also available: A. Giddens (ed.), *Sociology: Introductory Readings* (Cambridge, 1997). An important and influential discussion of the three 'founding fathers' of sociology is provided in A. Giddens, *Capitalism and Modern Social Theory: An Analysis of the Writings of Marx, Durkheim and Max Weber* (Cambridge, 1992 edn). Good overviews of different theoretical traditions are provided in: Randall Collins, *Four Sociological Traditions* (Oxford, 1994), T. Noble, *Social Theory and Social Change* (Basingstoke, 2000) and M. Waters, *Modern Sociological Theory* (1994). R. Stones (ed.), *Key Sociological Thinkers* (Basingstoke, 1998) is a useful collection containing 21 essays on the most influential social thinkers. An important discussion of the inseparability of the disciplines of history and sociology from the perspective of a sociologist is provided in P. Abrams, *Historical Sociology* (Shepton Mallet, 1982). The relationship between totality, structures and the individual is brilliantly captured in C. Lloyd, *The Structures of History* (Oxford, 1993), and his *Explanation in Social History* (Oxford, 1986). Good, general, introductions to postmodern thought are provided by H. Bertens, *The Idea of the Postmodern: A History* (1995) and T. Woods, *Beginning Postmodernism* (Manchester, 1999).

Raymond Williams, *Keywords* (1988 edn) remains an important and useful discussion of the meaning of significant terms in social and cultural theory. Nigel Rapport and Joanna Overing, *Social and Cultural Anthropology: The Key Concepts* (2000) contains useful discussions of the most influential ideas in that particular field, while Andrew Edgar and Peter Sedgwick, *Cultural Theory: The Key Thinkers* (2002) contains introductory essays on a number of the theorists discussed in the current text.

Naturally, as part of their remit, guides and primers for the study of history, contain full reference to social history, as with J. Black and D.M. MacRaild, *Studying History* (Basingstoke, 2000), J. Tosh, *The Pursuit of History* (2000) and A. Marwick, *The New Nature of History* (Basingstoke, 2001), make regular mentions. E.H. Carr, *What is History?* (2001 edn), R.J. Evans, *In Defence of History* (1998), and G.R. Elton, *The Practice of History* (Oxford, 2002 edn) contain important philosophical discussion of the impact of the social sciences upon history. The new edition of P. Burke (ed.), *New Perspectives on Historical Writing* (Oxford, 2001 edn) does likewise. Marnie Hughes Warrington, *Fifty Key Thinkers on History* (2000) contains useful introductory essays on many of the historians discussed in the current text.

▶ Chapter 1 'Cinderella' Gets Her Prince? The Development of Social History

Harold Perkin's 'What is social history?', *Bulletin of the John Rylands Library*, 36 (1953) provides a still useful measure of how far social history had yet to travel as well as how much it has changed in the time since Perkin first wrote. Useful brief accounts are: J.C.D. Clark, 'What is social history ...?', in Juliet Gardiner (ed.), *What is History Today?* (Basingstoke, 1988) and P. Cartledge, 'What is Social History Now?' in D. Cannadine (ed.), *What is History Now?* (Basingstoke, 2002).

Lloyd's *Structures of History*, noted earlier, has excellent chapters on the traditions discussed in this chapter. The heavy influence of economic change remains with social history and the linkage is captured well in E. Roll, *A History of Economic Thought* (5th edn, 1992). For some reason, S. Pollard, *The Idea of Progress* (1968) is not much quoted but it, too, deals well with the mixture of social change and intellectual development which helped to shape historical research. The importance of positivism, for both sociology and social history, should be noted. For an overview of such linkages, see S. Gordon, *The History and Philosophy of Social Science* (1991) and P. Halfpenny *Positivism and Sociology: Explaining Social Life* (Unwin, 1982). It is important, too, that further reading entails the examination of classic works of social history, too. If early social history was in some ways defined against J.H. Clapham, then his *Economic History of Britain* (3 vols. 1926–38) should be considered. G.D.H. Cole and R. Postgate, *The Common People 1746–1945* (2nd edn, 1946), remains a useful and rich account of a Leftist perspective from the inter-war period, republished many times. G.M. Trevelyan, *English Social History* (1941), remains a classic account if its type; a key moment before British Marxism took hold. For the pivotal moment in the development of the latter, we still have to consult the preface of E.P. Thompson, *The Making of the English Working Class* (1963), which influenced more than a generation of social historians. Keith Wrightson, *English Society, 1580–1680* (2003 edn), like Thompson's account, contains a brilliantly clear evocation of a particular kind of social history. The impact of the British Marxists has been the subject of much work. H.J. Kaye, *The British Marxist Historians: An Introductory Analysis* (Basingstoke, 1995 edn), is regarded as a standard account, and has the advantage of examining most of the important contributors, chapter by chapter. M. Perry, *Marxism and History*, however, contains a more pungent analysis of their works. One strain of their approach is also considered in F. Krantz, *History From Below: Studies in Popular Protest and Popular Ideology* (1988 edn). When it first appeared, F.M.L. Thompson, *The Cambridge Social History of Britain, 1750–1950*, 3 vols (Cambridge, 1990), was criticised for its lack of a unifying theoretical framework, but it does provide some excellent examples of social history *as practised*. The impact of E.P. Thompson and others of his ilk upon American scholars can be seen in H.W. Gutman, *Work, Culture and Politics in Industrializing America* (1966). J.A. Henretta, 'Social history as lived and written', *American Historical Review*, 84, 5 (1979) succeeds in pulling the threads together and provides an international perspective so often lacking elsewhere.

The gender dimension had an early champion in the form of Ivy Pinchbeck, *Women Workers and the Industrial Revolution, 1750–1850* (1930). In Britain, Sheila Rowbotham is the name most closely associated with the sustained attempt to write women back into history that came out of the second wave of the women's movement in the late 1960s and early 1970s. Rowbotham's seminal work, *Hidden from History* (1973), can be said to have really initiated the study of women's history in this country. The year after *Hidden from History* was published in the UK, Lois Banner published *Women in Modern America: A Brief History* (New York, 1974). For a sharp if brief survey of the development of women's history and its evolution into gender history see Joanna Alberti, *Gender and the Historian* (Harlow, 2002).

▶ Chapter 2   Fruit of a 'special relationship'? Historical Sociology

Several works which discuss the development and meaning of social history, not least the marriage between sociology and history. One of the best starting points, from a historical perspective, remains C. Lloyd, *Explanations in Social History* (Oxford, 1988 edn), while P. Abrams, *Historical Sociology* (Shepton Mallet, 1982) offers a discussion of the relationship between history and sociology from the perspective of a sociologist. The best wide-ranging yet concise analysis is found in P. Burke, *History and Social Theory* (Oxford, 1992 edn). C. Wright Mills, *The Sociological Imagination* (Oxford, 2000 edn), although essentially a discussion of trends in 1950s American sociology, still offers a useful discussion of the relationship between the individual and society, and a reasoned plea for the connection of history and sociology. P. Abrams, 'History, sociology and historical sociology', *Past and Present*, 87 (1980), D. Smith, 'Social history and sociology – more than just good friends', *Sociological Review*, 30 (1982), and G. Stedman Jones, 'From historical sociology to theoretical history', in *British Journal of Sociology*, 27 (1976), provide still relevant overviews of the development history and the linkage with sociology. Important differences of opinion and position can be found in J.H. Goldthorpe, 'The uses of history in sociology: reflections on some recent tendencies' *British Journal of Sociology*, 42, 2 (1991) and J.M. Bryant, 'Evidence and explanation in history and sociology: critical reflections on Goldthorpe's critique of historical sociology', *British Journal of Sociology*, 45, 1 (1994). E.J. Hobsbawm, 'From social history to the history of society', *Daedelus*, 100 (1971) engages with debates about the nature of social history. Hobsbawm's essay was reprinted in M.W. Flinn and T.C. Smout, *Essays in Social History* (1974), a collection which provides useful case studies of seminal social history at that point. An imperious overview of the post-1945 social history project can be found in J.A. Henretta, 'Social history as lived and written', *American Historical Review* (1979). Examples of historians in action in the field of social history can be found in A.Green and K. Troup (eds), *The Houses of History: A Critical Reader in Twentieth-Century History and Theory* (Manchester, 1999). The most comprehensive survey of works by historical sociologists is: D. Smith, *The Rise of Historical Sociology* (Philadelphia, 1991).

▶ **Chapter 3   'A mass of factors and influences?' Systemic, 'Total' and 'Comparative' Histories**

Much of the best material on this subject stands at polar opposites: large-scale studies, such as Braudel's own *Mediterranean*, which we have mentioned many times; or shorter, analytical expositions on theories and problems, usually in article form. Consulting the prefatory comments of Braudel's major studies (*Mediterranean* and *Civilisation and Capitalism*) would benefit any reader interested in 'histoire totale'.

Important works on Braudel, his method and influence, include H. Trevor-Roper, 'Fernand Braudel, the *Annales* and the Mediterranean', *Journal of Modern History*,

44 (1972); J.H. Hexter, 'Fernand Braudel and the *Monde Braudellien*', *Journal of Modern History*, 44 (1972). A review essay containing much useful material on the *Annales* and the comparative dimension, is D. Smith, 'History, geography and sociology: lesson from the Annales School', *Theory, Culture and Society*, 5 (1988). Similarly, the method and application of another of great *Annaliste* E. Le Roy Ladurie warrants consideration by those wishing to move from a superficial appreciation of comparison to a deeper meaning, wherein the actual application of the method can be noted. See particularly his *Peasants of the Languedoc* (1974), which is best read in conjunction with his two contributions to historiography and the art (and science) of history: *Territory of the Historian* (Brighton, 1979) and *Mind and Method of the Historian* (Brighton, 1981). In all these works, there is an inevitable blending *histoire totale* and comparative history.

Moving on to the sociologists and other social theorists who have sought to deal with either the totalising vision or the comparative aspect (or, in some cases, both), one of the key works remains C. Tilley, *Big Structures, Large Processes, Huge Comparisons* (New York, 1984), which began life as a paper and grew. In our chapter we make much of G. Arrighi's, *The Long Twentieth Century* (1994). This is because Arrighi so consciously sets out to frame his analysis as a totalising enterprise; yet, at the same time, he explains his framing and theorising with great clarity. This book is large and heavy going but it can profit the dipper as well as the deep and complete reader; it functions as a route map as well as highly original piece of research. We made mention of the West German 'New Social History' (*Gessellshaftgeschichte*) approach, which drew inspiration from Max Weber and apart from Jürgen Kocka, whose work on the social history of the bourgeoisie is of vital importance (see, e.g. *Bourgeois Society in the Nineteenth Century*, 1993), another interesting and incisive contribution is H. Ulrich-Wehler, 'What is the 'History of Society', in *Storia Della Storiographia*, 18 (1990). This, in turn, can be read in conjunction with an essay that puts perhaps a more Anglo-Saxon spin on many of the issue raised by Ulrich-Wehler and others: Eric Hobsbawm, 'From social history to the history of society', *Daedelus*, 100 (1971), which was reprinted in M.W. Flinn and T.C. Smout, *Essays in Social History*, (Oxford, 1974).

Unlike Braudel, perhaps, Bloch is remembered more for his contribution to comparative history than to total history. His own research-based works, *Royal Touch* (1924) and *Feudal Society* (1940), are, like Braudel's *Mediterranean*, important original contributions in this area. For Bloch's contribution to the consideration of this core theoretical and methodological issue, it is advisable to consider first 'A contribution towards a comparative history of European society', in his *Land and Work in Medieval Europe: Selected Papers by Marc Bloch* (1967), trans. J.E. Andersen, and then to examine that work in the broader context of his *The Historian's Craft* (Manchester, 1992). The application of macro-sociological analyses to 'real' historical problems is essential to 'proper' comparative history. After nearly forty years,

Barrington Moore Jnr, *Social Origins of Dictatorship and Democracy: Lord and Peasant in the Making of the Modern World* (1966), remains an important signpost on the road to comprehension. Newer and equally highly structured and theoretically and methodologically sharp is T. Skocpol, *States and Social Revolutions: A Comparative Analysis of France, Russia and China* (Cambridge, 1990).

Many papers and articles exist in which the comparative method is partly or wholly framed. Written a quarter of a century ago, and approaching the subject with a scepticism born from an interest in cultural history rather than sociological theory, T. Zeldin, 'Social history and total history', in *Journal of Social History*, 10 (1976), is nevertheless important and revealing. A long, at times over-complex essay on the subject can be found in A.A. Van Den Brambussche, 'Historical explanation and the comparative method: towards a theory of the history of society', *History and Theory*, 28, 1 (1989). The first section, which discusses critical philosophy, seems not to be relevant to the discussion. But the remaining sections are deep and sharp. There is no escaping the importance of the *Annales* contribution, and so W.H. Sewell, 'Marc Bloch and the logic of comparative history', *History and Theory*, 6 (1967) offers a characteristically original, intelligent essay. Also important is T.T. Skocpol and M. Somers, 'The uses of comparative history', *Comparative Studies in Society and History*, 22, 2 (1980). Like Van Den Brambussche, Tilly and Sewell, Skocpol and Somers seek to model comparative history into a number of types and instances. A short essay which actually applies the comparative method, both lucidly and in a highly relevant way, is Nancy L. Green, 'The comparative method and post-structural structuralism: new perspectives for migration studies' in J. Lucassen and L. Lucassen (eds), *Migration, Migration History, History: Old Paradigms and New Perspectives* (Berlin, 1997).

▶ Chapter 4   Social Structure and Human Agency in Historical Explanation

The issue of structure and agency in social theory is discussed in most general sociology textbooks. A very useful brief overview of the issues is David F. Walsh 'Structure/Agency' in C. Jenks (ed.), *Core Sociological Dichotomies* (1998). A more detailed discussion of the way various key social theorists have viewed the concept of 'society' is provided by D. Frisby and D. Sayer, *Society* (London, 1986). D. McLellan, *The Thought of Karl Marx* (Basingstoke, 1995 edn) is an excellent introduction to Marx's ideas, containing extensive extracts from Marx's original writings. A. Giddens (ed.), *Emile Durkheim: Selected Writings* (Cambridge, 1972), is a good collection of Durkheim's work, with an introductory essay by Giddens. H.H. Gerth and C. Wright Mills (eds), *From Max Weber: Essays in Sociology* (1991 edn), is an important anthology of that author's work, which also contains a useful introductory essay.

D. Forgacs (ed.), *A Gramsci Reader: Selected Writings 1916–1935* (1988), is a comprehensive selection of Gramsci's writings, which also includes a glossary of key terms used in his work. Some of Althusser's most influential writings appear in: Louis Althusser, *Lenin and Philosophy and other Essays* (New York, 1971). A good selection of Foucault's writings, with an introductory essay, is P. Rabinow (ed.), *The Foucault Reader: An Introduction to Foucault's Thought* (1991). P. Cassell (ed.), *The Giddens Reader* (Basingstoke, 1993) provides the same for Anthony Giddens. Giddens' own *The Constitution of Society: Outline of the Theory of Structuration* (Cambridge, 1984) is not only a comprehensive statement of his own theoretical position, but also offers critical evaluations of a number of other significant social theorists. J. Goudsblom and S. Mennell (eds), *The Norbert Elias Reader* (Oxford, 1998) offers a good introduction to writings of that author.

► Chapter 5   Ideology, *Mentalité* and Social Ritual: From Social History to Cultural History

There are a number of scene-setting works which provide the vital first step for those wishing to probe more deeply into the meeting place of social and cultural history. The first text to recommend is Lynn Hunt (ed.), *The New Cultural History* (Berkeley and Los Angeles, 1990): not only is Hunt's own contribution clear and lucid but she pulls together a number of eminent writers who state the case for the new cultural history in their own terms whilst reflecting upon the canonical works of such writers as E.P. Thompson and N. Zemon Davis. Thompson's *Making of the English Working Class* is listed later. His collection of essays, *Customs in Common* (1991), is also vital. On Thompson, see E.K. Trimberger, 'E.P. Thompson: understanding the process of history' in T. Skocpol (ed.), *Visions and Methods in Historical Sociology* (Cambridge, 1984). On Davis, see her collection, *Society and Culture in Early Modern France* (Stanford, CA, 1975). For a consideration of Thompson and Davis together, see Suzanne Desan, 'Crowds, community and rituals in the work of E.P. Thompson and Natalie Davis', in Hunt (ed.), *New Cultural History*. Hunt's first volume was then followed up by an authoritative addition to the body of scholarship Victoria E. Bonnell and Lynn Hunt (eds), *Beyond the Cultural Turn* (1999).

Another important work, here, is Roger Chartier, *Cultural History* (1988). Unsurprisingly, Peter Burke has made a significant contribution in this area, too. His *New Perspectives on Historical Writing* (Oxford, 1991) contains a very useful introduction and several chapters that discuss themes examined in this chapter of our book. P. Burke (ed.), *Varieties of Cultural History* (Oxford, 1997), is more directly and generally relevant, demonstrating a prodigious range of scholarship, drawing upon the many traditions that helped to shape cultural history. A little-known essay which deserves to be more widely appreciated is W. Scott, 'Cultural history at the crossroads: a local experience and a personal view', *Tidskrift Kultur Studier*, I: *Cultural Change in Theory and Practice* (May 1995). Scott also applies his philosophy in an important essay on the French Revolution: W. Scott, 'Reading/writing/killing: Foucault, cultural history and the French Revolution', *Arcadia: Zeitschrift führ Allegemeine und Vergleichende Literaturwissenschaft*, 33 (1998).

Important intellectual contributions to our understanding of culture, especially collective mentalities, include: M. Bakhtin, *Rabelais and his World* (Cambridge, MA, 1978) and R.G. Collingwood, *The Idea of History* (Oxford, 1946; 1992 edn). S. Vice, *Introducing Bakhtin* (Manchester, 1997), provides an excellent introduction to Bakhtinian thought, while P. Morris (ed.), *The Bakhtin Reader: Selected Writings of Bakhtin, Medvedev and Voloshinov* (2002) is an important anthology of writings by the 'Bakhtin circle'. The important anthropological contribution of Claude Lévi-Strauss is discussed in numerous texts, with C.R. Badcock, *Lévi-Strauss: Structuralism and Sociological Theory* (1975) proving to be very useful. Clifford Geertz, 'Deep play: notes on the Balinese cockfight', in his *The Interpretation of Cultures: Selected Essays* (1993 edn), has also been hugely influential.

European scholarship has long contributed to developing notions of cultural history and the history of cultures. Students would benefit from at least dipping into Jakob Burkhardt, *The Civilisation of the Renaissance in Italy* (New York, 1961 edn) and J. Huizinga, *The Waning of the Middle Ages* (1924; 1990 edn), not least the introductions to both books. Again, the *Annales* contribution looms large. Its contribution both to social and cultural history is cogently overviewed in Peter Burke, *The French Historical Revolution: The Annales School, 1929–89* (Oxford, 1990). The original idea is often the best, and major *Annalistes* endeavours of the first generation still stand the test of time. These include Marc Bloch, *Royal Touch* (1924; London, 1973) and Lucien Febvre, *The Problem of Unbelief in the Sixteenth Century* (1942; Cambridge, MA, 1983).

The tensions between mentalities' perspectives and the Marxist-inspired approach ('history from below') are important. E.P. Thompson, 'History From Below', *Times Literary Supplement* (1966), offered a clarion call to historians of the working class and it remains a useful starting point. A fuller treatment can be found in J.A. Sharpe, 'History from below' in Peter Burke (ed.), *New Perspectives on Historical Writing* (Oxford, 1991): an excellent and wide-ranging account. A fuller account still can be found in a volume dedicated to Hobsbawm: Frederick Krantz, *History From Below: Studies in Popular Protest and Popular Ideology* (1985). The preface of E.P. Thompson, *The Making of the English Working Class* (1963; 1968 edn) remains one of the most brilliant short statements of the mood and meaning of 'history from below': almost every paragraph contains phrases that have become part of the mental furniture. Crowd action, we explained, was an important focus for such historians, and several works by George Rudé remain important, *The Crowd in the French Revolution* (1959), *The Crowd in History* (1964) and *Protest and Punishment: The Story of the Social and Political Protesters Transported to Australia, 1788–1868* (Oxford, 1978). On the 'history from below' approach to labour history, readers should consult E.J. Hobsbawm, *Labouring Men: Studies in the History of Labour* (1964; 1968 edn), and almost any title in Christopher Hill's huge output of books, but *The World Turned Upside Down* (1972) is one to begin with. Approaching such matters from a more 'marxisant' perspective, the prolific and original Raphael Samuel produced many essays and collections that still stimulate the reader today. Perhaps two volumes, the second published posthumously, characterise the things he was working on late in life. *Theatres of Memory* (1994) and *Island Stories* (1998), contain many essays which address issues, people and groups at the margins of history; but they contain much else besides, and represent a good way of working backwards into Samuel huge corpus of works

The mentalities approach is analysed with great poise in Burke, in his article 'Strengths and weaknesses of the history of mentalities', *History of European Ideas* (1986). *Annales* scholarship in the 1960s and 1970s led the way in the study of mentalities and a number of texts are required reading. An excellent, and explicit, statement on the psychological dimension of cultural history can be found in R. Mandrou, *Introduction to Modern France, 1500–1640* (1961) and his *Magistrates and Sorcerers in Seventeenth-Century France* (1968). Some of the greatest work was by E. Le Roy Ladurie, including *Montaillou* (1975; 1978 edn) and *Carnival in Romans* (1979; 1981 edn). Similarly important, though looking at the earlier period, J. Le Goff, *Medieval Civilisation* (1964; 1988 edn). More modern works of European scholarship, which are shaped explicitly by the cultural turn in historiography, demonstrate a more than residual *Annales* influence. Those which offer both case studies of cultural history, and a consciously stated framework for such study, include C. Ginsburg, *The Cheese and the Worms: The Cosmology of a Sixteenth-Century Miller* (1976; 1992 edn). A connection between English and French scholarship is never better demonstrated than in one of the finest historical works of the twentieth century: K. Thomas's *Religion and the Decline of Magic* (1971; 1991 edn). Similarly, an important Euro-American endeavour, drawing heavily upon Clifford Geertz's anthropology, can be found in R. Darnton, *The Great Cat Massacre and other Episodes in French Cultural History* (1984), which, like Ginzburg's study, benefits from a conscious framing of the issues and philosophies in its introductory section.

For a general discussion of the development of women's history: see G. Holloway 'Writing women in: the development of feminist approaches to women's history' in W. Lamont (ed.), *Historical Controversies and Historians* (1998). For a comprehensive survey of the development of women's history and its evolution into gender history see: J. Alberti, *Gender and the Historian* (Harlow, 2002). C. Hall and L. Davidoff's *Family Fortunes: Men and Women of the English Middle Class 1780–1850* (1987) is an exemplary study of gender relations. J.W. Scott's poststructuralist approach to gender history can be traced in her *Gender and the Politics of History*

(New York, 1988), which gathered together several of her influential essays. This collection has subsequently been issued in a new edition with additional material: *Gender and the Politics of History: Revised Edition* (New York, 1999).

The postmodernist direction, that is, 'linguistic turn', in post-social cultural history has generated something larger than a little cottage industry. What Lynn Hunt and others spotted in the 1980s, Gareth Stedman Jones had begun to sketch a little earlier. Jones had begun his career as a labour historian, writing an impressive book, *Outcast London* (1971; 1986). From there, he began to question the materialist perspective of the (largely) Marxist social and labour historians, developing the ideas through an important study, *Languages of Classes: Studies in English Working Class History* (Cambridge, 1983). At about the same time, Richard Price and Patrick Joyce engaged in a lengthy debate in the pages of the journal *Social History*, which began to mark out the fault lines of class, for and against. Debates have also raged, from time to time, in *Past and Present, Social History* (again), *Journal of Modern History*, and *Storia Della Storiographia*. The individual contributions are too numerous to list, but Keith Jenkins has produced an effective distillation of the various confluences: *The Postmodern History Reader* (1997). This is a very good collection, which can usefully be read alongside his other works. The case for history as it is, and always was, is made by R. Price, 'Postmodernism as theory and history' in J. Belchem and N. Kirk (eds), *Languages of Labour* (Aldershot, 1997), in a volume which is more generally useful. Readers wishing to consider further the impact of postmodernism in the field of social history will need to read works of the French school, notably those of Foucault, Derrida and Barthes. C.O' Farrell's *Foucault: Historian or Philosopher?* (Basingstoke, 1989), provides an excellent summary of Foucault's work, as well as discussing his reception by historians. Hayden White is also influential, and his two major works: *Tropics of Discourse* (Baltimore, 1978) and *Metahistory: The Historical Imagination in Nineteenth-Century Europe* (Baltimore, 1987) are required reading. Postmodernists working in Britain have also made a continuing contribution to the field over the past ten years or so. Useful and important texts include: K. Jenkins, *On What is History from Carr and Elton to Rorty and White*, (1995), A. Munslow, *Deconstructing History* (1997), B. Southgate, *History: What and Why?* (1996). For a comprehensive critique of many aspects of postmodernism see: A. Callinicos, *Against Postmodernism: a Marxist Critique* (New York, 1999 edn), while Nicos Mouzelis *Sociological Theory: What Went Wrong?* (1995) provides an excellent analysis of the postmodern critique of conventional social theory. Whilst no trumpeter for postmodernism, Willie Thompson's new study, *Postmodernism* (2004), offers an effective analysis of many of the debates at the heart of this chapter.

For those who moved from orthodox (political, economic, often Marxist) social history, exciting new fields opened up. An early pioneer in marking out a new focus on the culture of working-class life was John Walton. See, for example, *The Blackpool Landlady: A Social History* (Manchester, 1978); *The English Seaside Resort: A Social*

History 1750–1914 (Leicester, 1983); and *Fish and Chips and the British Working Class 1870–1940* (Leicester, 1992). For the clearest examples of a direct switch from the 'social' to the 'cultural' we can cite Bill Lancaster, whose first major publication was a study of labour politics – *Radicalism, Cooperation and Socialism: Leicester working-class politics 1860–1906* (Leicester, 1987) – but who moved on to produce *The Department Store: a Social History* (Leicester, 1995). A similar trajectory was followed by Geoffrey Crossick whose earliest work was a classic of labour history, *An Artisan Elite in Victorian Society: Kentish London 1840–1880* (1978), but who also went on to work on the consumption side, producing *Cathedrals of Consumption: The European Department Store 1850–1939* (Aldershot, 1999), edited with S. Jaumain.

Index